The Presidential Debates:
Issues and Questions for
the 2016 Elections
and Beyond

The Presidential Debates: Issues and Questions for the 2016 Elections
and Beyond

Edited by John Norton Moore

CAROLINA ACADEMIC PRESS
Durham, North Carolina

ISBN 978-1-61163-918-6
LCCN 2016935752

CAROLINA ACADEMIC PRESS, LLC
700 Kent Street
Durham, North Carolina 27701
Telephone (919) 489-7486
Fax (919) 493-5668
www.cap-press.com

Printed in the United States of America

Contents

The Presidential Debates

Focusing The Presidential Debates[1]

John Norton Moore[2]

Introduction and Overview of Issues Facing the New President

The Constitution of the United States begins with a powerful statement of national aspirations: "**We the people** of the United States, in Order to form a more perfect Union, establish Justice, insure domestic Tranquility, provide for the common defense, promote the general Welfare, and secure the Blessings of

---

1. The papers, and videos of the press conferences, associated with this initiative are posted on an initiative website at: www.FocusingThePresidentialDebates.com

2. Professor of Law, the University of Virginia. Formerly the Chairman of the Board of the United States Institute of Peace, a United States Ambassador, Chairman of the National Security Council Interagency Task Force on the Law of the Sea (coordinating eighteen federal agencies), and Deputy Special Representative of the President for the Law of the Sea Negotiations, among six presidential appointments. Professor Moore also served as Co-Chairman with the Deputy Attorney General of the United States of the first talks between the United States and the USSR on the Rule of Law (Moscow and Leningrad 1990), Consultant to the Arms Control and Disarmament Agency (1987-91), Chairman of the American Bar Association Standing Committee on Law and National Security (1982-86), Counselor on International Law to the Department of State (1972-73), and Chairman of the Governance & Ethics Committee of Freedom house, among other governmental and private sector assignments. He is the initiator and original draftsman for Freedom House of what subsequently became the Community of Democracies. He is also the 2013 recipient of the American Bar Association's Morris I. Liebman Award in National Security Law. Most recently, he won Bronze as a member of the United States Masters Bench Press team in the 2015 World Championships.

The views expressed in this paper are solely those of Professor Moore, and this project is not associated with the University of Virginia or any governmental or other organization with which he is or has been affiliated. Unless otherwise stated, the views of individual paper presenters are their personal views.

Liberty to ourselves and our Posterity, do ordain and establish this Constitution for the United States." That document and its subsequent Bill of Rights,
built on the genius of our founders, have produced the greatest success in history. But two hundred and twenty-six years after ratification of the Constitution our Nation faces grave challenges; challenges which could severely erode
that singular success. At the same time, the Nation has exceptional opportunity; opportunity which could make the Nation even stronger.

Which path is taken largely depends on the choices we make now, and our
leadership in implementing those choices.

Once again this Great Nation has embarked on a journey to elect a new President. The candidates have come forward and the debates are under way. It is in
the interest of all Americans that the candidates and their debates seriously address the grave national challenges and opportunities now before the Nation.
We cannot afford politics as usual, with candidates vying to be the most immoderate in their Party. The challenges are unforgiving and the opportunities
fleeting.

The experts participating in this initiative are deeply concerned about the
problems facing this Great Nation and have come together to present suggestions and raise questions for the Presidential candidates; Republican and Democrat alike. The papers being distributed to the Press today are being sent to
each of the declared candidates in both parties. The campaign organization of
each candidate, as well as the Democratic National Committee and the Republican National Committee, have also been notified of this initiative and invited to send a representative to the press conferences.

Each paper reflects the view of the presenter. There has been no effort to coordinate views; nor is any presenter responsible for the views expressed by
other presenters. Some of these papers may appeal more to Democrat candidates and some may appeal more to Republican candidates. The subjects, however, have been chosen for their national importance, and the presenters for
their recognized expertise.

It is hoped that as the debates progress in and between both parties that the
candidates, and the Nation more broadly, will reflect on the range of serious problems and will consider the questions and/or specific recommendations presented in these papers. We here today are not able to individually participate in
the debates, but we hope to be heard by the candidates and the American people through the great institution of America's free press. It is in that spirit that
we have invited you today to this press conference at the National Press Club.

America is, and must always remain, a land of opportunity for all, regardless of ethnicity, gender, color, or religion, a leader in the struggle for peace and
justice, a beacon of hope to the world, and the home of the free. We must

never forget that America's true greatness lies in is national values and its un-quenchable spirit.

Priority National Problems and Opportunities

A partial list of critical national problems and opportunities includes:

- Restoring the American economy to substantially higher levels of sustained economic growth. This growth goal is critical for our effectiveness in meeting almost all other national goals and must be one of the Nation's highest priorities;
- Restoring the United States military and defense communities to robust strength;
- Promoting a more stable world, and reducing threats from rogue actors and terrorist groups;
- Enhancing United States credibility and effectiveness in foreign affairs;
- Reducing and controlling the national debt;
- Reforming the Social Security System for greater effectiveness and long-term economic health;
- Reforming Obamacare (ACA), Medicare, and Medicaid for greater effectiveness in meeting national health goals and long-term economic health;
- Reducing taxes on Americans and American corporations,[3] and more effectively controlling the regulatory burden on American business as critical elements in restoring growth;
- Reforming immigration policy to ensure that America will have border security and adequate enforcement, that immigration policy will support American business and the economy, that there will be a one-time path to legal status for the many whose presence is benefiting the Nation, and that going forward immigration policy, like all national policies, will be guided by the rule-of-law;
- Reforming the criminal justice system by reducing incarceration for non-violent offenders and paring back overly broad use of the criminal justice system in non-violent offenses. At the same time, we may need even tougher laws for the most serious categories of repeat violent offenders, shooting homicides, and terrorism;

---

3. America's corporate tax rate of 35% (rising to as high as 39% including state taxes) compares with a rate of 20% in the United Kingdom, 17% in Singapore, 15% in Canada and Germany, and 12.5% in Ireland). This huge rate differential creates a powerful incentive for American firms to relocate abroad.

- Reducing crime through enhanced education against crime in our school systems, and more effective "community policing" through engaging the police more actively and directly with the communities they protect. The homicide rate in many of our major cities has surged recently, and it is our minority communities most at risk from any breakdown in mutual trust. Effectively reducing crime requires leadership from both police and the communities they serve. Recent events in Ferguson, Baltimore, and elsewhere suggest that we need to review both the adequacy of police training, and the adequacy of citizen training in supporting our police departments and their vital mission to protect the community. The police, and the communities which depend upon them, are inevitably linked. When that link becomes frayed, both the police and the communities they serve are harmed;
- Embracing modern medical science in settings where a more robust national research program targeting a particular disease holds promise both for enhanced cure offering better relief to millions of Americans, as well as substantial cost savings for the Nation. Arthritis, and other musculoskeletal conditions, which are the top causes of disability among United States adults, meet these conditions and could well serve as an initial focus for a new national "targeting disease" initiative. If successful, perhaps Alzheimer's and serious mental illnesses could be next;
- Adopting a comprehensive energy policy leading to energy independence for America;
- Rebuilding our crumbling infrastructure of roads, bridges, dams, airports and the power grid. Not only are thousands of "high hazard" dams and "deficient" bridges dangerous, but collectively our inadequate infrastructure has been estimated to cost the Nation a quarter trillion dollars a year, or more, in wasted time and fuel from road and airport congestion, and power outages;[4]
- Enhancing educational opportunities for all Americans, and more effectively meeting skills-based educational needs in the workplace;
- More effectively promoting abroad the core American values of democracy and the rule of law;

---

4. Perhaps an increased federal gasoline tax, at a time of a dramatic decrease in the price of gasoline, would now be possible as a targeted way of facilitating national infrastructure repair of highways and bridges. Such a tax would not only fund infrastructure, but also reduce carbon emissions and place the tax squarely on the principal users of the infrastructure. Similarly, a small user tax for airports and power consumption could assist with airport and power grid infrastructure.

- Reenergizing our national commitment to protection of the environment, but as with all governmental actions, doing so through cost-benefit effective measures;
- Ending tax and other laws discriminating against the family. Government actions should only strengthen and support the family;
- Paying greater attention to "right-sizing" government and reducing "government failure;" including revitalizing the role of the states in our federal system; and
- Assisting the process of forming a new Administration by streamlining
  the appointment and confirmation process.

To review this list is to appreciate the enormous challenge faced by the next President of the United States. The discussion which follows, built around the national objectives set forth in the Preamble to the American Constitution, is offered to provide greater granularity on some of the principal challenges and opportunities set out above.

To Promote the General Welfare

The most serious challenge facing the Nation is restoring a more robust growth rate. In recent years we have become mired in a low growth trajectory. The resulting costs are immense; fewer good jobs, a growing deficit, crumbling infrastructure, stagnant wages, a widening wealth gap, a shrinking military, diminishing opportunity to support the environment, and less American influence abroad. Virtually every major national objective is touched by this poor economic performance. As such, improving our growth rate is the Nation's number one problem. We can and must do better! The good news is that even small differences in growth rates make large differences when compounded through time. Thus, to move from a 2% growth rate to a 3% growth rate will make the Nation as a whole 27% richer than it would otherwise be in just 25 years. In a generation (50 years) the Nation as a whole would be 63% richer at the 3% rate. To raise the growth rate to 4% would in 25 years make the Nation as a whole 62% richer. And in a generation the 4% rate would make the Nation 164% richer. The rate of sustained economic growth matters.

Enhancing America's Growth

Though economics, like all social sciences, can be fuzzy at the edges, we know generally what works to promote growth and what works to retard growth. Lower taxes, particularly income and corporate taxes, profoundly affecting incentives to work and save, encourage growth.[5] Higher taxes depress growth. Higher taxes on dividends and capital gains, doubly suppresses growth in depressing savings and investment. While environmental, safety, and other regulations are necessary to address market externalities, excessive regulation depresses growth. High quality education encourages growth. Reducing trade barriers enhances growth (though America needs much stronger engagement with China on "non-tariff barriers," such as "anti-trust" and other domestic laws used by China and other trading partners to reduce the competitiveness of American companies). Facilitating small business encourages growth, as small business is, in reality, the large backbone of the economy. Facilitating women's access to the work force encourages growth. Repairing our crumbling infrastructure would enhance efficiency and encourage growth. And a climate of economic uncertainty, or perceived governmental hostility to business, can retard the "animal spirits" necessary for innovation. The paper by John H. Cochrane on "Economic Growth" addresses more fully how our Nation can meet its critical national need of enhancing growth.

Tax Fairness

There is a core misunderstanding about taxes in America; a misunderstanding which must be forthrightly addressed if we are to restore robust growth. The political rhetoric that the income tax unfairly favors the wealthy is not just false; the reality is quite the opposite. Our political history is one of imposing income taxes on a smaller and smaller base of the population; a path ultimately risking third-world out-of-control expenditures, as removal of political inhibitions on raising taxes leads political elites to support larger and larger expenditures. If we continue to focus on raising taxes as the solution to national problems we doom the Nation to subpar growth.

With respect to "fairness," according to the Internal Revenue Service, as of 2012 (with taxes even more progressive since then) the top 1% of tax payers paid 38.1% of the federal income tax, the top 10% paid 70.2%, the top 25% paid 86.4 %, and the top 50% paid 97.2%.[6] In contrast, according to the Urban

---

5. A legislative change permitting American corporations to bring back their very substantial earnings now parked abroad, and which were already taxed once abroad, would generate billions in stimulus for the American economy.

6. Figures are for the tax year 2012. IRS, Statistics of Income Division, Individual Income Tax Shares, 2012, *available at* http://www.irs.gov/pub/irs-soi/soi-a-ints-id1506.pdf.

Institute, in 2013 the bottom 43% of taxpayers paid no federal income tax at all.[7] With a combined state and federal tax rate approaching 50% in some states, such as California and New York, the income tax is a serious drag on growth. Moreover, the recent effort to raise taxes on dividends and capital gains is doubly unfair as the taxpayer will have first paid taxes on the wages she earned and then will be taxed again on the fruits of her decision to invest rather than to immediately spend her wages. Thus, saving and investment, actions critically needed for economic growth, are disfavored in tax policy over immediate consumption. And America's top corporate tax rate is one of the highest in the world; again serving as a drag on investment and growth.

Sometimes the argument is made that to ascertain overall tax fairness we must include not just the income tax but also payroll taxes. Adding payroll taxes and income taxes together does give a better picture of the total tax burden on lower income workers. But it is a false comparison, as payroll taxes are for the purpose of "entitlements" for the individual worker paying into the system; "entitlements" principally of Medicare and Social Security. Income taxes, in contrast, go to pay all of the myriad costs of government, such as defense and education, and are in no way "entitlements" for the taxpayer.

The tax code is also enormously complex, and compliance costs for business and individuals to file their taxes is yet another drag on growth. Further, these compliance costs are on top of the economic reality that an income tax depresses growth as compared with a consumption tax raising the same revenue. Ideally, America should adopt a simplified flat tax system, or perhaps eliminate the income tax completely in return for a National Sales or Value Added Tax (VAT).[8] Opposition from entrenched special interests to such approaches, however, is so substantial that possibly the best "tax reform" achievable in the short run may be to reduce the top rate, including "Obamacare surcharges," to 33% and the tax on long term capital gains and dividends to 15%, again including "Obamacare surcharges." No one should be required to pay more than one-third of their income in federal taxes; a rate comparable or higher than taxes owed under feudalism.[9] We should remember that federal income taxes are on top of

---

7. Estimated for tax year 2013. Urban Institute and Brookings Institution, Tax Policy Center, Tax Notes, September 30, 2013, *available at* http://www.taxpolicycenter.org/Uploaded-PDF/1001697-TN-who-pays-no-federal-income-tax-2013.pdf.

8. Progressivity can be built into a national sales tax or VAT through such means, for example, as exempting food, clothing, housing and medical services.

9. Indeed, according to the *Wikipedia*, Villiens and Serfs under feudalism "usually paid 10% of their income to the Church and 10% to the feudal lord." *See* https://simple.wikipedia.org/wiki/Feudalism.

state income taxes, property taxes, and a host of other federal, state and local taxes. A top 15% rate on capital gains and dividends would give a kick start to capital formation, another key component of growth. Moreover, dividends have already been taxed once at the corporate level.

In contrast, the recent proposals made by some candidates to dramatically increase the top income tax rate, or the capital gains tax rate, would slow an already sputtering economy and are neither the route to fairness, nor the route to reducing the wealth gap. Recent proposals to boost the earned income tax credit for childless low-wage workers, however, could both encourage employment and strengthen the safety net.

Yet another of the myths about the federal tax system is that it is just one big "loophole" for the wealthy. To the contrary, the tax code has been designed to capture revenue. Not surprisingly, it contains numerous loopholes for the Government specifically designed to raise revenue regardless of their obvious lack of "fairness." Thus, the "alternative minimum tax," which at its inception was designed to hit the "wealthy" taxpayer who was using abusive tax shelters, today treats all state income taxes paid as though they were an abusive tax shelter and effectively removes the deduction for state income taxes paid. Excuse me? Paying your state income taxes owed is an abusive tax shelter? The capital gains tax applies fully to all gains but limits deduction of losses to $3,000 per year. If the taxpayer has a good year and sells capital investments for a substantial profit the Government makes out nicely, thank you. But if the taxpayer has substantial capital losses, even to the point of being poorer at the end of the year, the Government still taxes all income but the $3,000 loss, as though the taxpayer had "income" when her net worth actually declined. And the tax code no longer permits "income averaging" which was a fairer method of taxation letting a one-time windfall be averaged over a number of years. Instead the Code now taxes a one-time windfall at a top rate as if the windfall were the normal annual income of the taxpayer.

Further, as the paper on "Controlling the Deficit" by Peter Ferrara shows, the federal deficit has not arisen because the Nation has decreased taxes. Rather, the deficit is a product of a prodigious increase in federal spending; particularly the increase in "entitlement" expenditures resulting from President Johnson's "Great Society" programs, and other more recent increases in "entitlement" expenditures under both Republican and Democrat Presidents. Increasing taxes is not the way to increase growth, is not the way to enhance fairness, and is not the way to effectively address the low growth "widening wealth gap." Grover Norquist will present a paper on Tax Policy, more specifically addressing "What Tax Reform Should Look Like Under the Next President."

Social Security Optionality: Reducing The Wealth Gap

One of the most important papers is that by Peter Ferrara on "Social Security Optionality: Reducing the Wealth Gap." It is generally understood that, at minimum, the Social Security system can and must be adjusted to prevent the bankruptcy looming at the end of its current trajectory. This could be done, for example, by raising payroll taxes, by raising the retirement age and/or lowering benefits. There are simply fewer and fewer Americans supporting more and more retirees and changes must be made to avoid running short of funds to pay promised benefits as early as 2028 or 2033. But this way of focusing on the social security "problem" completely misses both the core of the "problem" and the compelling social security "opportunity." It also calls for a wrongheaded additional burden either on senior citizens or workers.

The core of the Social Security problem is not averting bankruptcy, though substantial changes would be necessary even to meet that objective, but the terrible job the system does for working Americans who pay into the system. Even if Social Security continues to pay all promised benefits, the real rate of return on the taxes paid into the system still would be less than 1%. Social Security is not a savings and investment system, but rather a tax system with those taxes returned with only a slight real rate of return, and no guaranty or ownership entitlement at all.

The "raising taxes and lowering benefits" route to Social Security "reform" also misses the Social Security "opportunity." That opportunity is to give American workers under age 40 the opportunity to opt into a private investment account into which their Social Security taxes would be deposited and invested and which they would own. Their investments would then compound through time like a normal retirement account. A two-earner middle income couple at standard long term investing returns would retire after a lifetime under this approach with an account estimated at over a million dollars which they would own. Their account would pay them at least double the traditional Social Security return while still letting them leave the full account to their children if they so choose. There is no magic here. The great difference in rate of return is achieved by a simple shift from a tax and pay system to a normal savings and investment retirement system.

The return would go up dramatically; at least quadrupling the Social Security 1% return to a 4-6% return, if not higher, as has traditionally been the investment return over the last 200 years. This is nothing more than the TIAA/CREF retirement system used by universities and hospitals in the United States for many years. Nor is this new or untested. When other nations such as Chile have shifted to this approach, despite shortcomings and problems, the returns have gone up and workers have flocked to the new system. Moreover, a guaranteed Social Security type minimum return could be built into the system if desired, restrictions on investments could be imposed to avoid high risk investments, and to protect choice and current expectations the system should be offered as an option. Anyone 40 or under who wished to remain in the old system could do so or they could opt for the new system. Finally, the change can be made while fully protecting retirement obligations of those over 40 in the system without raising payroll taxes, reducing benefits, raising the retirement age, or means testing recipients, as are the usual suggestions for "Social Security reform."

Social Security obligations, if meaningful, are already obligations of the Nation, so the transition can be funded either through general revenues or issuance of long term bonds without truly increasing national obligations. The long term beneficial economic effects for the Nation of this change in the Social Security system—increasing personal savings, increasing capital available for investments in America, decreasing the "wealth gap," strengthening the family, and ultimately even decreasing the deficit and increasing tax revenues as income is generated from the new wealth—will hugely outweigh the interest payments on 50 year bonds issued periodically to pay for the transition, should that modality of financing the transition be chosen. There is no single policy change this Nation can make to more effectively reduce the wealth gap and provide working families a real chance at wealth creation. Social Security "optionality" for reducing the wealth gap is the most obvious "low hanging fruit" available to America. It is literally a kick at American workers and their families and the worst of "old thinking" to demagogue Social Security optionality.

Targeting Disease

America also has important opportunities not yet addressed in the Presidential debates; opportunities with great meaning for millions of Americans. Medical research has come to the point that we may be able to much more effectively target disease through greater specific support. The national debate has focused on access to medical care; but what if medical science has progressed on certain disease processes that a major directed effort, perhaps one disease process at a time on cures or treatments deemed promising, could dramatically reduce the incidence of the disease? As will be discussed in the "Right-Sizing Government" paper, basic research will be underfunded by markets because it is a "positive externality" in economic theory. There is, then, a case for government in filling this need. Our government, of course, through the National Institutes of Health, already makes substantial commitments to basic research in dealing with diseases; cancer, heart disease, aids, Alzheimer's, and other diseases. But if the cost to the Nation of certain diseases, through lost work and medical payments, is larger than the likely cost to better understand and cure the disease, and the science is promising enough to make that calculation, then it may be time to consider a national "moon shot" at curing, or at least better controlling, certain diseases. Indeed, perhaps if such a targeted approach is successful, the Nation might target one disease after another where the science suggests that the national savings from cure or better control would exceed the cost of the basic research. And, of course, a wonderful byproduct of any successes would be that millions of Americans would no longer be condemned to a lifetime of pain or disability. As an initial hypothesis for such a "targeting disease" approach, there is considerable evidence to suggest that arthritis and musculoskeletal diseases today meet the criteria for a major national effort.[10] Over fifty million Americans are affected by these diseases, more than twenty million have activity limitations from these conditions, and the direct and indirect economic cost in lost work and treatment costs is estimated to be over $200 billion per year. If a major research effort were able even to cut this cost in half, the yearly saving, repeated each year into the indefinite future, would be $100 billion.

Dr. Steven R. Goldring, MD, the Chief Scientific Officer Emeritus at the prestigious Hospital for Special Surgery in New York, has prepared a groundbreaking paper which should be considered carefully by all the candidates, discussing whether the cost of these diseases, the percentage of the American population affected, and the state of the scientific understanding, suggests that arthritis and musculoskeletal diseases would be a useful place to start in such a national "Targeting Disease" research initiative.

Immigration Reform

No nation can tolerate uncontrolled immigration. The Nation's borders must be secure and future immigration and legal status must be controlled by the rule of law rather than the clandestine crossing or the expired visa. Much of the effective enforcement will inevitably be internal and in this respect the E-verify system, an employment eligibility verification system, should be strengthened and expanded. We must also focus immigration enforcement not just on illegal border crossings but also on illegal visa overstays; a major source

---

10. Perhaps if this initial "Targeting Disease" program were a success, the Nation could take on other diseases whenever they met the same cost and science criteria, whether schizophrenia (which struck down my older sister in her late teens after a bright start as a National Merit Scholar), Alzheimer's, or other diseases.

of illegal immigration—including some of those who participated in the 9/11 attacks.[11] But when the borders are secure and internal enforcement more effective, some one-time mechanisms should be put in place to legally recognize the many individuals who have come to America to work, who have obeyed the law, who have paid taxes, some who may have gone to school in America, some who may even have served in the American military, and who seek legal status. America needs innovators and workers and our Nation traditionally has benefitted from immigration from every region in the world. Immigration policy should realistically take account of these economic needs of the Nation and of the reality that immigrants are embedded in our society in important ways.[12] In this respect, we should substantially increase the quota for highly skilled workers as we reexamine categories for lawful immigration. Though surrounded with greater controversy, we might also at least review putting in place a more realistic temporary program for certain agricultural workers; a program required to meet three conditions; first, that the demand cannot be met from American workers, second, that good working conditions and fair wages are mandated as part of the approval process, and third that the program is subject to a 100% departure check. Professor Peter Skerry, an expert on immigration policy, will explore in greater detail issues concerning Immigration Policy.

Other Challenges To The General Welfare

Many other important challenges relate to the general welfare and must also be addressed, though the experts here today have no detailed papers to offer at this time. These additional challenges include:

---

11. According to *The Economist*, the proposal to "build a wall on the Mexican border" and "deport all 11 million immigrants currently thought to be in American illegally," "[a]part from the misery this would cause, ... would also cost $285 billion, by one estimate—roughly $900 in new taxes for every man, woman and child left in ... America." *The Economist*, September 5, 2015, at 15. *See also* Steve Case, "Our Immigration Opportunity," *Washington Post*, at A21 cols 2-4 (Sept. 13, 2015). A wall would, of course, also not deal with a major part of the immigration problem; that of visa overstays.

12. The proposal to immediately deport the millions of immigrants thought to be in America illegally; that is, immigrants who arrived in America through either unlawful entry or overstaying a lawful visa (and their family members), would have a devastating effect on the economy, in addition to the human misery, and the permanent blight on America's conscience. Costs, among other direct and indirect costs of such a forced migration, would include a major loss of productivity for American employers, as well as the economic and human costs of an army of enforcement agents.

- **Supporting the family.** The family is the core of child development, social development and an important part of a healthy America. Yet a shocking number of our laws are anti-family; from the "marriage penalty" in the tax code, to the imposition of estate taxes on transfers at death to one's children. Is it in the National interest to encourage unlimited spending during one's lifetime, but to massively tax an already taxed lifetime accumulation passed to one's children at death?[13] America needs a governmental commission to not only examine anti-family laws, but to examine ways of encouraging stable family formation. The breakdown of the family is a serious national problem and one which has outsized impact on minority communities;

- **Regulatory reform.** As the paper on "Right-Sizing Government" will discuss, proper regulation is an important function of government in protecting the environment, safety, health, truthfulness of investment information, and soundness of the banking system, among other important functions. But special interest pleading, the inevitable governmental overreaction when legislating to resolve problems, and the democratic deficit inherent in the administrative state, can result in badly skewed regulation; regulation generating far greater costs than benefits. America needs a mechanism to swap out these costly regulations for likely more effective but less costly "second generation" regulations. As a start, a new President should task the Office of Management and Budget with conducting a careful agency-by-agency review of those regulations with largest economic effect, and then making recommendations to the President and the Congress, where possible, to swap out inefficient first generation regulations for more efficient second generation regulations, and to repeal altogether those regulations which review shows to be severely non-cost-benefit effective (when measured by their own objectives). An additional useful initiative would be to create a small government agency (with a maximum $20 million budget) which would be tasked with simply publicizing for the American people what it considers each year to be the ten costliest

---

13. Property, in the Anglo-American tradition, is a bundle of rights, privileges, powers and immunities with respect to an owned asset. The estate tax is not only anti-family, but it also removes one of the most important indicia of ownership; that is the ability of the owner to pass on the asset. Inheritance was a crucial feature in the development of property rights in the Anglo-American tradition; a tradition which revered the family. For the United States Government to dramatically impair that indicia of ownership is not only a detriment to family, it reduces an important indicia of ownership of the property owner herself. The cost of eliminating the estate tax would be less than 1% of federal revenues, and to eliminate the tax would have positive economic effects on jobs, hours worked, and wages.

(considering the overall costs of regulations which when measured by their own objectives are generating greater costs than benefits) regulatory decisions. We should also review the issue of "regulatory takings" to more fairly treat those whose property has been effectively "taken" through the regulatory process.[14] Yet another possibility, this one which might be considered a "nuclear" option in controlling non-cost-benefit regulations, would be to legislatively expand due process review by the federal courts to permit the courts to strike down administratively imposed regulations where a judicial determination is made that the regulation, by its own objective, generates costs exceeding at least three times the benefits, or some other ratio deemed by Congress as clear regulatory failure;

- **Energy policy.** In recent years "fracking" and other new techniques for producing oil and gas have turned America into a major energy producer. Given the importance to the Nation of ending massive transfers of American wealth to foreign oil producers it is strongly in the national interest to encourage, rather than discourage, energy development. Moreover, lower cost energy produced in America will assist American manufacturing and business in a globally competitive environment. America should aim for permanent energy independence. In contributing to that goal, alternative, non-fossil fuels such as wind, solar, and nuclear should be encouraged where cost effective or likely to become so in a reasonable period of time. One governmental failure from the past to be addressed is that of locating a permanent repository for civilian spent nuclear fuels. Solving this problem can only be accomplished by bringing together all the stake holders to reach an agreed solution; not by resuming the years and years of court battles going nowhere;

- **The environment.** Damage to the environment imposes real costs. Accordingly, we must protect the environment, both on land and at sea. "Negative externalities," imposing costs on the environment, whether from the private sector or the government, must be priced out through appropriate regulation or legislative mandate. Any such regulation, however, should be at least reasonably cost-effective and should not, as a cur-

---

14. When government can impose costs on private parties off budget through the exercise of its regulatory power, this can easily lead to inefficient actions, with costs being ignored. On the other hand, private actions harming others, such as nuisance, have no case for compensation from regulation. Further, much regulation has *de minimus* effect on the property owner, and to seek to compensate for all such government actions is simply not practical. The trick is to find the right balance to be legislatively implemented through some appropriate percentage reduction in value requiring compensation as a "regulatory taking."

rent Justice of the United States Supreme Court has noted for much such regulation which came before him while a Judge on the Fifth Circuit Court of Appeals, seek the last 10% of benefit at huge and unjustified economic cost.[15] The best scientific evidence is that global warming is real and that mankind's activities are at least a significant contributor. Absent the global warning "deniers" offering better science, they should stand down. But equally important, it is not clear that massive expenses incurred by America to seek to halt global warming will generate greater benefit (a benefit likely achieved simply through slowing global warming) than their considerable and immediate economic costs. Real jobs, real growth, real alternative expenditures, and other real consequences must be carefully weighed against the rush to view all energy policy through a lens of global warming and climate change. Likely, cost-benefit analysis would support some, but not all, proposals for dealing with global warming. In this connection, cost-benefit analysis should not be used, or viewed, as an "anti-environment" tool. Rather, sophisticated analysis, including values other than dollars alone, provides a needed rigor to avoid shooting ourselves in the foot;

- **Obamacare, Medicare, Medicaid and Health Access.** Obamacare (the ACA) has generated substantial opposition. It is highly complex, coercive, costly, job inhibiting for small business, and has still not brought medical insurance to all Americans.[16] Medicare and Medicaid, highly popular programs, have imposed large entitlement costs, costs that are projected to escalate through time without greater cost control. Medicaid, in a well-intentioned effort to control costs, has reduced payments to health-care providers so severely as to dramatically reduce those will-

---

15. Stephen Breyer, *Breaking the Vicious Circle: Toward Effective Risk Regulation* (1992). As one of many examples of non-cost-benefit regulations discussed by then Court of Appeals Judge Breyer (now Justice Breyer of the U.S. Supreme Court) the Judge presents the following example of an actual mandated PCB cleanup as "the problem of the last 10 percent:" "In 1990, in New Hampshire, $9.3 million was spent to remove the final little bit of highly diluted PCBs by incinerating the dirt. Without this expenditure, the dirt was 'clean enough for children playing on the site to eat small amounts of dirt for 70 days per year without significant harm.' The area was a swamp, so children did not play there. Future development was unlikely. Experts agree that the chemicals would evaporate by the year 2000. $9.3 million spent to protect non-existent dirt-eating children is 'the problem of the last 10 percent.'" *Id.* at 11-12.

16. One useful change which could be quickly implemented would be to relax the ACA regulations limiting the range of insurance plans which can be offered. *See* Joseph R. Antos, "Health Care Reform After the ACA," 370 *New England Journal of Medicine* 2259, 2261 (2014).

ing to serve Medicaid patients. Physicians, particularly primary-care physicians, and nurse practitioners are not being trained in adequate numbers. Paper work for health care providers is displacing critical time with the patient, whether driven by a commendable goal of better record keeping for patients, or less commendable goals of "cover you're a**" actions driven by litigation fear, or bureaucratic requirements for obtaining reimbursement imposed by insurance companies or the government. Accelerating concentration in health-care, as hospitals purchase physician practices and consolidate, will increasingly raise cost issues associated with dominant regional suppliers. Treatment of the mentally ill, with schizophrenics living in the streets, is a national disgrace. Because of an absence of sensible time limitations on assessing injury, as well as the failure to appropriately cap damage claims, the cost of medical insurance is out of control; particularly for those health care providers specializing in obstetrics. Americans support cost-effective preventive care, high quality medical care, and access to medical insurance for all Americans. How to achieve these goals at affordable cost for the Nation is enormously complex. It is recommended that, as a priority, the new Administration appoint a high-level Health-Care/Health-Cost Commission to make recommendations for a structure which would more effectively meet national health goals. Issues to be addressed should include all the above, as well as nationally portable major-medical policies for the individual, and enhanced preventive care for all.[17] America needs a carefully thought out approach to these difficult issues, not a 2,700 page bill unread by most who voted on it, however well intentioned;

- **Education.** High quality education is an important ingredient of personal development, personal success, aggregate economic growth, and, ultimately, good governance. Many factors go into producing high quality education. These include adequate funding, excellent teachers, starting early, small classes, and good facilities, among other factors. Parental involvement and parental choice also seem to correlate strongly with better educational results from our schools. Perhaps, however, it is time to consider, as well, setting up sophisticated programmed learning systems on the Internet in most educational subjects from beginner to advanced, so that anyone with access to the Internet, of whatever age, can pursue

---

17. For an interesting discussion of a "public utility" model, which might have a place in health-care reform, *see* Nicholas Bagley, "Medicine as a Public Calling," 114 *Michigan Law Review* 57 (2015).

education as desired.[18] Similarly, in areas where basic work skills are in short supply, perhaps more school system/industry partnerships in training could meet these skill needs. Economic theory also deserves a better place in our public school curriculum, including "public choice theory" which won the Nobel Prize in economics for Professor James M. Buchanan and which educates about "government failure," in parallel with "market failure." Good civic education should include a solid grounding not only in the strengths and weaknesses of both markets and government; it should instill genuine understanding as to the causes of both "market failure" and "government failure," and the resulting need for checks and balances, and constant vigilance on the exercise of power. Our school system is also missing an opportunity to "take a bite out of crime" by failing to systematically integrate anti-drug, anti-crime, pro-rule-of-law programs more effectively into the school system. In the past we have taken for granted that anti-crime socialization occurred in the family. But with contemporary stresses on the family, the schools need to supplement this traditional family training. Where such "rule-of-law" or "culture of lawfulness" programs are being taught in the public schools abroad, the results have been promising. Dr. Roy S. Godson, who has been a principal innovator of these "rule-of-law/anti-crime" programs is presenting a paper on their promise;

• **Responding to economic crises.** The 2008 financial crisis, like all deep economic downturns, has done lasting damage to the Nation; indeed to the world. How we handle such crises is an extremely important issue which needs careful preparation before the crises occur. Given the controversy surrounding the Dodd-Frank "Wall Street Reform and Consumer Protection Act of 2010,"[19] enacted in response to the 2008 crisis, it is imperative that a new Administration review the adequacy of mechanisms now in place and the cost/benefit effectiveness of Dodd-Frank.[20] While there is abundant blame to share with the private sector, it is imperative that we also not forget the governmental missteps contributing to the crisis. Surely, these include adoption, prior to the crisis, of the "mark-to-

---

18. The private sector has long since produced superb lectures on a wide range of subjects. *See*, for example, the lectures offered by The Teaching Company.

19. 2,300 pages long, and giving rise to thousands of pages of subsidiary regulations.

20. For a devastating critique of the broadly accepted narrative of market failure in the Great Depression and the 2008 Financial Crisis, as well as an exploration of the costs of much of the "regulatory reform" in response, *see* Paul G. Mahoney, *Wasting a Crisis: Why Securities Regulation Fails* (2015).

market" accounting requirements which had properly been abandoned after the Great Depression. Mark-to-market accounting distorts markets by exaggerating the effect upward of asset values during booms, and distorting real asset values downward during liquidity crises. The effect during the crisis of mark-to-market requirements for assessing bank capital under conditions of extreme illiquidity in the mortgage market was devastating. Similarly, government agencies promoted overly permissive mortgages in their support for increasing home ownership. We should not have let our understandable interest in promoting home ownership, which has many benefits including reducing the wealth gap, set aside appropriate standards for offering mortgages; a cost paid by the economy as a whole, as well as in devastating financial pain for the individual homeowner, when property prices went south.[21] Further, though controversial and "banned" by Dodd-Frank, we should examine, as an alternative crises mechanism, the use of government bridge loans for "too-big-to-fail" financial institutions in a crises meltdown threatening the economy as a whole. While we will never be sure, it is likely that had the Federal Reserve or the Treasury Department prevented the collapse of Lehman Brothers, Bear Stearns, and subsequent companies such as American International Group (AIG), through the use of bridge loans to meet the liquidity problems of these companies (with possible option kickers for the Government) that the taxpayer would have made out hugely,[22] and the resulting downward spiral of confidence in the overall economy might have been considerably lessened. Yes, such an approach poses a "moral hazard," potentially incentivizing sloppy risk performance.[23] But what is worse; a cascading crisis of confidence throughout the economy triggered by collapse of major financial institutions, or some "moral hazard" cost? In this connection, the economic value of an institution which continues to function is far greater than one put out of business. Just imagine, for example, the greater return to the taxpayer, and the lesser downward effect in financial markets, if the AIG liquidity crisis had been handled through a bridge

---

21. The housing crisis also had a devastating effect on minority wealth. *See* Michael A. Fletcher, "A Shattered Foundation," cols. 1-3 A1 (January 25, 2015).

22. The taxpayer ultimately made out extremely well in the 2008 financial crisis with respect to the pay back to the government at more than the cost of government financial loans and guarantees.

23. "Moral hazard" can also be significantly offset through appropriate individual penalties, or by Central Bank crisis lending at very high interest rates, rather than assuming the only antidote is permitting institutional collapse.

loan permitting full continued operation of one of the finest insurance companies in the world. The broadest issue here is not just an assessment of Dodd- Frank, but also the still developing international Basel rules on banking; indeed, ultimately the full national and international regulatory structure imposed on the banks. We can, of course, dramatically decrease the risk of bank failure by massive advance regulatory intervention through both Dodd-Frank and Basel banking rules. But at some point the costs to efficiency, competitiveness, and the economy may outweigh the benefits from further hikes down the regulatory risk reduction path,[24] compared to an after-the-fact liquidity mechanism. Dodd-Frank commits the Nation to a "risk reduction" regulatory path for too-big-to-fail financial institutions, as opposed to the Nation's previous understanding of meeting emergencies through using after-the-fact liquidity extensions from a Central Bank. Likely, this Dodd-Frank moment reflected a post-crisis political setting in which the "left" wanted more regulation, and the "right" abjured "bailouts," as inconsistent with free markets. We may, however, have made at least too one-sided a choice.[25] Finally, given the haphazard fiscal

---

24. See generally, "Risk-weighted capital: Whose model is it anyway?" *The Economist* 70, at 73 (Sept. 19, 2015).

25. A classic in economic theory, Walter Bagehot's "Lombard Street" essay, sets forth the alternative crises management approach followed for many years by central banks. "[T]he Bank of England ... must in time of panic do what all other similar banks must do; that in time of panic it must advance freely and vigorously to the public out of the reserve. And with the Bank of England, as with other Banks in the same case, these advances, if they are to be made at all, should be made so as if possible to obtain the object for which they are made. The end is to stay the panic; and the advances should, if possible, stay the panic. And for this purpose there are two rules: First. That these loans should only be made at a very high rate of interest. This will operate as a heavy fine on unreasonable timidity, and will prevent the greatest number of applications by persons who do not require it. The rate should be raised early in the panic, so that the fine may be paid early; that no one may borrow out of idle precaution without paying well for it; that the Banking Reserve may be protected as far as possible. Secondly. That at this rate these advances should be made on all good banking securities, and as largely as the public ask for them. The reason is plain. The object is to stay alarm, and nothing therefore should be done to cause alarm. But the way to cause alarm is to refuse someone who has good security to offer. The news of this will spread in an instant through all the money market at a moment of terror; no one can say exactly who carries it, but in half an hour it will be carried on all sides, and will intensify the terror everywhere. No advances indeed need by made by which the Bank will ultimately lose." *Id.* at 75-76 (Lexington, KY reprint). Walter Bagehot [1826-1877], an influential political and economic writer who in 1860 took over as editor-in-chief of *The Economist*, was, of course, principally focusing on the Bank of England.

In the panic of 2008, perhaps the Federal Reserve and the Treasury Department were

response to the crises of billions spent on allegedly "shovel ready" projects during the 2008 crisis, would it not make sense to adapt, going forward, one of the proposals from the Great Depression? That is, set up a small government agency (perhaps with a $20 million budget) which would in advance of crises compile a list of needed infrastructure projects (and engage in some appropriate contingent work); projects which would genuinely add to growth if implemented by Congress for needed fiscal stimulus during a future crises;

• **Providing a level playing field for our security markets.** America's stock exchanges and security markets are the most important and deepest security markets in the world. As such, they perform critical roles for the Nation, including facilitating investment and supporting retirement for millions of Americans. Maintaining the health of our security markets, including faith in their honesty, efficiency, and fairness, is essential. Modern technology, particularly high speed computers and high speed access, but also newer security derivatives, add substantial complexity in policing the health of these markets. The "flash crash" of 2010, and the recent "mini-flash-crash" of the summer of 2015, raise important questions as to the current regulatory structure for these markets, and whether we are providing a level and fair playing field. A new Administration should undertake a careful review of the health of our security markets; with a particular focus on the impact of new technology.

To Provide for the Common Defense

A second major grouping of challenges to the Nation are external, relating to national security and defense.[26] The world today has numerous serious chal-

---

concerned as to whether they had adequate legal authority. *But see section* 13(3) of the Federal Reserve Act. Perhaps also, Lehman Brothers and Bear Stearns simply could not offer what was felt to be adequate security. But did any concern about adequacy of security take account of the enterprise value of these investment banks as security for non-payment of loans? The author does not seek to second-guess the Federal Reserve or Treasury Department decisions, here, as he is simply not privy to the full 2008 context. He would, however, like to make a point that perhaps a mixture of emergency lending powers and risk reduction regulation might be a better approach than simply reliance on risk-reduction. Further, a relevant question in relying solely on regulatory risk reduction measures, quite apart from the added regulatory burden, is whether the triggering of too big to fail mechanisms, such as those set out in Dodd-Frank, will halt a panic or increase it? We should never forget that the principal objective here is to stop an economy wide panic!

26. For an excellent overview discussion of critical security and foreign policy choices facing a new American President see *Choices for America in a Turbulent World* (Rand Cor-

lenges; a rogue Russia under Putin's leadership waging unconventional war on Ukraine, bombing to support a genocidal regime in Syria, and threatening elsewhere; an Iran seeking to become a nuclear power and continuing its support for terrorism, destabilization of the Arab Middle East, and implacable hostility to Israel; an intransigent Israeli/Palestinian dispute; an unstable nuclear North Korea continuing to add to its nuclear arsenal; a China doubling down on assertiveness of its oceans claims against Japan in the East China Sea and its ASEAN neighbors in the South China Sea; an out-of-control series of cyberattacks against the West aimed largely at theft of both security and commercial information; a radical Islamist movement (ISIL) currently controlling large swaths of Iraq and Syria, dedicated to a new "Caliphate" setting aside national borders, and seeking to inspire terrorism in North Africa, Europe and America; and finally competing radical Islamist terrorist groups such as Al Qaeda supporting global terror, among more localized violent movements.

As though this panoply of threats is not enough, American credibility (and resulting ability to deter) has eroded through both Republican and Democratic Administrations. It is today clear that the War in Iraq was a serious miscalculation,[27] and a subsequent Administration has compounded the problem by walking away from a red line for Syria not to use chemical weapons in its civil war, not intervening in a timely manner in Iraq to prevent the virtual explosion of ISIL, failing to deter Putin in Ukraine, and concluding an arms agreement with Iraq opposed by a majority of the Congress and by both our Israeli and Arab allies in the Middle East. No one believes these issues are simple, or that they have obvious solutions. But whatever the rationale for these recent American actions, collectively they and other actions have eroded American prestige and credibility around the World. At the same time, budgetary constraints have harmed the readiness of the United States military while problematic ac-

---

poration, 2015). This is a first volume in a "Strategic Rethink" series from Rand). The preface to this volume appropriately notes that it "should be of interest to [among others] … the staff and advisers to the 2016 presidential candidates.…" *Id.* at *iii*.

27. There is no question that Saddam Hussein and his regime were thoroughly evil. The Hussein regime initiated aggressive wars against Iran and Kuwait, they committed horrific human rights abuses against Shia and Kurd populations in Iraq, they brutally tortured American POWs during the Gulf War, they attacked Israel with Scud missiles during the War, and they flaunted United Nations arms control inspections in the years after that War. But before the Iraq War, United States pressure had forced Iraqi compliance with much tougher on-site arms control inspections, and, according to George Tenet as then head of the CIA, at that time there was no credible threat from Hussein against the United States. The better course would have been to wait out the new much tougher on-site inspection regime while continuing economic sanctions against the Hussein regime.

tors, such as China and Russia, have continued to increase their military. Other problems in meeting these challenges have included repeated failures, from the Vietnam War, through the War in Afghanistan and the Iraq War, to the war against ISIL, to follow professional military advice for any necessary war fighting; an embrace during the George W. Bush Administration of a "torture-lite" policy which alienated America's allies and damaged the intelligence community; reduced effectiveness of the critical National Security Council system for coordinating United States policy on an interagency basis; absence of an effective structure to engender lasting and meaningful democratic governance in post-conflict settings such as Afghanistan and Iraq; and massive leaks in classified materials undercutting our ability to obtain crucial intelligence information and angering our allies.[28]

The Law Of The Sea

As another serious problem inhibiting effective United States engagement abroad, the Republican Senate caucus has acquiesced to an isolationist faction within the Party which has opposed United States adherence to the Law of the Sea Convention with a patina of canards that has to date blocked United States adherence. This Convention, supported by all American Presidents of both parties, the United States Military (and particularly the Coast Guard and the Navy), and American industry (including the oil companies and our one remaining deep seabed mining company), the environmental community, and meeting all of the conditions set by President Ronald Reagan, expands United States resource jurisdiction in an area greater than the Louisiana Purchase and the acquisition of Alaska combined. United States non-adherence to date, in the face of overwhelming international acceptance of the Convention, has cost United States leadership in oceans policy, a greatly weakened United States ability to engage in critical oceans issues affecting the Arctic Ocean and the South China Sea, and the loss of two of the four United States deep seabed mine sites with strategic mineral deposits of an estimated value of half a trillion dollars, while China and Russia move aggressively to lock up strategic deep seabed sites in America's absence.

---

28. As a consumer of intelligence information in the United States Government I was raised on a system of strict need-to-know. Somehow, the Nation lost its way in the wide sharing of intelligence after 9/11; an understandable reaction motivated by the need for sharing critical information across then government intelligence stovepipes. The Nation needs a more carefully thought out solution to these two real problems; protecting classified information and sharing across capabilities and agencies where needed.

China & The South China Sea

The South and East China Sea disputes are also a problem requiring early attention. The United States has a direct interest in protecting navigational freedom in the area and has important defense treaties with the Philippines and Japan. Every effort should be made to have China understand that its own interest lies, not in aggressive actions toward its neighbors, but in cooperative efforts with Japan and the ASEAN nations to peacefully resolve these island and oceans boundary disputes.

ISIL

The threat from ISIL, now controlling large swaths of both Syria and Iraq, is real. ISIL is destabilizing the Arab Middle East and parts of Africa, is breeding a global terrorist threat, and is working at generating violence in America and Europe. While ISIL likely could have been more easily stopped in its formative period, the challenge today is formidable. An early priority for the new President will be to explore the potential for a global or regional coalition, effective military options, and effective political options[29] to defeat ISIL. The difficulty of implementing an effective strategy should not be underestimated.

Russia & Ukraine

The crisis in Ukraine is also real and dangerous. Russia, under Putin, must be deterred from further escalating the crisis in the Ukraine, or elsewhere. If possible, and it may not be, Russia should also be brought back more effectively into détente. A carefully thought out combination of enhanced deterrence, including in Ukraine, and renewed diplomacy to explore possible areas of agreement, would seem required.[30] We should not forget that throughout the Cold

---

29. At this stage there are few attractive options, particularly political options, in the fight against ISIL. Though opposing the Iraq War, the author convened a group of experts in Washington D.C. when it became evident that the War would take place, to discuss a constitution for Iraq. At that time the author recommended a federal structure for Iraq, with separate areas of significant autonomy for Kurds, Sunnis and Shia, under a strong Iraqi central government. If there is any possibility of Sunni tribal leaders abandoning the extreme ISIL leaders, some alternative political mechanism might be needed, given the failure of the Iraqi Government to generate confidence in its Sunni population. A federal system for the Kurds, Sunnis and Shia, under a weakened central Iraqi Government, may be one of the few remaining political possibilities in taking on ISIL in Iraq.

30. Of these, the critical current need is for enhanced deterrence. No one should have illusions about the ease of restoring détente with Russia, but détente should remain on the table as a United States objective.

War America continued to negotiate arms control and other agreements with the then Soviet Union. Putin is playing an increasingly dangerous, and self-destructive, game in the Ukraine, in Syria, and in partnerships with China and Iran. Russia, a major nuclear power, must be an early and important focus of the new President.

North Korea

The increasingly erratic behavior of North Korea, another nuclear nation, will also require prompt and careful Presidential attention. The United States, in conjunction with the United Nations Security Council, which still guarantees South Korea against North Korean aggression, should send a clear deterrent message to the leadership of North Korea. It is an absence of deterrence which motivates the North to higher risk behavior. If, of course, North Korea can enter into useful discussions with South Korea such discussions should be encouraged. In addition to deterring North Korean aggression against its neighbors, America also has an important interest in discouraging North Korean export of its nuclear technology.

Iran

Though Iran is in focus as a result of the Iran Nuclear Agreement, Iran is one of the largest supporters of terrorism in the world today, including its support for Hamas, Hezbollah, militias in Iraq, the Houthi rebels in Yemen, the Bashar al-Assad regime in Syria, and at least past attacks against United States military directly in Lebanon and Iraq. An important challenge facing the new President is how to more effectively deter these seriously destabilizing actions by Iran. It is time to stop ignoring the Iranian commitment to terrorism! Nor is Iran's support for terrorism unrelated to Iran's deepening repression at home; yet another issue crying out for a strong American voice rather than a diminishingly audible murmur!

Supporting Democracy & The Rule Of Law Abroad

Finally, it is a sad reality that the period of rapid democratization following the 1990 collapse of the former Soviet Union, and the brief period of hope associated with the "Arab Spring," have given way to push-back by totalitarian and authoritarian leaders, civil wars supported by brutal totalitarian factions, and increasing repression in Russia, Iran, China, Venezuela, and many other countries. America faces a serious challenge in restoring the earlier global momentum toward democracy and the rule of law; a momentum so important for peace, human rights, economic development, and national well-being.

David J. Kramer, one of the world's top experts on democracy, human rights and the rule-of-law, will address this challenge.

General Recommendations

A few broad recommendations on these defense and foreign policy challenges include:

- **America must be engaged in the world and must lead.** The siren song of isolationism may be tempting but is a formula for decline. America must provide the leadership for a more peaceful and stable world;
- **America must keep its word and be true to its allies.** Deterrence against security threats depends heavily on a reliable America. Once credibility is lost, it is difficult to regain, and the loss makes for a riskier world;
- **America must never engage in foreign wars when better options are available.** The great destructiveness of war, the human cost, and the unpredictable nature of war, suggest that, except in defense against attacks on America or our allies, or severe threats against the Nation or our allies, the Nation should proceed with the greatest caution in committing the United States military to foreign wars. Short of war America has a broad panoply of foreign policy tools, including providing leadership to principally affected nations, economic sanctions, logistics support, training and intelligence support;
- **Once a war is undertaken, America should fight to win, and win decisively.** The President is the constitutionally designated Commander-in-Chief. War-fighting decisions should be based on professional military advice, vetted throughout the course of the war, directly with the President;
- **The United States military requires increased support now.** Readiness, following years of conflict in Afghanistan and Iraq, has dropped substantially while the threat, including the geographic range and combat mode of potential engagement, has increased. According to the National Defense Panel, commissioned by Congress to review the 2014 Quadrennial Defense Review, our military faces "major readiness shortfalls that will, absent a decisive reversal of course, create the possibility of a hollow force...."[31]
- **Ideas matter. America, working with its allies, must engage robustly in the political struggle against destructive ideologies such as that of Al-Qaeda,**

---

31. William J. Perry and John P. Abizaid, *Ensuring a Strong U.S. Defense for the Future: The National Defense Panel Review of the 2014 Quadrennial Defense Review*, Washington, D.C.: United States Institute of Peace, July 2014, at 36. *See also* Robert H. Scales, "Our Army is breaking," *The Washington Post* cols. 2-4, at A13 (August 2, 2015).

Boko Haram, and ISIL. And our own engagement, whether on the battlefield or in the war of ideas, must adhere to our values of human rights, the rule of law and religious freedom;

- **The level of cyber-attacks against America and American industry is out-of-control and must be deterred.** Deterring such attacks, with closer cooperation of both government and industry, is a priority;[32]

- **Economic sanctions today are light years ahead of economic sanctions of old and if used effectively can be a distinctive tool of American foreign policy.** Global trade, and financial transactions implemented through the global banking system, among other interactions, are essential for modern nations. When America is successful in coordinating such sanctions with the European Union, China, Russia and the United Nations, as it was in sanctions against Iran, the potential to enforce compliance with the non-proliferation treaty (the NPT) and to end support for terrorism is great. We should not underestimate the potential for such measures as an alternative to use of force when they are broadly implemented internationally and are maintained with strength and determination.[33] We should not have abandoned these sanctions against Iran without insisting on full compliance with the NPT and full compliance with the non-use of force norms of the Charter;

- **The recent nuclear deal with Iran is weak.** It should not have permitted Iranian enrichment given the past Iranian violations of the Non-Proliferation-Treaty (the NPT), and despite the agreement's safeguards, it is likely inherently unverifiable should Iran be committed to a nuclear bomb. It is too narrow in failing to focus, as well, on compliance by Iran with the fundamental non-use of force norms embodied in Article 2(4) of the United Nations Charter with respect to all of Iran's neighbors, including Israel. It is weakness, not strength, for the Group of 5 plus 1, under United

---

32. According to *The Economist*: "If Chinese spies broke into an American Government building and stole important documents, or were seen planting explosives in the electric grid, uproar or worse would ensue. Yet state-supported Chinese hackers have, officials say, been getting away with the digital equivalent for years, with notably little response." *The Economist*, "Cyber-security Trouble Shooting," Sept. 12, 2015, at 27. Cyber-security includes, among other issues, espionage, theft of commercial secrets, and "digital" as a weapon for intimidation or destruction.

33. Smart sanctions, when levied against individual human rights violators and purveyors of terror, as opposed to sanctioning an entire country, also have demonstrated considerable effectiveness. There is pending in the Congress a bi-partisan "Global Magnitsky Human Rights Accountability Act" which, if enacted, would provide America with an even sharper tool against these individual bad actors.

States leadership, to mobilize enormous sanctions pressure on Iran but to apply none of that pressure to Iran's continuing support for terrorism around the world.[34] The global concern that Iran not obtain a nuclear bomb is, of course, strongly related to Iran's support for terrorism and its blatant threats of aggression. These are not "separate" issues. Unfortunately, by concluding the agreement as a fait accompli, whatever the vote in the Congress the Administration will have left the United States isolated in any future effort to roll back the agreement. What can be done is enhanced military support to Israel and American allies in the Gulf, and coordination with America's allies to make it clear to Iran that future cheating by Iran with the agreement, including its NPT pledge not to develop a bomb, will be met by whatever actions are necessary, including the use of force, to uphold the NPT and decisively prevent an Iranian nuclear bomb. To add to the deterrent effect of such a United States pledge, and thus reduce the risk that an actual use of force would be required, Congress should enact a joint resolution making "No Iranian Nuclear Bomb" a national policy;

- **America should work internationally to hold terror states accountable through civil damages for the killing and destruction they cause.** The rule of law generates a right to seek civil damages against those who unlawfully kill or destroy the property of others. Yet we continue to provide sovereign immunity to the purveyors of terror around the world; insulating them from suit in domestic courts. A protocol to the twelve international anti-terrorism Conventions, already in force for the United States, which would extend the current criminal penalties under those Conventions to include civil judgments against the purveyors of terror, such as Iran and its leaders today, is now available. This protocol should be actively supported by the United States. Billion dollar judgments against terror-nation assets around the world, and those of their leaders, are potentially one of our most effective tools in the fight against terror;[35]

---

34. The deal to "normalize" relations with Cuba is also weak. Diplomacy is our most important path to resolving international differences. But when America negotiates, it should do so with strength and appropriate bottom line goals. Negotiating with the Castro regime may be a useful strategy, but a deal should have required real concessions in liberalizing the regime, freeing political prisoners, and improving the plight of the Cuban people. A weaker deal simply perpetuates the Castro Gulag.

35. For a copy of this Draft Protocol to the United Nations Anti-Terrorism Conventions see John N. Moore, "Civil Litigation Against Terrorism: Neglected Promise" in *Legal Issues*

- **More effective engagement in the Israeli/Palestinian Conflict.** America has, in the past, played an important role in efforts at peace in this lingering conflict. Choices today, whether premised on a continuing status quo or a two-state solution, have become more difficult. It is likely that through time such choices will become even more difficult for both Israelis and Palestinians. As such, America should explore diplomatic openings offering promise while continuing to support Israel against aggression and terrorism;
- **More effective engagement in the United Nations.** The United Nations has serious problems, including its blatant discrimination against Israel. But the failure of more effective American engagement has only made matters worse and empowered our enemies. We need a tougher policy of engagement with the United Nations to support American foreign policy and American values, and those of our allies. In this connection, we should examine "collective security" generally with a view to greater before-the-fact deterrence, explore the Canadian initiative for a more effective stability force as an alternative to unilateral American action, engage more vigorously in diplomatic lobbying in capitals on UN issues, seek to end the Israel bias which cripples the UN in the Middle East, work to enhance a "democracy caucus" in the UN, and press for more effective UN engagement on promoting democracy and the rule of law;
- **America should deploy an effective anti-ballistic missile system, whether land-based or mobile sea-based, to protect against rogue-nation ballistic missile threats.** Unlike the era of the ABM Treaty with the USSR, when effective ABM systems required air bursts of nuclear warheads, effective non-nuclear ABM technology is now virtually on the shelf, particularly for mobile sea-based systems.

Admiral Dennis C. Blair, the former Commander-in-Chief of the United States Pacific Command and, more recently, the Director of National Intelligence in the Obama Administration, will present a paper on these critical defense and security issues. He will be followed by Professor Chester A. Crocker, one of the Nation's preeminent experts in foreign policy, a former Assistant Secretary of State for African Affairs, and the former Chairman of the Board of Directors of the United States Institute of Peace, who will present a paper on foreign policy issues facing the Nation and questions for the candidates on those issues.

---

in the Struggle Against Terror, J.N. Moore and R.F. Turner, eds., Durham: Carolina Academic Press, 2010, at 231.

To Establish Justice & Insure Domestic Tranquility

America has serious problems with its justice system. Too many Americans are in jail serving long sentences for non-violent crimes, nevertheless there is still too much violent crime, especially gang-related shootings in our largest cities, and our police are not always adequately funded or adequately trained.[36]

Too Many In Jails And Prisons

The Nation's prison and jail population has more than quadrupled since 1980. With less than 5% of the world's population the United States has nearly a quarter of the World's prison and jail population. According to a recent Washington Post article, approximately 1 in 100 adults in America are behind bars.[37] The cost is great to house this many prisoners, but even greater in the loss of potential earnings power, higher unemployment rates, and damage to the families of the incarcerated. Moreover, we are using jails to house too many of our mentally ill, rather than providing effective medical treatment and care.[38] For

---

36. The justice system has other issues not discussed here. For example, civil forfeiture, morphing from the war on drugs to many other areas of criminal law enforcement, and permitting seizure of assets without judicial process, is greatly in need of review. Some twenty years ago, Congressman Henry Hyde, the Chairman of the House Judiciary Committee, wrote an important book on civil forfeiture abuses and their encroachment on property rights and civil liberties. Henry Hyde, *Forfeiting Our Property Rights: Is Your Property Safe From Seizure?* (Cato Institute, 1995). Subsequently, the abuses have gotten worse, leading to a recent *Washington Post* expose. *See* Michael Sallah, Robert O'Harrow Jr. & Steven Rich, "Stop and Seize," *Washington Post*, page A1 (Sept. 7, 2014). If police department budgets should receive any funding at all from civil forfeitures, which may be doubtful, it should be under careful controls to protect property rights of the innocent, require genuine due process for forfeitures, and protect associated civil liberties.

37. Sari Horwitz & Nikki Kahn, "Unlikely Allies," *Washington Post*, page A1, cols. 2-4 (Aug. 16, 2015) (A story about how left and right are coming together for sentencing reform.)

38. *See, e.g.*, Justin Volpe, "Jail is No Place for People with Mental Illness," *Washington Post*, at cols. 1-2, page B3 (Sept. 27, 2015). *See also* "Editorial: Jamycheal Mitchell's ghastly death," *Washington Post*, at cols. 1-3, page A22 (Oct. 4, 2015). "For want of an available bed in a state psychiatric hospital, Jamycheal Mitchell, a mentally ill young man in Virginia who shoplifted a soda and two snacks worth $5.05 from a 7-Eleven, wasted away behind bars for four months, all but ignored by jail staff who should have noticed his catastrophically deteriorating health. Incoherent, emaciated and filthy, he died in his cell in August. Police are now investigating." *Id.* at col. 1.

the world's leading democracy this silent blight of over incarceration is not just wrong, but a national scandal.

We have come to this sad state in part because of a genuinely difficult war on drugs, in part because of sentencing reforms aimed at encouraging uniform sentencing, in part because we have tended to criminalize every infraction whether or not violent, and in part because politics supports a message of "tough on crime;" thus supporting tougher and tougher criminal laws and sentencing. But what is really needed are more effective policies in preventing crime. We are also much overdue for a National Commission to review the sentencing guidelines for non-violent offenses to make sentences more appropriate for the crime. But the problem goes beyond sentencing and more effective crime prevention. We have made one non-violent offense after another subject to criminal penalties. Literally, we have piled law upon law, and embellished them with criminal sanctions and prison terms. This excessive criminalization too should be reviewed in light of penalties other than incarceration, and sanctioning approaches other than criminalization. Did the Nation really benefit from putting Martha Stewart in jail at enormous cost to the taxpayer rather than simply levying a large fine against her? Did the criminal charge against the accounting firm Arthur Andersen, a corporation rather than a person, serve the national interest when it destroyed one of the big five American accounting firms in 2002, putting over 80,000 innocent employees out of work for the asserted abuse by a few in their accounting for the bankrupt Enron Corporation?[39] Would a substantial fine, or license suspension of the individuals involved, as opposed to a corporate criminal sanction, have been more in the national interest? Have we applied criminal sanctions too broadly to the business world?

Further, Texas and other states, along with many other countries in the World, are exploring alternatives to lengthy incarceration.[40] Some of these approaches seem to be working well. A national criminal justice review should be looking carefully at all of these issues, more effective policies in preventing crime, sentencing reform, over criminalization, better alternatives for those needing psychiatric care, and alternatives to lengthy jail sentences. The paper by Harry R. Marshall, Jr., a former Senior Legal Adviser in the Criminal Division of the United States Justice Department, explores a range of these issues in reducing prison populations.

---

39. The criminal conviction of the Arthur Andersen firm was subsequently set aside by the Supreme Court. But this came too late to save the reputation of the firm itself.

40. See, e.g., Reid Wilson, "Juvenile prison populations fall as states' changes take effect," The Washington Post cols. 1-3 A5 (February 1, 2015).

Reducing Crime And Enhancing Community/Police Relations

Despite previously unprecedented levels of incarceration, the Nation still has a serious crime problem, a problem particularly acute in victimizing minority communities in major cities. This blends with too few resources for police departments, too little community understanding of the difficulties faced by the police, and sometimes inadequate police training, to generate the witches' brew of disorders and reduced trust between the police and the residents they serve—a toxic brew seen recently in Ferguson, New York, Baltimore, and other cities. This too is a major national problem, and a complex one, which must be addressed. Quite possibly we must enact even tougher laws for repeat violent offenders or firearm homicides. But the problem will not be solved simply by increasing incarceration rates.

Two of the papers being presented in this initiative address these intertwined problems of enhancing police and community relations. Collectively, these papers address likely the most effective avenues to crime prevention; much more effective anti-crime pro rule-of-law education of our youth, and "community" or "relational policing," much more effectively engaging the police and the community it serves. The first paper, mentioned briefly above in the discussion of education, is the paper by Dr. Roy S. Godson on "Education against Crime: Fostering Culture Supportive of the Rule of Law." If we were able to better instill an anti-crime message in our public schools, a message rooted in powerful information about the costs to the perpetrator, the victim, the city, minority communities, and society in general, we would be reaching the most important point for crime control—that is, the belief system of the individual.[41] Dr. Godson has pioneered the teaching of these innovative programs around the world. They deserve a trial in America.

The second paper; that by Chief Timothy J. Longo, Sr., the nationally respected Chief of Police of Charlottesville, Virginia, addresses "Relational Policing," a title the Chief believes better addresses needed engagement than "Community Policing." Chief Longo's paper addresses how greater police involvement directly with residents in a community can both assist the police and lead to safer communities. More effective policing will likely require higher police budgets for more old-fashioned "walking the beat," more police, higher salaries for police, community youth programs run by the police, greater police training

---

41. While not offering a panacea for mass killings; killings which are all too frequently committed by mentally ill shooters, a major anti-crime educational initiative just might help to reduce the frequency of these atrocities. *See also* the work of the Duke University School of Medicine Professor, Dr. Jeffrey Swanson in mental illness and the prevention of gun violence.

(particularly in settings involving potential use of deadly force), and other modalities of engendering greater interaction and greater trust between the police and the community which they protect. But the reduction in crime and enhanced respect for the police and the rule-of-law more broadly just might make it a bargain. While such programs are not new in America, their adoption on a larger scale could make a difference. This enhanced "Relational Policing," too, deserves a try.[42]

Strengthening The Judiciary

The courts are a crucial fundament of our rule-of-law democracy. We rightly believe that America has a criminal justice system rooted in fundamental protections for the accused. For the most part that is the case. Recent investigations, however, many triggered by newer DNA science, have demonstrated too many times where the innocent have been convicted. A review of these cases shows that most relate to issues of witness identification (frequently involving poor line-up or other witness identification missteps), junk science, incompetent representation, or over-zealous prosecution at the trial level. All of these issues can and should be addressed in a careful review by new Justice Department leadership (and the equivalent in all fifty states) to ensure that American courts remain the bastion of a free people. We must also ensure adequate public defenders to make our adversary system work as it was designed.

The Supreme Court of the United States has traditionally come under fire by those who disagree with its decisions. But the Supreme Court is a core institution of our great democracy. It is not designed to reflect the will of the majority, which is a principal role of the Congress, but rather to implement the rule-of-law in interpreting statutes and applying the Constitution of the United States (including the Bill of Rights) and its system of checks and balances. Some discourse about the Court seems to assume that its task is to clear the way for congressional action. A more Madisonian way of thinking about the Court, however, is that it is the principal bulwark in protecting the multiple protections for our freedoms which are built into the Constitution. The Court protects the separation of powers between the legislative and executive branches. It protects states' rights in our federal system. It protects the integrity of the electoral process. And it protects individual freedom as guaranteed in the Bill of Rights, including freedom of speech and the press as a crucial "fourth estate"

---

42. Some of this is already underway in Baltimore. See the story in the *Washington Post* of August 16, 2015, at page C1 "Mending Ties in Fractured City," featuring recent youth community engagement in Baltimore by Interim Police Chief Kevin Davis.

so necessary for effective governance. The Court does all of the above by applying the Constitution of the United States as the highest law of the land. As
a human institution the Court may sometimes get it wrong, and given its role
in protecting minority freedoms, it will frequently be criticized by the public.
But the alternative to the Court is a Westminster style democracy without the
checks and balances which remain the genius of our Constitution.

In its role in interpreting statutes, however, a strain of thought about interpretation is harming the work of the Court. It is an approach to interpretation which should, I believe, concern the Congress whose work is being
interpreted in these cases. This interpretive approach is also misleading some
to believe that the approach restrains the Court, when the opposite is true. Inevitably, legislation and regulations will be filled with semantic and syntactic
ambiguity.[43] This is simply the nature of ordinary language. Not surprisingly,
it is these ambiguities which make their way to the Court. As such, most interpretive decisions at the Supreme Court level can be reasonably argued for
either interpretation of the statutory language. It is simply myth to believe that
the language in these cases coming before the Court always carries a "plain and
natural meaning." The interpretive error is to argue in interpreting an Act of
Congress, as does at least one Justice of the Court in quite vehement language,
that it is impermissible to examine legislative history.[44] Instead, according to

---

43. It is theoretically possible to run a draft of statutory language through a computer
to identify syntactic ambiguities (that is, those ambiguities dealing with the logic of language) before a legislature acts. In reality, however, while perhaps possible at the edges as
an aide in the work of the legislature, such programs generate so many ambiguities as to make
the legislative process cumbersome. In any event, the present reality is that legislative language, like ordinary language, is filled with both semantic and syntactic ambiguity.

44. For a flavor of the debate within the Court on this interpretive issue *See, e.g., Bank
One Chicago, N.A. v. Midwest Bank & Trust Co.*, 516 U.S. 264, 276-83 (1996) (Stevens, J. concurring, debating with Scalia, J., concurring); *Wisconsin Pub. Intervenor v. Mortier*, 501 U.S.
597, 610-12 n.4, 616-23 (White, J., writing for the Court, debating with Scalia, J. concurring). The strongest "textualist" on the Court, opposed to the use of legislative history generally, is Justice Scalia. One of the most striking "textualist" statements in the work of the
Court is the statement in the statutory interpretation decision, authored for the Court by
Justice Scalia, in the case of *Republic of Iraq v. Beaty*. The opinion in *Beaty* actually states in
authorizing a retroactive removal of jurisdiction from the Federal Courts: "We cannot say
with any certainty (for those who think this matters) whether the Congress that passed the
EWSAA *would have wanted* the President to be permitted to waive § 1605(a)(7) (emphasis
by the Court)." *Republic of Iraq v. Beaty*, 556 U.S. 848, 860 (2009). As the numerous *amicus* briefs in this case show, there was abundant legislative (and executive) history, as well
as textual analysis, to rule out the interpretation of the statutory language chosen by the
Court. *See, e.g.,* "Brief for Tortured American Prisoners of War as *Amici Curiae* Supporting

this view, only the language of the statute is relevant. But modern linguistics makes it clear that language takes much of its meaning from context. Legislative history may well provide that crucial context. Moreover, surely the obligation of the Court in interpreting an Act of Congress is to carry out the intent or purpose of the Congress, not that of the Court. In its interpretive role, as opposed to its role in assessing constitutionality, the Court is subordinate to the legislature. If examining additional legislative history, that is examining the maximum context available, holds better promise in getting to the congressional purpose behind the language, then surely the Court is obliged to do so. The Court should always review, not only the full language itself of a legislative enactment, but the maximum context likely to assist in understanding the congressional purpose. Some legislative history, of course, is of dubious value and may only reflect the view of an individual member of Congress, or even that of a staff member. But the Court has plenty of intellectual firepower to give minimal, if any, weight to such legislative history. Of course, too much should not be made of this difference in legislative interpretation. For legislative history also will frequently not carry conviction for the Court as to the congressional purpose. But the bottom line is that when the Court is simply interpreting an Act of Congress it is obliged to carry out the legislative purpose, not whatever purpose the Court believes may be better. It is mythology, and a mythology counter to modern linguistics, to believe that ambiguous language alone

---

Affirmance," (*Republic of Iraq, Et Al., v. Robert Simon, Et Al*) (This *amicus* brief, submitted to the Court by the author as Counsel for *Amici*, shows that the textual provision in question was drafted by the Executive and presented to the Congress for enactment with a written statement from the Executive as to its purpose; a purpose which did not include the interpretation accepted by the Court, *id*. at 11). *See also* for a purely linguistic analysis of this case, the "Brief of Dr. Stephen Neale as *Amicus Curiae* in support of Respondents," (*Republic of Iraq, v. Robert Simon, Et Al*). This latter brief, applying modern linguistics, clearly shows that language heavily takes its meaning from context. "Linguistic theory, the philosophy of language and cognitive science provide a concrete framework, within which it is possible to articulate a principled rationale for determining the plain meaning of statutory language.

These 'linguistic tools' include the theories of grammatical structure, linguistic context and pragmatic inference. The absence of such a framework has hampered the Court's ability to provide rules in the consistent interpretation of the plain meaning of statutory language...." *Id*. at 4. The author had an office next to then Professor Scalia at the University of Virginia Law School, and is an admirer of much of the Justice's jurisprudence. Elsewhere the author defended the Justice against an unfair attack made on the Justice's approach to treaty interpretation. *See* John Norton Moore, Treaty Interpretation, the Constitution and the Rule of Law (2001). But the Justice, and those on the Court following him in not taking account of legislative history in statutory interpretation, are seriously mistaken.

holds the answer to interpretation, and thus that it is impermissible to examine legislative history. The rule-of-law requires that the language embodied in the Congressional enactment, as well as its full context, is the basis for statutory interpretation. The importance of this obligation to properly implement congressional purpose makes this more than simply a personal choice in legal philosophy.

To Secure the Blessings of Liberty

American values of freedom, democracy, human rights (including freedom of religion, freedom of speech and the press, and property rights, among other human rights), and the rule of law, matter. These are not just "American values," but values which have emerged from bitter human struggle and experience (for example, as in the events leading to the British Magna Carta) even before the adoption of these values in our Constitution. Moreover, they are values which work cross culturally around the world. The core political struggle throughout much of human history has been between a ruling "vanguard elite" on the one hand, leading to totalitarian and authoritarian regimes with their largely unchecked power, and "democracy" on the other hand, with leaders chosen through periodic free elections and an array of checks and balances on the exercise of power. While the former model features "rule-by-law," as well as rule by naked power, as interchangeable modalities for sending regime opponents to the gulag, the latter model features "rule-of-law" as a check on power, and strong protections for the individual.

Half a century ago the relative superiority of these models was debated. Today we know that, in the aggregate, democracy wins by virtually all major social indicators. Democracies as a whole have fewer aggressive wars (and virtually never fight other democracies), have higher economic growth (though China for some time has been an exception as it leaves behind the disastrous economic policies of the Mao era), greater protection of human rights, better environmental protection, less famine, fewer refugees fleeing, and better performance on a host of other social indicators. Not surprisingly, America has sought to support transitions to democracy and the rule of law. The record is clear, enhanced success for those nations making the transition as in much of Eastern Europe, and continuing failure for those such as Cuba, Iran, North Korea, Sudan, Syria, Venezuela, and too many others. For America to assist transitions to democracy not only assists millions beyond our borders to have a better life, but it also contributes to enhanced American economic growth and reduced risk of war.

The Community Of Democracies

One policy which might be explored to more effectively further democracy and the rule of law abroad would be to work more effectively within the United States created "Community of Democracies" to generate a powerful "democracy caucusing group" within the United Nations as a counterpart to existing "regional groups," or more narrow functional groups such as the "Group of 77" developing countries. We should also coordinate with the Community of Democracies on a robust global educational program about the importance of democracy and the rule of law.

An African Democracy Center

A second policy, which would assist in Africa against the inroads of ISIL, would be to coordinate with the European Union and the Organization of African Unity to establish a major democracy training center in Africa for the training of African officials across the Anglophone divide, in both English and French. The Center would be a permanent bricks and mortar facility designed to train thousands of African leaders in weekend seminars, speeches all over Africa, month-long courses, and full degree programs. The United States and the European Union might each put in about 50 million U.S. dollars equivalent over a span of the first ten years in establishing the Center, with future expenditures gradually transferred to the Organization of African Unity, or simply a coalition of African democracies.[45]

David J. Kramer, the former President of Freedom House, and a former Assistant Secretary of State for Human Rights in the George W. Bush Administration, will present a paper "Supporting Democracy, Human Rights and Rule of Law," setting out why and how the United States should continue to support these core American values of democracy and the rule of law as important United States foreign policy goals.

---

45. This is an initiative I first jointly developed with Ms. Fern Holland, one of my former law students at Georgetown, who was assassinated in Iraq while leading the American effort on training in women's rights. Subsequently, the Congress of the United States appropriated a million dollars to fund a grant, implemented through Freedom House, exploring the feasibility with African leaders of establishing such an Institute. The response from African leaders was positive and a new American Administration should undertake talks with the European Union as to jointly funding such an Institute. Because of the contribution made by Ms. Fern Holland to this project, I believe that an appropriate part of any such Institute, such as scholarships to attend the Institute, should be in her name.

To Form a More Perfect Union

"[T]here are more instances of the abridgment of the freedom of the people by gradual and silent encroachments ... than by violent and sudden usurpations."
James Madison, Speech in the Virginia Convention, 1788

"It is of great importance in a republic not only to guard the society against the oppression of its rulers, but to guard one part of the society against the injustice of the other part."
James Madison, The Federalist No. 51 (1788).

The great genius of the United States Constitution is that it is structured to control power with periodic popular elections of our leaders, separation of powers between the Executive, the Legislative and the Judicial branches, a federal system dividing powers between the federal government and the states, and, with the adoption of the Bill of Rights, robust protections of fundamental rights of the individual—protections safeguarded even from the wishes of a majority. In this structure the American Constitution has centrally embodied the core principals separating failed totalitarian and authoritarian governments from successful liberal democracies. Some, in response to contemporary difficulties in governance, would have us fundamentally rethink this system, perhaps shifting to a Westminster Parliamentary type system. Would it not be easier for a Government to make things happen in such a system? But our Constitution was not designed to be make things happen easily. It was designed to check power. Americans should start each day thankful for that genius of James Madison and the other founders of this great Nation.

Controlling Fiscal Irresponsibility

But America does have governance problems. As the Nobel Prize winning economist James M. Buchanan wrote in a paper presented in October 2005 in my seminar on "The Rule of Law: Controlling Government" at Virginia, "Fiscal irresponsibility stares us in the face and cries out for correction."[46] Writing a decade ago, Buchanan understood with great clarity that the Nation was embarked on a massive increase in spending. How much worse it has become since! Professor Buchanan also saw clearly that one of the paths to such spend-

---

46. James M. Buchanan, "Responsibility, Generality and Natural Liberty," (A paper delivered at the seminar on "The Rule of Law: Controlling Government," the University of Virginia School of Law (10/8/2005 draft).

ing was to focus the taxes necessary to pay for even a portion of this spending tsunami on a narrower and narrower base of the electorate. Doing so would postpone, or prevent altogether, the otherwise inevitable tax revolt. Addressing America's fiscal problems then requires both a focus on controlling spending and an end to populist efforts to narrow the tax base onto a minority referred to as "the wealthy." Sadly, the constitutional framers built in no direct checks on fiscal irresponsibility, and with the adoption of the Sixteenth Amendment in 1913 authorizing the income tax, a way was open to progressively narrow the tax base. The framer's original structure, of course, did not contemplate direct taxes on incomes opening a path to a progressive narrowing of the tax base; a core mechanism incentivizing out-of-control spending.

Professor Buchanan suggested that one way to get this fiscal irresponsibility under control was to adopt a principle of generality preventing government from taking any discriminatory measures. Under such a principle, if we had an income tax, all Americans would pay the same percentage of their income in taxes. While there is much to be said for this principle, which is a core principle of non-discrimination underlying the rule of law, it may be that the Nation has gone too far down the road of progressive income taxes to adopt such a principle, for example through a single flat-tax system, or even through an elimination of the income tax in return for a value added or national sales tax. As such, what is to be done? As a start either or both political parties might adopt a platform with a double pledge; first, pledging to work to reduce the deficit through spending reductions—aiming at a balanced budget within ten years, and second, pledging that the top income tax rate will never exceed 33% (with 15% as the top rate on dividends and long-term capital gains).[47]

Ultimately, it would be desirable to then adopt these principles as constitutional amendments, with, of course, the necessary requirement that the budgetary ceiling must be flexible in wartime. This "Fiscal Responsibility" Amendment, addressing both spending and taxing limits, would become the 28th Amendment to the Constitution (Amendment XXVIII). As an alternative, America might simply repeal the Sixteenth Amendment, authorizing "taxes on incomes," as an aberration inconsistent with the framer's Constitution. The lost revenue could be made up by a new federal sales or value added tax. Such a tax, on consumption instead of income, would both enhance economic growth, and abolish the complexity (with its substantial compliance costs), and supported special interests, of the current income tax code. The progressivity of such a

---

47. In this connection, long term means a year or longer. To extend this period as a requirement to qualify for the long term rate would generate even greater market inefficiencies than is caused by the tax distortion of the present one-year holding period.

consumption tax could easily be adjusted as desired by exempting food, clothing, housing and medical services from the tax, among other possibilities.
Moreover, a new "earned income credit" type safety net could be structured
to greatly simplify, and likely increase in doing so, current safety net programs
and payments.

Congress And The Budget

There is also a second serious governance problem. The Congress of the United
States has lost its way in implementing a normal budget cycle. In recent years,
the Congress has been unable to reach agreement on budget in a timely manner,
and the Nation has been run on continuing resolutions, or even equal percentage cuts across all programs whatever their relative priority or merit. The Nation
needs to return to a thoughtful budget process, with considered authorizations
and appropriations across the range of federal programs, and then enactment in
a timely manner. A major cause of the budgetary dysfunction, of course, has been
serious and important differences about controlling the national deficit. The President of the United States has also been a key player in this dysfunction. But the
occasion of a new Administration needs also to be an occasion for Congressional
leaders of both parties to come together to restore the normal budgeting process
and review other ways in which the work of the Congress might be facilitated.

Further, the Nation should not be threatened with government shut downs,
or credit downgrades, because of a Congressional or Presidential inability to
reach agreement on the budget. Nor does the gimmick of a vote on "the debt
ceiling" make sense after the Congress has already spent the money and borrowed to pay for it. This "debt ceiling" gimmick only casts shameful doubt on
America's willingness to live up to its existing debt obligations.[48] It should be
abolished as unfit for an honorable Nation.

Professional Military Advice

America has an additional governance problem as well, one which has come
about through repeated amendments to our defense structure—a gradual
change made without any real debate. We may have given the civilian Secretary of Defense too much authority in directing war-fighting once the Nation
commits, as opposed to greater reliance on professional military advice offered
directly to the President as the constitutional Commander-in-Chief. Most

---

48. And, of course, a fight over the "debt ceiling" adds to volatility in our financial markets, as well as contributing to potential credit downgrades for the Nation, thus doubly
shooting America in the foot.

Americans are unaware that there was no Secretary of Defense in World War II. That War was successfully fought with military advice from our professional military directly to the President of the United States. It was only in the aftermath of World War II that we created a Department of Defense (a necessary structure for then needed integration and specialized services) and a civilian Secretary of Defense. The civilian Service Secretaries of the Army and the Navy have been removed from the war-fighting chain for some time. There is, of course, a second major role for all of the civilian Service Secretaries, and for the Secretary of Defense. That is, the awesome responsibility of administering the Defense Department, with all of its defense agencies, office of the Secretary, office of the Joint Chiefs, and Armed Services. Its administrative responsibility includes the acquisition of weapons systems, training, and management of ongoing intelligence.

The war-fighting record of too many civilian Secretaries of Defense has not been good. Secretary McNamara systematically ignored professional military advice during the Vietnam War. Many military professionals today believe that War was winnable with normal war-fighting modes as recommended at the time by United States defense and intelligence professionals: isolate the battlefield by cutting the Ho Chi Minh Trail (after the War a North Vietnamese General said cutting the trail, and thereby preventing the required logistics supply for 300,000 North Vietnamese fighters in the South, would have defeated the North's aggression against South Vietnam), dramatically reduce Soviet resupply to the North by mining Haiphong Harbor (later done), use normal strategic bombing of military sites in the North (later done), build up South Vietnamese forces (later done), and adopt a "take and hold" anti-guerrilla war strategy as opposed to the "attrition" strategy used by General Westmorland in the early years of the War (later done by General Abrams).[49] Even without isolating the battlefield by cutting the Ho Chi Minh Trail, the War was eventually ended with an honorable peace in the Paris Accords, only to have the Congress pull the plug on further assistance to South Vietnam as Watergate disintegrated the presidency. But whether or not the Vietnam War was winnable, the war fighting by America was badly mishandled in the early years of the War, costing thousands of additional casualties for American service personnel.

Subsequently, Les Aspen, the then civilian Secretary of Defense, rejected professional military advice with respect to Somalia as tendered by General

---

49. For a quarter century the author has co-taught with a Vietnam veteran one of the Nation's top seminars on the Vietnam War; a seminar which has repeatedly vetted these and other issues with many of the Nation's wartime leaders, as well as historians and military experts on the War.

Colin Powell, then Chairman of the Joint Chiefs of Staff, to send adequate armor in country to deal with the contingency of "Black Hawk Down." That contingency occurred, and the resulting fiasco absent adequate armor quickly ended the United States effort in Somalia.

The successful 1991 Gulf War reverted to the Military Chiefs working closely with the President of the United States and was an extraordinary success. Going forward to the Iraq War, Secretary Rumsfeld ignored professional military advice as to the forces necessary during the occupation phase. Further, the Chiefs were not consulted on the extraordinary decision to send all of the Iraqi Army home or the draconian De-Bathification program firing the civilians running the government ministries, military advice to isolate the battlefield through forces necessary to seal the borders with Syria and Iraq went unheeded, and "take and hold" was effectively instituted only after General Petraeus arrived in Iraq. War-fighting in dealing with ISIL also seems questionable but this may be due to direct limitations imposed by the White House itself, rather than recommendations from the civilian Secretaries.

Has this questionable war-fighting in numerous post World War II conflicts been simply a happenstance of the wrong civilian Secretaries? Perhaps. Is modern war-fighting too complex for the President not to have a civilian adviser on war-fighting, as well as on the Administrative chain of command? Quite possibly. Certainly, we must maintain solid civilian control of the military, both a fundamental condition of democracy, and a Constitutional mandate with the President as Commander in Chief. We do so even accepting that from time to time Presidents themselves may make mistakes. But equally, we must involve the President of the United States, the constitutionally charged official, in critical war-fighting decisions.

Emphatically this is not an argument to "let the generals run the war." Generals can be wrong and Presidents right, as seems to have been the case for Lincoln in the Civil War and Truman in Korea. But when the Nation is committed to war, we must ensure that it is the President, the constitutionally designated Commander in Chief, who personally focuses on the conduct of the war, and who is advised directly by the Nation's professional military leaders.

Perhaps a starting point would be for the Presidential candidates, or their parties, to pledge that their Presidency will request professional military advice prior to any American commitments and war-fighting decisions, and that during the course of any war they will meet at least once per month with the Operational Commander, the Chairman of the Joint Chiefs, and the Chiefs, for a discussion of progress in the war. If this informal pledge proves useful through time, then we can more clearly incorporate this consultation recommendation into the statutory base of the Defense Department as a follow on to the Gold-water/Nichols Act. Such an approach would not remove the civilian Secretary of Defense from also offering war-fighting advice to the President, but it would more clearly prevent professional military advice from being excluded in critical war-fighting decisions.

Staffing A New Administration

As one more issue worthy of review by the Presidential candidates, and their parties, the candidate ultimately elected will need to staff their Administration. Getting the right team, and surely that means nothing less today than the A-Team, will be difficult. Increasingly, we have adopted so many conflict-of-interest, disclosure, and pre-clearance laws that it is harder to get the A-Team to agree to serve, and even after agreeing, the clearance and Senate approval processes take too long. The result has been a huge delay in getting an administration up and running.[50]

As examples, according to the Congressional Research Service, in the 112th Congress (2011-13) the mean time to move from nomination to confirmation was 151 days. And for the 113th Congress (2013-15) the mean time to move from nomination to confirmation was 119 days. And this was after the already time consuming nomination process.[51]

This problem of getting a new administration up and running will be a problem for either party which wins the Presidency. Further, addressing the problem after the election is too late, as most of these requirements are embedded in legislation. Of course, we must protect the government against unfit nominations, and we must maintain clean and good government. These are critically important goals! But surely we can simplify the current morass of appointment laws, and hopefully find more flexible solutions to problems pre-

---

50. I am indebted to former Secretary of State George Shultz for reminding me of this important issue directly related to the Presidential election cycle. For the Secretary's discussion of the importance, and contemporary difficulty, of staffing our government with the A-team, as well as other suggestions for better governance, *see* Chapter 2 "Better Governance," in George P. Shultz, Issues on My Mind: Strategies for the Future 9- 25 (2013).

51. According to the *New York Times*, as of May 2, 2013, "One of the worst backlogs is at the State Department, where nearly a quarter of the most senior posts are not filled, including those in charge of embassy security and counterterrorism. The Treasury Department is searching for a new No. 2, the Department of Homeland Security is missing its top two cybersecurity officials and about 30 percent of the top jobs at the Commerce Department are still vacant, including that of chief economist." *The New York Times*, http://www.ny-times.com/2013/05/03/us/politics/top-posts-remain-vacant-throughout-obama-adminis-tration.html.

venting the Nation's best from accepting appointment. As an initial suggestion, it might be useful for House and Senate leadership, in both Democratic and Republican parties, to agree to convene hearings about the appointment and confirmation process to see what might be done on a genuine bi-partisan basis prior to a new administration. Perhaps such hearings, with adoption of a bi-partisan agreed statutory solution shortly thereafter, might be held in the spring of 2016, well before the Presidential election and the next transfer of power.

Right-Sizing Government

How do we make decisions as to the right size of government? For too long we have debated the proper size of government along a "left-right" spectrum tracing back to the French Revolution. But we have much better understanding of government today, in part based on a fuller understanding as to the functioning of markets as well as the functioning of governments; that is, the strengths and limitations of each. I will be presenting a paper entitled "Freedom and Authority: Right-Sizing Government" which will offer a few thoughts on this fundamental issue. Hopefully, the categorizations of "government failure" offered in this paper may serve as a useful check list for assessing government programs.

A Postscript for the Candidates and the Press

For The Candidates

Congratulations on your decision to run for the Presidency of this great Nation! The experts gathered in this initiative hope that you will find the issues discussed and recommendations made in these papers helpful as you address the major problems and opportunities facing the Nation. We know that you are in a tough political race which you want to win. But we would ask that you make known to the American people what you regard as the major national problems, and your specific solutions for addressing each of those problems. The candidate who wins should be the candidate offering the best solutions, not the best sound bites. Ultimately this race belongs, not to you, but to the American people. For it is America, and its future, which are at stake.

For The Press

We hope that as you write about the candidates, and possibly assist in preparing questions for them in the Presidential debates, you will find the issues discussed, the questions posed, and the recommendations made in the papers presented in this initiative helpful. We know that each of us, including the members of the press corps, has preferences, whether on candidate, party or issues. But we would ask that you drill down on each of the candidates as to their views on the full scope of problems facing the Nation. Ultimately, it is through interaction of the candidates with the media that the American voter will make a determination as to which candidate has "the right stuff." We are privileged in America to have a free and robust media. You, the Fourth Estate, are an essential check to ensure that we put only the best candidate in the weighty office of the American Presidency. That means that you, too, have a solemn responsibility to the Nation as the debates, and the campaigns, go forward.

Focusing the Presidential Debates Initiative

Participants

- Admiral Dennis C. Blair, "Defense & Security Policy: Time for a Strategic Approach." Admiral Blair is the former Commander-in-Chief of the Pacific Command, former Deputy Director of the CIA, and Former Director of National Intelligence. He is one of the most esteemed voices in the Nation on defense and security policy;
- Professor Chester A. Crocker, "Foreign Policy." Professor Crocker is Professor of Strategic Studies at Georgetown's Walsh School of Foreign Service, former Assistant Secretary of State for African Affairs, and former Chairman of the Board of the United States Institute of Peace. He is one of the most respected voices in the Nation on foreign affairs;
- John H. Cochrane, "Economic Growth." Cochrane is a Senior Fellow at the Hoover Institution at Stanford University, a Research Associate of the National Bureau of Economic Research, and a Distinguished Fellow and formerly Professor of Finance at the University of Chicago Booth School of Business. Many top economists have told me that if anyone can recommend policies effectively to move the Nation forward at a more robust and sustained growth rate it will be John H. Cochrane;
- David J. Kramer, "Supporting Democracy, Human Rights and the Rule of Law." David is a former Assistant Secretary of State for Democracy, Human Rights and Labor, former Deputy Assistant Secretary of State for European and Eurasian Affairs, and former President of Freedom House. He is a top national leader in promoting democracy, human rights, and the rule of law;
- Dr. Steven R. Goldring, MD, "Targeting Disease: Musculoskeletal Conditions." Dr. Goldring is the Chief Scientific Officer Emeritus, and Richard

L. Menschel Research Chair, at the Hospital for Special Surgery in New York, Professor of Medicine at the Weill Cornell College of Medicine, former Professor of Medicine at Harvard Medical School, and former Chief of Rheumatology at Beth Israel Deaconess Medical Center. No one has a better understanding of what might be done to more effectively "target disease," starting with arthritis and related diseases, than Dr. Goldring;

- Harry R. Marshall, Jr., "Reducing Prison Populations: One of Many Needed Criminal Justice Reforms." Harry was a Senior Legal Adviser in the Criminal Division at the Department of Justice from 1991-2011, is an Adjunct Professor at the University of Virginia School of Law, and previously had a distinguished career as a Principal Deputy Assistant Secretary in the Department of State and as an ACDA Senior Attorney in the SALT Negotiations;

- Grover Norquist, "What Tax Reform Should Look Like Under the Next President." Grover is President of Americans for Tax Reform, a former economist at the U.S. Chamber of Commerce, and a former Commissioner on the National Commission on Restructuring the Internal Revenue Service. He is nationally prominent for his work to hold down taxes and reform the tax code;

- Peter Ferrara, "Social Security Optionality: Reducing the Wealth Gap," and "Controlling the Deficit." Peter is Director of the International Center for Law and Economics. He served as a senior staff member in the Reagan White House Office of Policy Development, and as an Associate Deputy Attorney General of the United States under President George H.W. Bush. He is the top expert in the world on meaningful Social Security Reform;

- Dr. Roy S. Godson, "Education against Crime: Fostering Culture Supportive of the Rule of Law." Dr. Godson is Professor of Government Emeritus at Georgetown University and former President of the National Strategy Information Center. He has pioneered the teaching of courses in public schools against crime and in support of the rule of law and is the leader internationally in this effort;

- Professor Peter Skerry, "Immigration Policy." Professor Skerry is Professor of Political Science at Boston College and a Nonresident Senior Fellow at the Brookings Institution. His research focuses on social policy and immigration, among other issues. He has been a Fellow at the Woodrow Wilson International Center for Scholars in Washington, D.C., and served as Director of Washington Programs for the University of California at Los Angeles' Center for American Politics and Public Policy, where he also taught political science. He was formerly a Research Fellow at the American Enterprise Institute, and Legislative Director for Senator Daniel Patrick Moynihan. He serves on the Editorial Board of the Journal of American Politics;

- Chief Timothy J. Longo, Sr., "Relational Policing." Chief Longo is the Chief of Police of the City of Charlottesville, Virginia. He is entering his 34th year in law enforcement and is nationally-recognized in the areas of police ethics and professional standards. He holds a law degree from the University of Baltimore, and from 1981-2000, he served on the Baltimore police force, where he commanded several divisions. Since 2001 he has served as Chief of Police for the City of Charlottesville, Virginia; and

- Professor John Norton Moore, "Introduction and Overview of Issues Facing the New President," and "Freedom and Authority; Right-Sizing Government." Professor Moore is the Walter L. Brown Professor of Law at the University of Virginia and directs both the Center for National Security Law and the Center for Oceans Law and Policy at Virginia. Formerly he served as a United States Ambassador, and as Chairman of the Board of the United States Institute of Peace. Much of his research has focused on democracy, the rule of law, and controlling government failure, as well as participating in founding the field of National Security Law. Professor Moore initiated this project and extended an invitation to the other participants.

Brief Biographies of the Participants

Admiral Dennis C. Blair

"Defense and Security Policy"

Admiral Blair is the former Commander-in-Chief of the Pacific Command, former Deputy Director of the CIA, and Former Director of National Intelligence. He is one of the most respected voices in the Nation on defense and security policy.

John H. Cochrane

"Economic Growth"

Mr. Cochrane is a Senior Fellow at the Hoover Institution at Stanford University, a Research Associate of the National Bureau of Economic Research, and a Distinguished Fellow and formerly Professor of Finance at the University of Chicago Booth School of Business. Many top economists have indicated that if anyone can recommend policies effectively to move the Nation forward at a more robust and sustained growth rate it will be John H. Cochrane.

Professor Chester A. Crocker

"Foreign Policy"

Professor Crocker is Professor of Strategic Studies at Georgetown's Walsh School of Foreign Service, former Assistant Secretary of State for African Affairs, and former Chairman of the Board of the United States Institute of Peace. He is one of the most respected voices in the Nation on foreign policy.

Peter Ferrara

"Social Security Optionality—Reducing the Wealth Gap" and "Controlling the Deficit"

Mr. Ferrara is Director of the International Center for Law and Economics. He served as a senior staff member in the Reagan White House Office of Policy Development, and as an Associate Deputy Attorney General of the United States under President George H.W. Bush. He is one of the top experts in the world on meaningful Social Security Reform.

Dr. Roy S. Godson

"Education Against Crime"

Dr. Godson is Professor of Government Emeritus at Georgetown University and former President of the National Strategy Information Center. He has pioneered curricula development and teaching to counter crime and in support of the rule of law in public schools and other sectors, and he is the leader internationally in this effort.

Dr. Steven R. Goldring, MD

"Targeting Disease—Musculoskeletal Conditions"

Dr. Goldring is the Richard L. Menschel Research Chair at the Hospital for Special Surgery in New York, Chief Scientific Officer Emeritus of the Hospital for Special Surgery, Professor of Medicine at Weill Cornell College of Medicine, former Professor of Medicine at Harvard Medical School, and former Chief of Rheumatology at Beth Israel Deaconess Medical Center. No one has a better understanding of what might be done to more effectively "target disease," starting with arthritis and other musculoskeletal conditions.

David J. Kramer

"Promoting Democracy, Human Rights and the Rule of Law"

Mr. Kramer is a former Assistant Secretary of State for Democracy, Human Rights and Labor, former Deputy Assistant Secretary of State for European and Eurasian Affairs, and former President of Freedom House. He is currently Senior Director for Human Rights and Democracy at the McCain Institute for International Leadership. Mr. Kramer is a top national leader in promoting democracy, human rights, and the rule of law.

Chief Timothy J. Longo, Sr.

"Relational [Community] Policing"

Chief Longo is the Chief of Police of the City of Charlottesville, Virginia. He is entering his 34th year in law enforcement and is nationally-recognized in the areas of police ethics and professional standards. He holds a law degree from the University of Baltimore, and from 1981-2000, he served on the Baltimore police force, where he commanded several divisions. Since 2001 he has served as Chief of Police for the City of Charlottesville, Virginia.

Harry R. Marshall

"Reducing Prison Populations"

Mr. Marshall was a Senior Legal Adviser in the Criminal Division at the Department of Justice from 1991-2011, is an Adjunct Professor at the University of Virginia School of Law, and previously had a distinguished career as a Principal Deputy Assistant Secretary in the Department of State and as an ACDA Senior Attorney in the SALT Negotiations.

Professor John Norton Moore

"Introduction and Overview of Issues Facing the New President" and "Freedom & Authority: Right-Sizing Government"

Professor Moore is the Walter L. Brown Professor of Law at the University of Virginia and directs the Center for National Security Law at Virginia. Among six presidential appointments, he has served as a United States Ambassador, as a Deputy Special Representative of the President, and as Chairman of the Board of the United States Institute of Peace. He has also been a Fellow at the Woodrow Wilson International Center for Scholars in Washington, DC, and served as the Co-Chairman with the Deputy Attorney General of the United States of the first talks between the United States and the then U.S.S.R. on the Rule of Law. Much of his research has focused on democracy, the rule of law, and controlling government failure, in addition to his work in founding the field of National Security Law. It is his invitation which has brought these twelve prominent Americans together in this initiative on "Focusing the Presidential Debates."

Grover Norquist

"Tax Reform"

Mr. Norquist is President of Americans for Tax Reform, a former economist at the U.S. Chamber of Commerce, and a former Commissioner on the National Commission on Restructuring the Internal Revenue Service. He is nationally prominent for his work to hold down taxes and reform the tax code.

Professor Peter Skerry

"Immigration Policy"

Professor Skerry is Professor of Political Science at Boston College and a Nonresident Senior Fellow at the Brookings Institution. His research focuses on social policy and immigration, among other issues. He has been a Fellow at the Woodrow Wilson International Center for Scholars in Washington, D.C., and served as Director of Washington Programs for the University of California at Los Angeles' Center for American Politics and Public Policy, where he also taught political science. He was formerly a Research Fellow at the American Enterprise Institute, and Legislative Director for Senator Daniel Patrick Moynihan. He serves on the Editorial Board of the Journal of American Politics.

Part One:
Economic Growth and
Domestic Policy

Introduction — Economic Growth and Domestic Policy

John Norton Moore

Once again this Great Nation has embarked on a journey to elect a new President. The candidates have come forward and the debates are under way. It is in the interest of all Americans that the candidates and their debates seriously address the grave national challenges and opportunities now before the Nation. We cannot afford politics as usual, with candidates vying to be the most immoderate in their Party. The challenges are unforgiving and the opportunities fleeting.

The experts participating in this initiative are deeply concerned about the problems facing this Great Nation and have come together to present suggestions and raise questions for the Presidential candidates, Democrat and Republican alike. The papers collected here have also been sent to each of the declared candidates in both parties. The campaign organization of each candidate, as well as the Democratic National Committee and the Republican National Committee, have also been notified of this initiative and were invited to send a representative to the press conferences.

Each paper reflects the view of the presenter. There has been no effort to coordinate views; nor is any presenter responsible for the views expressed by other presenters. Some of these papers may appeal more to Democratic candidates and some may appeal more to Republican candidates. The subjects, however, have been chosen for their national importance, and the presenters for their recognized expertise.

It is hoped that as the debates progress in and between both parties that the candidates, and the Nation more broadly, will reflect on the range of serious problems and will consider the questions and/or specific recommendations presented in these papers. We are not able to individually participate in the debates, but we hope to be heard by the candidates and the American people through the great institution of America's free press.

All of the expert papers and videos of the presentations are online at the Initiative website, www.focusingthepresidentialdebates.com.

Priority National Problems and Opportunities

A partial list of critical national problems and opportunities includes:

- Restoring the American economy to substantially higher levels of sustained economic growth. This growth goal is critical for our effectiveness in meeting almost all other national goals and must be one of the Nation's highest priorities;
- Restoring the United States military and defense communities to robust strength;
- Enhancing United States credibility and effectiveness in foreign affairs;
- Reducing and controlling the national debt;
- Reforming the Social Security System for greater effectiveness and long-term economic health;
- Reforming Obamacare (ACA), Medicare, and Medicaid for greater effectiveness in meeting national health goals and long-term economic health;
- Reducing taxes on Americans and American corporations, and more effectively controlling the regulatory burden on American business as critical elements in restoring growth;
- Reforming immigration policy to ensure that America will have border security and adequate enforcement, that immigration policy will support the economy, that there will be a one-time path to legal status for the many whose presence is benefiting the Nation, and that going forward immigration policy, like all national policies, will be guided by the rule-of-law;
- Reforming the criminal justice system by reducing incarceration for non-violent offenders and paring back overly broad use of the criminal justice system in non-violent offenses;
- Reducing crime through enhanced education against crime in our school systems, and more effective "community policing" through engaging the police more actively and directly with the communities they protect. The homicide rate in many of our major cities has surged recently, and it is our minority communities most at risk from any breakdown in mutual trust. Effectively reducing crime requires leadership from both police and the communities they serve. For the police, and the communities which depend upon them, are inevitably linked. When that link becomes frayed, both the police and the communities they serve are harmed;
- Embracing modern medical science in settings where a more robust national research program targeting a particular disease holds promise both for enhanced cure offering better relief to millions of Americans, as well as substantial cost savings for the Nation;

- Adopting a comprehensive energy policy leading to energy independence for America;
- Rebuilding our crumbling infrastructure of roads, bridges, dams, airports and the power grid;
- Enhancing educational opportunities for all Americans, and more effectively meeting skills-based educational needs in the workplace;
- More effectively promoting abroad the core American values of democracy and the rule-of-law;
- Reenergizing our national commitment to protection of the environment, including addressing the problem of global warming, but as with all governmental actions, doing so through cost-benefit effective measures;
- Ending tax and other laws discriminating against the family. Government actions should only strengthen and support the family;
- Restoring a normal budgeting process in the Congress of the United States;
- Paying greater attention to "right-sizing" government and reducing "government failure;" including revitalizing the role of the states in our federal system; and
- Assisting the process of forming a new Administration by streamlining the appointment and confirmation process.

To review this list is to appreciate the enormous challenge faced by the next President of the United States.

I now briefly review the issues of promoting economic growth, immigration policy, targeting disease, Social Security optionality, tax policy, and "right-sizing" government.

Promoting Economic Growth

The most serious challenge facing the Nation is restoring a more robust growth rate. In recent years we have become mired in a low growth trajectory. The resulting costs are immense; fewer good jobs, a growing deficit, crumbling infrastructure, stagnant wages, a widening wealth gap, a shrinking military, diminishing opportunity to support the environment, and less American influence abroad. Virtually every major national objective is touched by this poor economic performance. *As such, improving our growth rate is the Nation's number one problem.*

The good news is that even small differences in growth rates make large differences when compounded through time. Thus, to move from a 2% growth rate to a 4% growth rate will make the Nation as a whole 62% richer than it would otherwise be in just 25 years. In a generation (50 years) the Nation as a whole would be 164% richer at the 4% rate. The rate of sustained economic growth matters!

Though economics, like all social sciences, can be fuzzy at the edges, we know generally what works to promote growth and what works to retard growth. Lower taxes, particularly income and corporate taxes, profoundly affecting incentives to work and save, encourage growth. Higher taxes depress growth. Higher taxes on dividends and capital gains, doubly suppresses growth in depressing savings and investment. While environmental, safety, and other regulations are necessary to address market externalities, excessive regulation depresses growth. High quality education encourages growth. Reducing trade barriers enhances growth (though America needs much stronger engagement with China and others on "non-tariff barriers," such as "anti-trust" used by our trading partners to reduce the competitiveness of American companies). Facilitating small business encourages growth, as *small* business is, in reality, the *large* backbone of the economy. Facilitating women's access to the work force encourages growth. Repairing our crumbling infrastructure would enhance efficiency and encourage growth. And a climate of economic uncertainty, or perceived governmental hostility to business, including populist attacks on "wall street," can retard the "animal spirits" necessary for innovation.

The deficit and the national debt are critical problems. So too is the serious underfunding of our defense and foreign policy establishments. Both problems are joined at the hip with the growth problem. For enhancing the national growth rate to generate substantially increased revenues is the only good answer to these and many other national problems arising from our serious fiscal problems.

The paper by John H. Cochrane on "Economic Growth" addresses more fully how our Nation can meet its critical national need of enhancing growth. John Cochrane is one of the top economists in the Nation on promoting growth. I would urge anyone interested in this issue; the single most important issue facing the Nation, to read the excellent paper by Mr. Cochrane.

Immigration Policy

No nation can tolerate uncontrolled immigration. The Nation's borders must be secure and future immigration and legal status must be controlled by the rule of law rather than the clandestine crossing or the expired visa. We must also focus enforcement not just on illegal border crossings but also on illegal visa overstays; a major source of illegal immigration—including some of those who participated in the 911 attacks. But when the borders are secure and internal enforcement more effective, some one-time mechanism should be put in place to legally recognize the many individuals who have come to America to work, who have obeyed the law, who have paid taxes, some who may have gone to school in America, some who may even have served in the American military, and who seek legal status. America needs innovators and workers and our Nation traditionally has benefitted from immigration from every region in the world. Immigration policy should realistically take account of the economic needs of the Nation and of the reality that immigrants are embedded in our society in important ways.

The proposal to build a "Wall" and immediately deport the millions of immigrants thought to be in America illegally (and their family members), would have a devastating effect on the economy, in addition to the human misery, and the permanent blight on America's conscience. Costs of such a forced migration would include a major loss of productivity for American employers, as well as the economic and human costs of an army of enforcement agents. Nor would the "Wall" address the reality that perhaps as many as 40% or more of illegal immigrants are here because they have overstayed their visas.

Professor Peter Skerry, one of the Nation's top experts on immigration policy, explores in greater detail issues concerning Immigration Policy.

Targeting Disease

America also has important opportunities not yet addressed in the Presidential debates; opportunities with great meaning for millions of Americans. For example, medical research has come to the point that we may be able to much more effectively target disease through greater specific support. The national debate understandably has focused on access to medical care; but what if medical science has progressed on certain disease processes that a major directed effort, perhaps one disease process at a time on cures or treatments deemed promising, could dramatically reduce the burden of the disease? As is discussed in the "Right-Sizing Government" paper, basic research will be underfunded by markets because it is a "positive externality" in economic theory. There is, then, a case for government in filling this need. Our government, of course, through the National Institutes of Health, already makes substantial commitments to basic research in dealing with diseases; cancer, heart disease, aids, Alzheimer's, and other diseases. But if the cost to the Nation of certain diseases, through lost work and medical payments, is larger than the likely cost to better understand and cure the disease, and the science is promising enough to make that calculation, then it may be time to consider a national "moon shot" at curing, or at least better controlling, certain diseases. Indeed, perhaps if such a targeted approach is successful, the Nation might target one disease after another where the science suggests that the national savings from cure or better control would exceed the cost of the basic research. And, of course, a wonderful byproduct of any successes would be that millions of Americans would no longer be condemned to a lifetime of pain or disability.

As an initial hypothesis for such a "targeting disease" approach, there is considerable evidence to suggest that arthritis and musculoskeletal diseases today meet the criteria for a major national effort. Over fifty million Americans are affected by these diseases, more than twenty million have activity limitations from these conditions, and the direct and indirect economic cost in lost work and treatment costs is estimated to be over $200 billion per year. If a major research effort were able even to cut this cost in half, the *yearly* saving, repeated each year into the indefinite future, would be $100 billion.

Dr. Steven R. Goldring, MD, the Chief Scientific Officer Emeritus at the prestigious Hospital for Special Surgery in New York, has prepared a groundbreaking paper which should be considered carefully by all the candidates, discussing whether the cost of these diseases, the percentage of the American population affected, and the state of the scientific understanding, suggests that arthritis and musculoskeletal diseases would be a useful place to start in such a national "Targeting Disease" research initiative.

Social Security Optionality: Reducing the Wealth Gap

One of the most important papers is that by Peter Ferrara on "Social Security Optionality: Reducing the Wealth Gap." It is generally understood that, at minimum, the Social Security system can and must be adjusted to prevent the bankruptcy looming at the end of its current trajectory through either raising taxes or lowering benefits. There are simply fewer and fewer Americans supporting more and more retirees and changes must be made to avoid running short of funds to pay promised benefits.

The core of the Social Security problem, however, is not averting bankruptcy but the *horrible* job the system does for working Americans who pay into the system. Even if Social Security continues to pay all promised benefits, the real rate of return on the taxes paid into the system still would be less than 1%.

The "raising taxes and lowering benefits" route to Social Security "reform" also misses the Social Security "opportunity." That opportunity is to give American workers age 40 and under the opportunity to opt into a private investment account into which their Social Security taxes would be deposited and invested and which they would own. Their investments would then compound through time like a normal retirement account. A two-earner middle income couple at standard long term investing returns would retire after a lifetime under this approach with an account of substantial value which they would own. Their account would pay them *at least double* the traditional Social Security return while still letting them leave the full account to their children if they so choose. There is no magic here. The great difference in rate of return is achieved by a simple shift from a tax and pay system to a normal savings and investment retirement system. An owned private retirement account is nothing more than the model followed by the TIAA/CREF retirement system used by universities and hospitals in the United States for many years.

There is no single policy change this Nation can make to more effectively reduce the wealth gap and provide working families a real chance at wealth creation. Social Security "optionality" for reducing the wealth gap is the most obvious "low hanging fruit" available to America. It is literally a kick at American workers and their families and the worst of "old thinking" to demagogue Social Security optionality.

Tax Policy

There is a core misunderstanding about taxes in America; a misunderstanding which must be forthrightly addressed if we are to restore robust growth. The political rhetoric that the income tax unfairly favors the wealthy is not just false; the reality is quite the opposite. Our political history is one of imposing income taxes on a smaller and smaller base of the population; a path ultimately risking third-world out-of-control expenditures, as removal of political inhibitions on raising taxes leads political elites to support larger and larger expenditures. If we continue to focus on raising taxes as the solution to national problems we doom the Nation to subpar growth.

With respect to "fairness," according to the Internal Revenue Service, as of 2012 (with taxes even more progressive since then) the top 1% of tax payers paid 38.1% of the federal income tax, the top 10% paid 70.2%, the top 25% paid 86.4 %, and the top 50% paid 97.2%. With a combined state and federal tax rate of approximately 50% in some states, such as California and New York, the income tax is a serious drag on growth. And America's top corporate tax rate is one of the highest in the world; again serving as a drag on investment and growth and sending American corporations abroad.

The tax code is also enormously complex, and compliance costs for businesses and individuals to file their taxes are yet another drag on growth. Further, these compliance costs are on top of the economic reality that an income tax depresses growth as compared with a consumption tax raising the same revenue. Ideally, America should adopt a simplified flat tax system, or perhaps eliminate the income tax completely in return for a National Sales or Value Added Tax (VAT).

The recent proposals made by some candidates to increase the top income tax rate, or the capital gains tax rate, would slow an already sputtering economy and are neither the route to fairness, nor the route to reducing the wealth gap. No one should be required to pay more than one-third of their income in federal taxes; a rate comparable or higher than taxes owed under feudalism. We should remember that federal income taxes are on top of state income taxes, property taxes, and a host of other federal, state and local taxes.

Yet another of the myths about the federal tax system is that it is just one big "loophole" for the wealthy. To the contrary, the tax code has been designed to capture revenue. Not surprisingly, while including the infamous loopholes for the taxpayer, it also contains numerous *loopholes for the Government* specifically designed to raise revenue regardless of their obvious lack of "fairness." For example, the "alternative minimum tax or AMT," which at its inception was designed to hit the taxpayer who was using abusive tax shelters, today treats all state income taxes paid as though they were an abusive tax shelter and, where the AMT is triggered, effectively *removes the deduction for state income taxes paid.* Excuse me? *Paying your state income taxes is an abusive tax shelter?* As another example, the capital gains tax applies fully to all gains but limits deduction of losses to $3,000 per year. If the taxpayer has a good year and sells capital investments for a substantial profit the Government makes out nicely, thank you. But if the taxpayer has substantial capital losses, even to the point of being poorer at the end of the year, the Government still taxes all income but the $3,000 loss, *as though the taxpayer had "income" when her net worth actually declined.*

Further, as the paper on "Controlling the Deficit" by Peter Ferrara shows, the federal deficit has not arisen because the Nation has decreased taxes. Rather, the deficit is a product of a prodigious increase in federal "entitlement" spending resulting from President Johnson's "Great Society" programs, and other more recent increases in "entitlement" expenditures under both Republican and Democrat Presidents.

Increasing taxes is not the way to increase growth, is not the way to enhance fairness, and is not the way to effectively address the low growth "widening wealth gap." Grover Norquist will present a paper on Tax Policy, more specifically addressing "What Tax Reform Should Look Like under the Next President."

"Right-sizing" and Enhancing the Functioning of Government

Americans should start each day thankful for that genius of James Madison and the other founders of this great Nation. But America does have governance problems. The most serious is controlling fiscal irresponsibility. There is also a second serious governance problem. The Congress of the United States has lost its way in implementing a normal budget cycle. As one more issue worthy of review by the Presidential candidates, and their parties, the candidate ultimately elected will need to staff their Administration. Getting the right team, and surely that means nothing less today than the A-Team, will be difficult. Increasingly, we have adopted so many conflict-of-interest, disclosure, and pre-clearance laws that it is harder to get the A-Team to agree to serve, and even after agreeing, the clearance and Senate approval processes take too long. The result has been a huge delay in getting an administration up and running.

*Let us remember that America is, and must always remain, a land of opportunity for all, regardless of ethnicity, gender, color, or religion, a leader in the struggle for peace and justice, a beacon of hope to the world, and the home of the free. We must never forget that America's true greatness lies, **not** in its wonderful "spacious skies ... amber waves of grain ... and purple mountain majesties," but **in its national values and its unquenchable spirit.***

Economic Growth

John H. Cochrane[1]

Prepared for the Focusing the Presidential Debates Initiative

Growth Is Central

Sclerotic growth is the overriding economic issue of our time. From 1950 to 2000 the US economy grew at an average rate of 3.5% per year. Since 2000, it has grown at half that rate, 1.7%. From the bottom of the great recession in 2009, usually a time of super-fast catch-up growth, it has only grown at 2% per year.[2] Two percent, or less, is starting to look like the new normal.

Small percentages hide a large reality. The average American is more than three times better off than his or her counterpart in 1950. Real GDP per person has risen from $16,000 in 1952 to over $50,000 today, both measured in 2009 dollars. Many pundits seem to remember the 1950s fondly, but $16,000 per person is a lot less than $50,000!

If the US economy had grown at 2% rather than 3.5% since 1950, income per person by 2000 would have been $23,000 not $50,000. That's a huge difference. Nowhere in economic policy are we even talking about events that will double, or halve, the average American's living standards in the next generation.

---

1. John H. Cochrane is a Senior Fellow of the Hoover Institution, Stanford University. This essay is copyright © John H. Cochrane.

This essay was prepared as a contribution to "Focusing the Presidential Debates." Other essays and information can be found at www.FocusingThePresidentialDebates.com.

This essay may evolve over time, so please post or pass on links rather than copies of the file, http://faculty.chicagobooth.edu/john.cochrane/research/papers/cochrane_growth.pdf or http://faculty.chicagobooth.edu/john.cochrane/research/papers/cochrane_growth.html instead.

2. The numbers are based on real gross domestic product, series GDPCA, and total population, series POP, from the St. Louis Fed FRED database. Growth rates are continuously compounded, i.e., log.

Even these large numbers understate reality. GDP per capita does not capture the increase in lifespan—nearly 10 years—in health, in environmental quality, security and quality of life that we have experienced. The average American today lives far better than a 1950s American would if he or she had three rather than one 1950s cars, TVs, telephones, encyclopedias (in place of internet), or three annual visits to a 1950s doctor.

But even these less quantified benefits flow from economic growth. Only wealthy countries can afford environmental protection and advanced health care. We can afford to worry about global warming. India worries about 600 people per toilet, emphysema from burning cow patties, and easily treatable parasitic infections. Our ability to defend freedom around the world —even if we are wise enough to do it sensibly—depends on robust economic growth. If GDP had grown at 2%, not 3.5%, we would only be able to afford half the military we have today. The immense improvements in the quality of goods and many services we have today are part of the engine of economic growth.

Looking forward, solving almost all our problems hinges on reestablishing robust economic growth. Tax revenue equals tax rate times income, and growth determines how much income there will be. The amount of tax revenue our government has available to pay off debt and to pay the ballooning Social Security and health care expenses depends almost entirely on economic growth. Larger tax rates can't come close to raising that much money.

For example, the Congressional Budget Office, making its regular gloomy analysis of the US long-run budget outlook, assumes 2.2% growth from now until 2040.[3] But if GDP grew by 3.5% instead, even with no structural reforms at all, GDP in 2040 would be 38% higher, tax revenues would be 38% higher, and a lot of the problem would go away on its own. A 38% increase in federal revenue by higher tax rates or a 38% cut in spending are unlikely. Conversely, if GDP only grows 1%, GDP and tax revenues will be 26% lower than the CBO forecasts, which will force a fiscal crisis.

38% more income—or 26% less income—drives just about any agenda one could wish for, from strong defense, to environmental protection, to the affordability of social programs, to the welfare of any segment of the population, to public investments, health, and fundamental research.

And 3.5% is only a return to the post-WWII norm. Pre-2000 economic policies were not ideal. If we achieve 4% or more growth, even greater benefits occur.

---

3. Congressional Budget Office, June 2015 Long-Run Budget Outlook, Table A-1 p. 112.

The Source of Growth

Over long periods of time, economic growth comes from one source: productivity, the value of goods and services each worker can produce in a unit of time.

In turn, productivity comes from new ways of doing things: New ideas, at heart; new inventions, new products, new processes, new technology; new ways of organizing companies; new and better skills among workers. Southwest Airlines figuring out how to turn a plane around in 20 minutes, and Wal-Mart mastering supply logistics, are as much productivity growth as installing scanners or ATMs. Workers who know how to use computers rather than shovels produce a lot more per hour.

Higher productivity typically comes from new companies, which displace old companies —and displace the profits of their owners, and the healthy pay and settled lives of their managers and workers. Southwest enters and either displaces the legacy carriers—Pan Am and TWA—or forces wrenching changes for survivors such as American and United. A&P displaced mom and pop stores. Walmart displaced A&P. Amazon may displace Walmart. Nobody likes the process. Everyone needs the results.

Nothing other than productivity matters in the long run. A factor of three increase in income in 50 years, and the much larger rise in income and health since the dawn of the industrial age, pales relative to unions bargaining for better wages, progressive taxes or redistribution, monetary, fiscal or other stimulus programs, minimum wage laws or other federal regulation of labor markets, price caps and supports, subsidies, or much of anything else the government can do.

More people working, and working longer hours, can improve income a bit, but soon runs in to an upper limit. Our grandparents worked long hours, but were much worse off than we are.

Saving, investment and capital formation can improve income a bit, but its benefit is limited as well. A 1950 worker working with twice as many 1950 machines produces much less than a modern worker using current technology. Only new ideas, new products, new technologies, new organizations, and new skills produce such huge increases in prosperity.

In this context, the decline of US GDP growth coincides with more worrying changes. Productivity growth is declining. New business formation is sharply down. Mobility of people from job to job has declined.

Restoring Growth: A General Strategy

A debate rages among economists why America's growth has slowed. Most commentators advocate one side of that debate, and advocate strong policies according to their favorite theory. Lots of new ideas and grand policy programs are being dreamed up. Someone putting together a policy program might feel they have to choose a side in that debate, or they might wish to let that debate settle, to identify the most important policies.

Either approach is, I think, a mistake, given the urgency and magnitude of the problem, and given the likelihood that such a highly politicized economic debate will come to useful resolution anytime soon.

Let us instead work on the simple, common-sense things that everyone knows are broken, everyone understands are retarding growth, and that when fixed can increase growth. As opposed to looking for big magic bullets, new and clever theories, and ignoring the simple problems staring us in the face.

Will this approach restore 3.5% growth? Will it bring us to 4% or more growth? Well, really, it doesn't matter. When we have a big problem, and we know simple steps will help that problem, we should take those steps. We should do so, especially, because most of these simple steps can be taken at no fundamental economic or other cost.

Our economy is like a garden, but the garden is choked with weeds. Rather than look for some great new fertilizer to throw on it, why don't we get down on our knees and pull up the weeds? At least we know weeding works! For another metaphor, our economy has become like a hoarder's house. For a while he could get through the passages and keep life going, but now the junk is closing in. Well, rather than read the architectural magazines about just what the perfect house will look like, let's get to work cleaning up the mess.

Politics

Alas, such a common-sense, weed-the-garden program has little attraction to many ambitious politicians. Many politicians want a big new program, big new laws and initiatives—a New Deal, a Fair Deal, a Great Society. They don't see cleaning up the mess left behind by their predecessors as the way to getting one's face carved on Mt. Rushmore, let alone to win an election. Economists like big new ideas and programs too. Nobody got a Nobel Prize for saying, let's take Adam Smith's 250-year-old classics to heart.

But it is a big idea, a big program, and one that needs and will reward the courageous leadership of great politicians. Everybody has to give up their little deal, protection, tax break and subsidy; everyone has to allow their businesses or profession to be open to competition. Each person must understand that the small loss that he or she will experience directly will be more than made up by everyone else giving up theirs. Politically, rather than fall back on "I'll support your little deal, you support mine," everyone has to become part of the coalition that supports reform — "no, I'm not getting mine, so I'm not going to support you getting yours."

Forming such a coalition and keeping it together is hard. It is the essence of what great politicians can achieve.

Cleaning out the weeds also needs a large effort of simple governance. The President has to revisit and rewrite the mass of executive orders and memos. The Congress has to get serious and pass laws that are actually laws, not thousand page instructions for agencies to figure things out. It has to get around to repealing laws everyone understands are bad — the Jones act restricting shipping, the ban on oil exports, and so on — and reforming laws that everyone understands need to be reformed. It needs to actually follow its own budget law. The heads of agencies will have to renew the staff and reorient them to growth-oriented policy, and undertake a sweeping house-cleaning of regulations and procedures. They will have to implement managerial techniques such as pervasive cost-benefit analysis, regular retrospective review, and sunsets.

All of this is hard too. But it is the basic work of competent, growth-oriented government.

It is tempting to cast the question before us as growth vs. redistribution, or growth vs. inequality, as the rhetoric of redistribution and inequality pervades the arguments from those who want to continue the policies that are strangling growth.

But giving in to that rhetoric is a mistake. The US, in fact, has one of the most progressive tax systems in the world. And the relatively minor costs of government assistance to truly poor, needy, mentally ill or disabled people are not major impediments to growth. The weeds choking the economy represent cronyist redistribution to wealthy people, well-connected industries, and other powerful groups such as public employee unions, and large transfers among middle income people (Social Security and Medicare). They are not, by and large, the result of genuine and effective redistribution from rich to needy poor.

When the average person (voter) expresses concern over inequality, what they really mean is that they are concerned that average people are not getting ahead economically. If the average person were getting ahead, whether some big shot CEOs fly on private jets or not would make little difference. Conversely, the average voter, if not the average left-wing pundit, does not support equality of misery. If the average person continues to do poorly, it would bring them little solace for the government to tax away the lifestyles of the rich and famous.

Long-term robust economic growth is the only way to deliver sustained improvements in the lot of average Americans, and the less fortunate in particular. Redistributing Marie Antoinette's jewelry did little for the average French farmer.

The golden rule of economic policy is: Do not transfer incomes by distorting prices or slowing competition and innovation. The golden rule of political economics seems to be: Transfer incomes by distorting prices and regulating away competition. Doing so attracts a lot less attention than on-budget transfers or subsidies. It takes great political leadership to force the political process to obey the economic rule.

Regulation

The vast expansion in regulation is the most obvious change in public policy accompanying America's growth slowdown. Most recently, under the Dodd-Frank act and the ACA or Obamacare, these two large segments of the economy have seen radical increases in regulatory intervention. But environmental, labor, product, and energy regulation have all increased dramatically as well.[4]

Sometimes, regulation slows growth in return for public benefits, such as environmental protection or transportation safety. One can argue whether it does so efficiently, but there is a purpose.

Most economic regulation, however, is specifically designed to slow growth. The purpose of most economic regulation is to transfer money to a specific group of people, companies, or industry. It does so by slowing down new entrants, impeding competition, mandating uneconomic actions or cross-subsidies, slowing innovation, turning off price signals, distorting incentives, and encouraging waste. These *are* the tools of economic regulation, and they all impede economic growth.

People often complain that there are too many rules and regulations, or that the cost of filling out forms is too high, that there is too much red tape, that there are too many lobbyists, or that the direct measurable costs on industry are too large. The economic impact of regulation goes far beyond these standard complaints. The overwhelming cost of regulation is the economic dislocation: companies not started, products not produced, innovations not innovated, people not hired, costs not slashed, prices too high. And growth too slow. Just because it's harder to measure these costs does not mean that these are not the overwhelmingly more important costs, and the costs that we need to address.

---

4. Technically, "regulation" means rules written by independent administrative agencies, such as the Environmental Protection Agency, the Federal Aviation Administration or the Federal Reserve. Congress delegates authority to these agencies to write the actual rules. These rules have the force of law, and can carry criminal penalties including jail time, even when no intent to violate rules is alleged. Most economic regulation takes this legal form, but a great deal remains actual laws. I will use "regulation" a bit loosely to refer to both legal forms of government intervention in the economy.

Economic regulation has left behind the rule-of-law framework that many Americans suppose governs their affairs. In the popular imagination, regulation is about rules, and there are just too many of them. In many areas, however, the regulations are so vast, so complex, self- contradictory and so vague, that they basically give the regulators free rein to do what they want. In many cases, there is not a set of rules that you can read and comply with. You need to ask for preemptive permission from a regulator, who determines if your project can go ahead. Delay in getting needed approval is as good as denial in many cases. Projects that cost millions cannot bear years or often decades of delay in getting approvals.

In other cases, vague and expansive laws and regulations give regulators ammunition to pursue a few selected victims, to extort big settlements or send a few examples to jail. And by doing so to frighten the others into following the regulators' commandments. In many areas just about everyone is in technical violation of some law or regulation.

We are used to the right to see evidence against us, challenge witness testimony, and appeal decisions to an independent and higher court. These rights often do not apply to regulations, where the agency is prosecutor, police, judge, jury, and executioner all wrapped in one. The methods for determining an "abusive" practice or "discriminatory" outcome are not revealed ahead of time so that people could structure their actions in accordance with the rules.

Much of this state of affairs is Congress' fault, for writing long vague bills which devolve legal power to the agencies. But in an increasing trend, regulatory agencies are going far beyond even the clear limits of their statutory authority and writing rules or commanding outcomes clearly far beyond the plain language of the law. The EPA's expansion of carbon regulation and the definition of wetland are good cases in point.

The popular debate is about "more" vs. "less" regulation. Regulation is not more or less, regulation is effective or ineffective, smarter or dumber, full of unintended consequences or well-designed, captured by industry or effective, based on rules or based on regulator whim, accountable or arbitrary, evaluated by rigorous cost benefit standards or by political winds, distorting economic activity or supporting it, and so forth.

So "de-regulation" is also an inappropriate slogan. "Smart regulation," or "growth-oriented regulation" are much better descriptors of what needs to be done.

Finance

Financial regulation, even more transparently than other regulation, is just about who gives money and who gets money.

Under the Dodd-Frank act, a highly regulated industry has become suffo-
catingly regulated. The Federal Reserve embeds hundreds of employees at each
major bank, who pass judgment on every decision. The justice department
and SEC routinely pursue banks and other financial institutions for multibil-
lion dollar settlements, and now will pursue individuals with criminal charges.
The fixed costs of running a compliance department are so high that it is nearly
impossible to start a new financial company in the US. Just one new bank has
been chartered since the passage of Dodd-Frank.

The parts of the financial system that failed and were bailed out in 2008—
Fannie and Freddie, commercial banks—were already among the most highly
regulated businesses in America. Regulation did not fail for being absent. Regulation failed for being ineffective.

Alas, the basic structure of the Dodd-Frank act simply doubles down on the
same basic design that has failed again and again: The government guarantees
a wide swath of debt, by promise (deposit insurance) and by ex-post bailout.
An army of regulators tries to keep banks and other financial institutions from
exploiting the guarantee and taking too much risk, and clairvoyantly to forecast
panics and take action to stop them. That's like sending your brother in law to
Las Vegas with your credit card, but asking his kids to keep an eye on him.

Like much else in America, our government works to cross purposes. It
subsidizes debt with tax deductibility, deposit insurance, too big to fail guarantees, regulatory preference for holding short-term assets, liquidity rules,
credit guarantees, Fannie and Freddie, the home mortgage interest deduction,
community reinvestment act, student loan programs and so forth. And then
it tries to regulate against using debt with bank asset regulation, stress tests,
consumer financial protection, macro-prudential policy, and so on.

The alternative is clearly laid out in many sources: Risky investments must
be largely financed by issuing equity, not by borrowing very short term money.
When that happens, the mass of regulation is simply not needed in order to
stop financial crises. Then we will "only" face the task of removing needless
regulations whose main purpose is to create subsidies and protections for various clienteles.

Health

The ACA, thousands of pages of law, tens of thousands of pages of regulations, and even more decision-making power by newly empowered regulators,
such as the thousands of waivers given to individual companies, represents an
enormous increase in federal intervention in the market for health care and
health insurance. Like finance, health was already highly regulated. And like

finance, most of the ACA simply doubled down on the same basic regulatory structure that had caused so many pathologies before.

The central problem of preexisting conditions was an artifact of regulation. In the ideal form of health insurance, you buy cheap catastrophic insurance when young, but the insurance policy can follow you as you age, change jobs, and move from state to state, and does not radially increase premiums if you get sick.

Why don't we have that ideal insurance? Because previous rounds of regulation outlawed it. In the 1940s the US government allowed tax deductions for employer-provided group insurance, but not employer contributions to individual insurance or individuals' contributions to such insurance. By laws, insurance is not portable across state lines. Thus, there is no reason for anyone who might get a job or move to buy long-term individual insurance that protects against the emergence of pre-existing conditions. In response to the pre-existing conditions problem, the ACA forces community rating—everyone pays the same price—tries to mandate healthy people to buy insurance, and steps up pressure on employer provided group plans, which are the source of the problem.

Similarly, once insurance was tax deductible, there was an incentive to salt it up. You would not buy car insurance that "paid for" oil changes—especially if you had to deal with insurance paperwork each time. But with a tax deduction it's worth buying health insurance that "pays for" routine small expenses. Then the government (state and local too) instituted mandates that insurance must "pay for"—and, of course, charge premiums to cover—all sorts of additional procedures, which makes insurance too expensive.

We need to allow simple, portable, largely catastrophic, lifelong, guaranteed-renewable health insurance to emerge. Right now it's illegal. To the extent that the government wishes to subsidize health insurance—and it should—then it should give straightforward vouchers, which people can use to buy insurance, or to fund health savings accounts. Such vouchers should take the place of Obamacare, Medicaid, and Medicare.

Health care and insurance is not just distorted from the demand side—too many people paying with someone else's money. The supply side is ossifyingly restricted as well. New hospitals, new clinics that specialize in cheaply providing one service well, new doctors, new nurses, new insurance companies, all find a wall of laws, regulations, and officials blocking their path. For a reason: To maintain the profits of and cross-subsidies provided by the existing incumbents. Non-profit status itself blocks efficiency: you can't take over an inefficient non- profit, and non-profits can't issue equity to make important investments. In reducing the cost and improving the quality of health care, efficiency is far more important than trying to avoid a competitive rate of return to owners.

Energy and Environment

There are few places in the American government where one can witness inefficiency and growth-sapping regulatory bungling on the scale seen in our energy and much (not all) environmental regulation.

Like much else in America, our government pursues conflicting aims. It tries to subsidize and drive down the price of energy. And then it tries simultaneously to regulate against our using energy in a hundred different ham-handed ways, from mileage standards for cars, energy efficiency standards for windows and appliances, special parking places for electric vehicles, $7,500 tax credits to subsidize $100,000 Tesla cars bought by Silicon Valley zillionaires, hundreds of annually extended tax credits for various energy boondoggles, and so forth.

The poster child for inefficiency may well be the mandate for gasoline producers to use ethanol. Corn ethanol, it turns out, does nothing to help the environment: It takes nearly as much petroleum energy to produce it as it contains, in the form of fertilizer, transport fuel and so on; it uses up valuable land, which directly emits greenhouse gases, and contributes to erosion and runoff; it drives up the price of food. The only thing sillier was the mandate to include cellulosic ethanol, because the government mandated a technology that simply did not work.

If you were wondering why we do this, it should come as no surprise that corn is produced by big companies in Iowa. If you need more evidence, note that the US also has heavy restrictions on the importation of sugar cane ethanol—as we restrict all sugar cane imports—which actually might be of some environmental benefit. The planet, of course, does not care whether corn is grown in Iowa or sugar cane in Brazil. Corn growers and sugar producers do care.

A litmus test for a presidential candidate ought to be the willingness to stand up in Iowa and say, "Ladies and Gentlemen, a huge government subsidy for corn ethanol is a rotten idea."

Similarly, if you thought that subsidized production of photovoltaics and the various subsidies to putting solar cells on your roof, including the requirement that your fellow citizens buy electricity back from you at retail prices, are about the environment, you will be puzzled by our government's heavy import restrictions on cheap Chinese made solar cells. Obviously, mother nature cares not where the cells are produced. Mother politics does.

Energy and transportation policy seem to indulge flights of magical thinking. California, facing a drought, and not having built water projects in decades, is going to spend well over $60 billion dollars on a high-speed rail line. This is advanced in the cause of carbon emission reduction. And quite literally, the case has been made that by building the rail line, we will lower global temperatures, and increase rainfall. If on a dollars per ton of carbon saved the rail line fails elementary cost-benefit analysis, on dollars per drop of water created, it fails the magic vs. reality test.

As this example makes clear, the federal government is not alone. State and even local regulation is partly to blame as well.

Strong zoning laws forbid people from building houses near where they work, and forbid them from building workplaces near where people live, and from building shops near either. An electric car driving 60 miles is much less energy efficient than living in a high-rise apartment, in a mixed residential/commercial neighborhood, and walking!

A growth-oriented, and anti-cronyist energy policy is pretty simple. To the extent that the government wishes to reduce carbon emissions, impose a simple and straightforward carbon tax. In return, eliminate *all* the detailed mandates, subsidies, quantity regulations, and boondoggle unprofitable projects. If energy costs more, people will quickly figure out on their own what makes sense.

Energy is an economic paradox, as it is so highly regulated, with so much government picking of technologies, but simultaneously has such a flat long-run supply curve and there are so many technological alternatives. A large price of polluting energy is the most efficient way to induce clean energy innovation; far more efficient than massive amounts of federally subsidized research and development to financially unprofitable businesses and bureaucrats picking technologies. And price-induced behavior changes can reduce usage much more easily than mandating fancier technologies. Paying some attention to turning off the lights when you leave the room is more efficient than mandating LED bulbs and leaving the lights on.

If you are serious about carbon, let the words "nuclear power" pass your lips. We have sitting before us a technology that can easily supply our electricity and many transport needs, with zero carbon or methane emissions. New designs, if only they could pass the immense regulatory hurdle, would be much safer than the 1950s Soviet technology that failed at Chernobyl or the 1960s technology that failed at Fukushima. We are now operating antiques. And even with this rate of accident, nuclear power has caused orders of magnitude less human or environmental suffering than any other fuel.

Similarly, the most environmentally friendly way for people to live is in tightly packed cities, fed by genetically modified foods which yield more per acre of farmland and require fewer fertilizers and pesticides, from laser-leveled fields run efficiently by large corporations in the highest productivity locations. Federal policies to the contrary are not just anti-growth, they're anti-environment too. When federal policy can say these things in public, it will have a bit more standing to invoke the name of "science."

Environmental policy at a minimum needs a far more frequent application of cost-benefit analysis!

As important as carbon may be, our environmental policy has become obsessed with this one danger. But slow warming and sea level rise in 100 years are not the only, or possibly the main, environmental danger we face.

Most of the large species going extinct—elephants, rhinos, lions, and so forth, to say nothing of the more numerous and less photogenic—will go extinct from human predation, poaching, and loss of habitat long before climate has any effect on them. Most of the world faces environmental problems far more pressing than climate. And by focusing on climate, our government is spending far too little time, research and money on small but catastrophic dangers such as global pandemics, crop failures, animal diseases, and so on. As in finance, the unexpected and swift dangers are more likely to cause a crisis than the slow moving widely anticipated ones.

Taxes

Perhaps one economic issue just about every corner of the political spectrum can agree on is that our tax code is a massively complex and broken mess, needing reform.

Practically everyone agrees on the basic structure of a growth-oriented tax reform: Lower marginal rates—the extra amount of taxes you pay on an extra dollar of income determines the disincentive to earning that income. To raise revenue at lower marginal rates, broaden the base, i.e., remove exemptions and loopholes. And massively simplify the code.

Admittedly, not everyone agrees that tax reform should be oriented to growth. The voices for higher taxes argue for redistribution or decapitation—removal of high incomes, even without benefit to lower-income people—freely admitting the growth consequences of high taxes are at least not positive. They just view distributional goals as more important than growth.

Often, however, tax reform proposals sacrifice too quickly the principles of what a good tax system should be with perceived political accommodations to powerful interest groups. Economists should not play politician. We should always start with "in a perfect world, here is what the tax code should look like," and accommodate political constraints only when asked to. Political constraints change quickly. Economic fundamentals do not.

Herewith, then, a brief reminder of basic principles:

The right corporate tax rate is zero. Corporations never pay taxes. Every dollar of taxes that a corporation pays comes from higher prices of their products, lower wages to their workers, or lower returns to their owners.

Which one, depends on who can get out of the way. While it is politically tempting to suppose that wealthy stockholders bear the burden of corporate taxation, they are in fact the most likely to be able to avoid taxation. While imposing a corporate tax may hurts existing stockholders, by lowering the value of the stock, there is no reason new investors will give the corporation money unless they can get the same after-tax return they can get elsewhere, and in particular abroad. Thus, new investment dries up until the company can pay the same after-tax return to its investors—by raising prices, lowering wages, or reducing scale to generate greater before-tax profits. In addition, these days the owners and investors of corporations are as much your and my pension fund as they are rich individuals.

For all these reasons, eliminating the corporate tax is as likely to be more rather than less progressive. The higher prices a corporation charges hurt everyone. The lower wages corporations pay hurt workers. The income it passes along to its owners is subject to our highly progressive tax system.

A growth-oriented tax system taxes consumption, not income. When we tax income that is saved, or the investment income that results from past saving, we reduce the incentive to save, invest, start companies and build them, vs. enjoy consumption immediately. One of the first theorems you learn in an economics class on taxation is that the right tax on rates of return is zero.

A person-based consumption tax can be progressive. It is useful to collect the basic tax as a VAT. Then people in higher brackets can declare income and receive credit for investments.

The estate tax is a particularly distorting tax on saving and investment. One may sympathize with the moral judgment that rich kids don't "deserve" inherited wealth. But the point is on the incentives of the giver. The tax code should not give strong incentives to middle-age people to stop building their businesses, investing their money, spend their money on round the world cruises and their time with tax lawyers. Nor should it force the breakup of privately held businesses to pay taxes. Maybe the kids don't deserve it, but if people cannot provide better lives for their children, we remove one of the strongest and oldest human incentives for economic activity.

Taxing corporations rather than people and taxing income rather than consumption is behind many complexities of the tax code. For example, right now the corporate and individual tax rates must be at roughly the same level. If we tax corporate income less, then people rush to incorporate themselves. If we tax personal income less, the opposite. But if we tax consumption and not income, then there is no tax benefit to incorporating yourself. As another example, we only need special health savings accounts and college savings accounts because we tax income. If we taxed consumption we would just save for health, college, and retirement as we do everything else.

In partial recognition of the distortions caused by taxing rates of return, our tax code includes an absurdly complex web of ways of getting around capital income taxes, from IRAs, Roth IRAs, 527(b), 401(k), special tax treatment of pension funds and life insurance, lower rates for long-term capital gains, and the various trust shenanigans of the estate tax. Removing the attempt to tax investment income would make all of these complex structures irrelevant. Then they can be removed, greatly simplifying the code.

The economic distortions of the tax system result from the *overall* marginal tax rate, not each tax alone. The economic distortion due to taxation does not care that there are separate federal, state and local taxes. The economic distortion is the sum of all these. Start by producing one dollar more of value for your employer. Now subtract the corporate income tax, the payroll tax (Social Security, Medicare, etc.), your federal, state, and local income taxes; the investment taxes, capital gains taxes or estate taxes paid between earning and consuming, and the sales taxes, excise taxes, property taxes, gas taxes and so forth that you pay when you buy something, to see how much of value you actually get in return for the dollar of value you provided to your employer. That's the overall marginal tax rate.

Far too much tax discussion considers federal income taxes alone as if the others did not exist. They do exist. I only half-jokingly suggested an alternative *maximum* tax.[5] Add up all the taxes you pay, including all the taxes companies whose stock you own pay, to any level of government. If it's above some high number—say, 70%—you're done and have to pay no more.

When we say broaden the base by removing deductions and credits, we should be serious about that. Thus, even the holy trinity of mortgage interest deduction, charitable donation deduction, and employer provided health insurance deduction should be scrapped. The extra revenue could finance a large reduction in marginal rates.

Why? Consider the mortgage interest deduction. Imagine that in the absence of the deduction, Congress proposes to send a check to each homeowner, in proportion to the interest he or she pays on money borrowed against the value of the house. Furthermore, rich people, people who buy more expensive

---

5. *Wall Street Journal*, April 14 2013, http://faculty.chicagobooth.edu/john.cochrane/research/papers/ Alternative_maximum_tax_WSJ.pdf.

houses, people who borrow lots of money, and people who refinance often to take cash out get bigger checks than poor people, people who buy smaller houses, people who save up and pay cash, or people who pay down their mortgages. A rich person buying a huge house in Palo Alto, who pays 40% marginal income tax rate, gets a check for 40% of his huge mortgage. A poor person buying a small house in Fresno, who pays a 10% income tax, gets a check for 10% of his much smaller mortgage. There would be riots in the streets before this bill would pass. Yet this is *exactly* what the mortgage interest deduction accomplishes.

Charitable donations follow the same logic. Suppose Congress proposed to match private charitable donations with federal dollars. Rich people get 40% match, but poor people only get 10%. Not only would that cause riots, but then there would be a much closer eye on just what "charities" mean in today's America if they received direct checks from the Treasury. We may moan at the complexities of federal expenditures, but there is at least some oversight. Charities spend tax money largely in the dark. The shenanigans of the Clinton foundation are only the most recent visible example of how "nonprofits" are often the latest scam in the American legal system. Notice how every sports star or celebrity has a charitable foundation? They are great ways to escape estate taxes and investment taxes as well as campaign finance laws. Your kids can serve as the executives of the foundation.

Yes, universities (such as my employer) may suffer. Well, I started this essay with the idea that everyone must give up their little subsidy so that the rest will give up theirs. So too must academics.

Americans remain generous. Even without a tax incentive, Americans will give to worthy causes, as they give now to political campaigns. Worthy charities, such as my employer, may even gain by substitution away from tax and political scams.

In sum, the ideal tax system taxes people, it taxes consumption not investment income, and it taxes at a very low rate with a very large base.

The Political Debate on Taxes

Why is this so hard? Because our political debate mixes different goals.

The central goal of a growth-oriented tax system is to raise the revenue needed to fund necessary government spending at minimal distortion to the economy, and in particular minimizing the sorts of distortions that impede the growth process.

A first objection comes from those who want to pair reform of the code with substantial rises in overall revenue. This has been the main stumbling block to tax reform under the Obama Administration.

Second, our tax code mixes raising revenue with a host of special provisions designed to encourage specific activities and transfer income to specific groups or businesses. Objections come from those who what to preserve one or another subsidy, deduction, or exemption.

Third, our tax code mixes raising revenue with efforts to redistribute resources across income and various demographic classes.

The result is paralysis. The answer lies in separating the arguments. One could go so far as to separate the actual legislation.

First, we should discuss the *structure* of the tax code separately from the proper *level* of revenues. Let us agree that we will eliminate deductions and exemptions and have three brackets. Start with a revenue-neutral code. But agree that we can separately and much more frequently adjust the rates, which adjust the overall level of revenues.

Second, we should separate the tax code from the subsidy and redistribution code. Let us agree, the tax code serves to raise revenue at minimal distortion. All other economic policy goes into the subsidy code. And subsidies should be on-budget and explicit. So, you want a subsidy for home mortgage interest payments? Sure, let's talk about it. But it will be an on-budget expense—we will send checks to home buyers if we do it. You want to give $7,500 to each purchaser of electric cars? Sure, let's talk about it. But it will be an on-budget expense. We will send $7,500 checks electric car purchasers if we do it.

Yes, advocates will object. Congress is not at all likely to appropriate money in this way! Tax credits and deductions are very useful for hiding things like this. But again, honest political leadership should say, if we have to hide what we're doing from the American people, then we shouldn't be doing it. Or, we should structure it in a way that is acceptable.

This discussion reflects another reality: The size of the US government is vastly greater than we think. It looks like federal spending is only about 20% of GDP. But each deduction and mandate is the same thing as a tax and a subsidy. By bringing each deduction and tax credit on budget, we can correctly see exactly the size of our government, and more wisely vote on that size.

Even if my dream of putting all subsidies on budget fails, they should at least be conceptually separate parts of the tax code, and debated separately. The key is to keep the basic tax code focused on raising revenue at smallest possible economic distortion, and to argue separately about subsidies.

The art of politics is, of course, bundling things in a way to get deals done. But it is clear that the current bundling is producing paralysis. Those on the left that wish to raise revenue suspect that those who wish to reform the tax code will not later allow a discussion on revenue, so they must hold reform hostage. Likewise with those who want subsidies. Rather than produce another bundled mess, a great politician should be able to promise an honest hearing on revenue and unpalatable subsidies to get a clean growth-oriented reform.

Redistribution by our federal government fails because of its similarly chaotic approach. Discussions of progressivity consider redistribution through the federal income tax code forgetting about the smorgasbord of social programs and other taxes. Social Security, Medicaid, food stamps, unemployment insurance, and so on and so on all overlap to an incoherent mess. These should be condensed into one coherent approach to helping lower-income Americans. You can redistribute, if desired, by checks as well as by differing tax rates.

The central problem is again the tension between economics and politics. When a growth-oriented economist writes about taxes, the most important question is the distortion. What economic decision is distorted by taxes? If you produce $2 for your employer but only receive $1 in value, does that distort your decision to work, to take a job, or to invest in the skills needed for the job? Who gets how much money is really not that important to growth.

When the political system discusses taxes, the only question is who gets how much money, subdivided into minute income, geographic, racial and industry categories. Nobody pays attention to the distortions. But the distortions lower growth, and it is the job of wise political leadership to move the public discussion in that direction.

The current tax discussion understates, I think, the importance of simplicity in the tax code. A simple code makes its incentives transparent. A simple code vastly reduces compliance costs. And most of all, a simple code is much more clearly fair. Americans now look at the tax code and suspect — often rightly — that rich smart people with clever lawyers are getting away with things. Our voluntary tax code depends vitally on removing this suspicion. The Greek equilibrium in which each person cheats because he knows everyone else is cheating, corrosive far beyond its effect on revenue, can break out here too.

Tax lawyers and economists often come up with complex schemes to achieve parts of the principles I advocate, without doing much violence to the current code. I think this is a mistake. People who look forward to late March and early April each year as a time to show their hard-won expertise should remember how much the rest of the country hates the experience.

For example, rather than eliminate the corporate tax, some economists advocate having corporations notify each stockholder how much tax is paid on his or her behalf, and then the stockholder can deduct the corporate tax payments from his or her individual taxes. That achieves the same economic result, if the costs of filling out forms are zero.

But that setup is disastrous for commitment and simplicity. The corporate tax remains, and arguments about just what corporations can and can't deduct, which income where they pay taxes on remain firmly in place. With the corporate tax system still in place, we are a sneeze away from limiting or removing the pass-through. And one cannot ask for a way that smacks more of a handout to "the rich," hiding its effect of lowering product prices or raising wages. The code is only simplified if the corporate tax is eliminated. (And, if the government wants to subsidize R&D, energy investments, or other activities, do so with on-budget subsidies, just like for people.)

As another example, it seems politically easier to leave in place cherished deductions like health insurance, home mortgage interest, and charity, but limit the total amount of deductions any one person can take. That achieves the economic purpose.

But this setup leaves intact a perpetual argument. Next year, let's renegotiate a higher limit. Or let's exempt my favorite deduction from the limit. As long as each deduction remains in place, so does the constituency in its favor, and so do all the thousands of pages of tax code each entails.

Zero is zero. If you don't kill a tax completely, it keeps coming back like zombies in a science fiction movie. If you don't kill a tax completely, you do nothing to simplification of the tax code.

Eliminating whole sections of the tax code, rather than nullifying them with clever schemes, has another important advantage. A growth-oriented tax code operates by incentives, but people have to understand the incentives. Tax economists tend to be ultra-rational, and figure that people will react to the actual financial incentive even if it is quite hidden. Of course, the point of hiding it—of offering corporate tax rebates, say, rather than eliminating the corporate tax, or sharply limiting deductions rather than eliminating them—is precisely to fool people politically into thinking the provisions are still there. Well, people so fooled may not see the economic incentive either. Behavioral economists who argue that only very clear, simple, provisions have the appropriate incentives have a point. And their point argues for a simple code full of zeros rather than a complex code that has the same set of economic incentives once an expert combs through it.

Debt and Deficits; Social Security and Medicare

Debt and deficits are a looming threat to growth. Read any one of the nonpartisan Congressional Budget Offices' long-term budget outlooks.

Our central problem is straightforward: promises to pay Social Security benefits, Medicare and other health care will soon overwhelm the US budget. Hidden mountains of unfunded pension liabilities, state debts, student loan debts, and debts the US will incur if another financial crisis, recession, or war face us, add to the risks.

Growth-oriented policy will do a lot to solve the debt and budget problem. Economic growth raises tax revenues without raising tax rates. Stagnant growth will make all these problems much worse.

Conversely, a looming debt crisis or the extreme taxes that would be needed to pay for an unreformed system will be strong drags on economic growth. So, setting long-run spending in order now is both necessary, and much easier than doing it later.

Indexing Social Security to price inflation rather than wage inflation takes care of much of the Social Security problem. Indexing it to the prices of things that old people actually buy helps even more. Changing the nature of health care support to vouchers, and enacting the other health care reforms mentioned above will give both better help to people in need and solve that budget problem. Both of these steps are much easier the sooner they are taken, so that nobody has to receive an actual cut in benefits.

An economist should emphasize the distortions to economic decisions embodied by these programs, not the cost per se. Programs are bad when they require taxes so large that the taxes kill growth, or when the incentives of the programs sap people's incentive to work, save, and invest. Social security should be converted to private accounts, not so much to save the government money as to ensure that each person knows that an extra hour of work, or extra effort made to learn a new skill or start a company, results eventually in greater resources for him or her, not just greater taxes.

Social Programs

From a growth perspective, the most important characteristic of social programs is also not so much their cost, as it is their disincentives and their ineffectiveness.

Most of our social programs phase out as income rises, often with hard steps at which if you earn one extra dollar you lose a large benefit. If you earn an extra dollar, you can lose health care subsidies, food stamps, Social Security, Medicare, disability payments, and a host of smaller subsidies from home heating oil subsidies, child care subsidies, transportation subsidies and even (in my home town) parking permit subsidies.

As usual in our weed-pulling exercise, there are so many programs and they interact in so many ways that adding them all up is hard. The broad picture though is that for many Americans there is close to a one for one tax rate from zero up to $60,000 per year in the form of reduced benefits.

The answer is not necessarily to be stingier. The answer, as elsewhere, is to design programs with more attention paid to marginal disincentives, and to design programs that fit together rather than assume each one acts in isolation.

One good way to eliminate marginal disincentives is more frequently to condition support on *time* rather than *income*. Unemployment benefits work to some extent this way. Yes, you lose unemployment benefits if you get a job, which provides a disincentive. But you can only earn unemployment benefits for a certain period of time.

It is surprising, in fact, that a society as fluid as ours conditions so much of its government activity on income, as if income were a permanent and innate characteristic. Income changes rapidly through time and over the life cycle.

Social programs are so expensive because most of them are middle class subsidies, not help for the truly poor and desperate. We need to spend more is on the truly unfortunate. Schizophrenics in the streets are unbecoming of a great nation, and helping them costs relatively little. They don't vote.

Labor Law and Regulation

Our government and politicians keep repeating how much they want to "create jobs" and help Americans to work.

A Martian, parachuting down and studying our economy would come to the opposite conclusion. There are few economic activities in which the government throws more obstacles than that of hiring someone.

Start, of course, with taxes: income taxes and payroll taxes are primarily taxes on employment. But the regulatory burdens of employment are larger still, as anyone who has tried to get a nanny legal will attest.

Minimum wages, occupational licensing, anti-discrimination laws, laws regulating hours people can work, benefits they must receive, leave they must be given, fear of lawsuits if you fire someone, and so forth all impede the labor market.

We are swiftly becoming a nation divided, as Europe is, between "haves" with expensive, highly regulated, full time jobs—that are inflexible for people who wish part time work—and often illegal, under the table, part time "gig" work.

Companies have innovated around many of these distortions with contract workers, but the current fight whether contract workers, independent contractors (Uber drivers) and franchisees must be considered employees of the parent company threatens to undo all of that, placing another huge wedge in the labor market and segregation between well paid, hard to get, full time jobs and a larger pool of unemployed.

America needs a vast deregulation of its labor market. I want to work for you, you want to pay me? Good enough.

The usual argument is that workers need protection of all these laws. Well, the supposed protections do cost economic growth, and they do reduce employment. How much do they actually protect workers? The strongest force for worker protection is a vibrant labor market—if you don't like this job, go take another. The tightly regulated labor market makes it much harder to get a new job, and thus, paradoxically, lowers your bargaining power in the old one. At a minimum let's revisit just how much protection is actually being given, and just what the cost in growth is, and whether it's worth it.

Immigration

"Give me your tired, your poor, Your huddled masses yearning to breathe free, ..."—Emma Lazarus.

* * *

"He has endeavoured to prevent the population of these States; for that purpose obstructing the Laws for Naturalization of Foreigners; refusing to pass others to encourage their migrations hither, ..."— Declaration of Independence.

Not anymore.

We can end illegal immigration overnight: Make it legal. The question is, on what terms should we allow legal immigration.

The immigration debate has nothing to do with who is allowed to come to this country. That's the tourist visa debate. The immigration debate is about who is allowed to work in this country, and, later, who is allowed to become a citizen. Our federal government has a massive program in place to stop people from working. That *is* immigration law.

Immigrants contribute to economic growth. Even if income per capita is unchanged, imagine how much better off our Social Security system, our Medicare system, our unfunded pension promises, and our looming deficits and debt would be, if America could attract a steady flow of young, hard-working people who want to come and pay taxes. Aha, we can attract them! They're beating the doors down to come. But then we keep them out.

Allowing free migration is, by many estimates, the single policy change that would raise world GDP the most. If you believe in free trade in goods, and free investment, then you have to believe that free movement of people has the same benefits.

The most common objection is that immigrants steal American jobs. No, they create American jobs, just as a higher birthrate of Americans would do. Every immigrant is as much a consumer of things we produce, a buyer of houses and cars, a starter of new businesses, as he or she is a worker. Immigrants come to do jobs that are available, not jobs that Americans don't have. They do work that complements those of Americans, and thus make Americans more productive and better off.

There is very little economic argument for keeping immigrants out of California from old Mexico that would not also apply to keeping immigrants to California out of New Mexico. (Or, as Oregonians, Coloradans, and Texans might wish, keeping Californians out of their states!)

We worry about immigrants using social programs. Fine, but why then is immigration skewed to family members, likely to use social programs, and excludes workers, least likely to use them? If the worry is that they'll go on welfare, why on earth do we *forbid* them from earning a living? If social program overuse is a worry, charge a $5,000 bond at the border, require proof of $10,000 of assets and health insurance, and anyone who is convicted of a felony goes home. This fear does not excuse our immigration system.

The status of the 11 million already here is a national embarrassment. 11 million people live in this country, work, pay taxes, buy food and cars and houses, and yet are deprived of legal protection, easily exploited by employers, afraid to even take airplanes, let alone not allowed to vote. If this were a racial minority, we would be scandalized.

But immigration law is so dysfunctional that we need not discuss radical programs. Let's fix the basic growth-killing pathologies that we all recognize need to be fixed.

Start by letting in people who obviously contribute to the American economy and society. Ambitious young people come to the US to get degrees in medicine, engineering, and business. They want to stay, work, buy things from our businesses and pay taxes. They want to start businesses and hire people. We kick them out. The H1B visa lottery should simply be abandoned. Any high-skill immigrant should be able to stay. Any high-wealth immigrant should be able to stay. Immigrants often start small businesses that serve poor areas. Anyone who starts a business should be able to stay. People who came at a young age, have been through American schools, served in the US military, and know no other country should be able to stay.

The immigration discussion is full of more nonsense than any other policy question facing the country. No, immigrants are in fact much less likely to commit crimes than Americans. No, terrorists come on tourist visas. They do not swim the Rio Grande and stop to pick vegetables for a few years before blowing things up. And we already spend more than twice—$13 billion dollars—on the border patrol than we do—$ 6 billion—on the entire FBI. They are "illegal" some say. Well, that's easy to fix. Change the law, and they will no longer be illegal! Constructing a great Ice Wall on the border with Mexico is a canard. Immigrants come on airplanes and overstay tourist visas.

As with taxation, the immigration debate needs to separate completely separate questions: Who is allowed to enter the country? Who is allowed to work here? These are completely separate issues. Restrictions on work do nothing to address security.

Immigration and growth feed each other. Immigrants help economic growth. But conversely, the lack of economic growth is feeding a misguided but understandable resentment towards immigrants.

Education

How often must commenters on all sides of the political spectrum complain that America's public schools are awful?

They are particularly awful for people of lower income, minorities and new immigrants. The problem is not money. Study after study shows that America spends as much or more money on education than other countries, and experiment after experiment has shown almost no effect of showering money on bad schools.

The culprit is easy to find: awful public schools run by and for the benefit of politically powerful teachers' and administrators' unions. (Don't forget the latter! Teachers account for only half of typical public school expenses.) Education poses a particularly large tradeoff between profits to incumbents and economic growth, since education lies at the foundation of higher productivity. In addition, the costs of awful schools fall primarily on lower-income people who cannot afford to get out of the system. It is one of the major contributors to inequality.

The solution is simple as well: widespread financing by vouchers and charter schools. As with health care, a vibrant market demands that people control their spending, and can move it to where they get better results. As with health care, the government does not have to directly provide a service in order to help people to pay for that service. But as with health care, a healthy market also demands supply competition, that new schools be allowed to start and compete for students.

Higher education has been relatively healthy in the US, but federal policy is busy making a mess of it. The correlation between more and more subsidy to higher education, the astronomical rise in tuition, and the leftward drift of campus politics towards support of a larger government is hard to miss. The federal government took over the student loan market, and is busy creating a new debt bomb that will likely end in another mass bailout. Immigration restrictions are making it harder for students to access this, one of our great export successes.

There is a strong correlation between college education and later income. That does not mean that more college education will automatically generate more individual income or more economic growth. To some extent, smart people who will earn more money anyway go to college, and smart people who know they will benefit from a college education go to college. To a greater extent, people who choose science, engineering, math, computer, or business majors go on to earn greater incomes. Those who study other subjects may profit personally from the experience, but generally do not go on to contribute as much to economic growth.

Loans that are forgiven if one does not earn a higher income, or forgiven for students who go in to non-profit, social work, government or other low-paying work, or who do not work at all, are particularly troublesome from a growth perspective.

Sweat the Little Stuff

Our growth needs to be revived by pulling a thousand little weeds. A selected few reminders and examples follow.

We still have agricultural price supports, tariffs and quotas for things such as sugar and oranges.

Trade is relatively free, but could be freer. And keeping trade open requires endless effort against the forces of protection.

The opponents of free trade, and immigration, adduce long-standing fallacies, that one must constantly fight. When, say, China, sends us cheap manufactured goods, they take dollars in return. Every one of those dollars ends up buying an American export, or invested in America. Trade is not a "competition," and our trading partners are not "competitors." We win in trade when American consumers get to buy things more cheaply. The point of trade is not to increase exports. When Germany sent Greece Porsches in return for worthless pieces of paper, it was Greece that came out ahead in the deal, not Germany.

That much of the nation's infrastructure is crumbling is a common observation. And infrastructure supports growth. Low interest rates are a particularly propitious time to build infrastructure.

So why is there less consensus for a large program to repair and build public infrastructure, including roads and bridges, but also bicycle paths, parks, airports, ports, and so forth? In large, part, I think, our government has squandered its people's trust in its ability to carry out infrastructure projects in a cost-effective, well-planned, and timely fashion. Instead, voters are used to reading about bridges to nowhere, high speed trains from nowhere to nowhere, billion dollar cost over runs, decade-plus waits for permits, massive consulting fees, and other pathology.

The process of infrastructure investment needs a complete overhaul. To mention just a few, it is no surprise that costs spiral when projects must pay "prevailing wages" and obey set-asides for specific contractors, or when environmental review takes years. It is no surprise that projects are not repaired when federal funds pay for new construction but not repair. Federal funding diverts resources to rail, a charming but very inefficient mode of transport, over freeways, airports, buses, bus lanes or bus rapid transit, or other needed modes. Real time tolling, private toll roads, and congestion pricing are easy ideas, used successfully in other countries, but almost never here.

So, yes, we need a growth-supporting infrastructure program. But our political leadership needs to show us it can construct infrastructure in a more competent, less politicized, way, focused on delivering the needed infrastructure at least cost to the taxpayer.

There Is Good Spending

I close this essay with two areas in which I think our Government could spend some more money, in ways that would enhance economic growth.

Our legal and criminal justice system is clearly becoming dysfunctional. This system is trapping many people already struggling with poor schools and job prospects. That we spend tens of thousands of dollars to house prisoners and next to nothing to train them to succeed when they exit guarantees their return. Even doubling resources, so that crimes in poor neighborhoods are routinely solved, so that people accused of crimes have speedy trials and reasonable representation, not life-destroying years waiting for cases to be heard, so that people who are imprisoned receive some basic help in dealing with the outside world, would cost little compared to the trillions we spend on middle-class social programs.

The war on drugs is a massive failure. Not only is it leading to mayhem in poorer areas of the US, it is causing narco-states, corruption, violence, and poverty in our neighbors, and driving much immigration pressure. Al-Qaeda, the Taliban, and ISIS earn lots of money from drug trafficking. Legalization would drive them out of business far more effectively than war.

The federal government has a role in financing basic research. Yes, 95% of funded research is silly. Yes, the government allocates money inefficiently. Yes, research should also attract private donations. But the 5% that is not silly is often vital, and can produce big breakthroughs. Like the military, there are a few things the federal government must do. We are falling behind on basic research investments.

More

And FDA approvals take forever. And patent law is a mess leading companies to spend too much time on lawsuits. And anti-trust law is completely outdated, just throwing sand in the gears. And the NLRB and EEOC are making a mess of labor markets. And the FCC is going to turn the internet into the 1965 French telephone company. And... well, this could go on pretty much forever.

There are a lot of weeds. Just turn to the Hoover research website http://www.hoover.org/ research, especially Economic Policy, Education, Energy Science & Technology and Health care tabs. Turn to Cato's website http://www.cato.org/_and browse down the "Research Areas" tabs, especially the Education, Energy and Environment, Finance, Health Care, Regulatory studies, Tax and budget, and Trade and Immigration tabs. I have kept this essay deliberately free of a forest of numbers and citations for easy reading, but the numbers and citations are easy to find.

This essay summarizes some of my own earlier writings on many of these issues, all available at http://faculty.chicagobooth.edu/john.cochrane/. For more on regulation, see "The Rule of Law in the Regulatory State." For more on health care and insurance see "After the ACA: Freeing the Market for Health Care" and "Health Status Insurance." On financial reform (alternatives to Dodd-Frank) see "Towards a Run-Free Financial System."

Immigration Policy

Peter Skerry[1]

Prepared for the Focusing the Presidential Debates Initiative

Immigration is woven into the warp and woof of America's self-understanding in a way that is true of few other nations. In our schools and around our dinner tables, the topic invariably leads to allusions to the Statue of Liberty welcoming immigrants to this haven of opportunity and freedom, or to the contributions that immigrants have made and continue to make to our nation's pluralist tapestry, the vibrancy of our cities, the creativity of our arts and popular culture, and the dynamism of our economy. Yet at the same time, immigrants have been regarded—today and in our past—as threats to those same valued features of our national life. Indeed, in the on-going debate, immigrants have been depicted as a drain on our fiscal resources, a production factor of dubious benefit on which sectors of our economy have become unduly dependent, a strain on our neighborhoods and communal institutions, a challenge to our cultural cohesion, and even a threat to our way of life.

So, immigration is a highly complex policy issue, or set of issues, that arouses intense emotions. In the policy arena it also calls upon the technical and analytic skills of lawyers, economists, historians, sociologists, and social policy analysts. To be sure, in the broad national debate over immigration, especially in the media, advocates on all sides of the issue routinely resort to emotionally evocative appeals to conscience, faith, national security, and American exceptionalism. Yet it is striking how quickly these aspects of this issue get stripped away the closer we get to the legislative debate in Washington, where our political and business elites have long and skillfully endeavored to reduce immigration to its more manageable economic and fiscal dimensions. Indeed, if there is any "Washington consensus" to be discerned in this contentious policy domain, this is it.

---

1. Professor of political science, Boston College; Senior Fellow, Kenan Institute for Ethics at Duke University.

This phenomenon is not hard to understand. The fiscal and economic impacts of our immigration policy—the demands immigrants place on social programs at various levels of government or the benefits they afford specific business sectors or economic strata—may be technically complex to ascertain, but they are also easier to quantify, analyze, and assess than the more emotion-laden and diffuse impacts of immigration on American social, cultural, communal, and political processes.

Then, too, the overwhelming majority of immigrants (excepting of course refugees, whose particular plight is highlighted by the recent news from Europe) come here either directly or indirectly (that is, to join their families) in search of economic opportunity. Moreover, the technical prowess and professional prestige of economists in policy circles affords their analyses of these processes great visibility. And in any event, business and other economic interests are typically well-defined, highly organized, and for the most part well-represented among our political institutions and elites.

None of this is news to the millions of Americans frustrated with our immigration policies, especially those populist voices pressing Republican elites to stop kowtowing to entrenched business interests. Less noted is the surprisingly business-friendly posture of liberals engaged in the immigration debate. In part, this is because when liberals support business pleas for increased levels of immigrant labor (as they invariably do), it is in part because they have confidence in the institutions of the administrative state, which have been fashioned, largely by them, to monitor and discipline the market behavior of firms. In any event, it is ironic to see liberals, who are inveterately dubious of business claims when it comes, for example, to tax or environmental policy, accept on their face the demands of those same parties for immigrant workers.

Of course, many—arguably most—Americans do not share the faith of liberal (or for that matter many conservative) elites in the ability of administrative agencies to regulate markets and firms. Indeed, Americans instinctively distrust the lawyers and technocrats who populate these agencies. And so do the populists now surging through the Republican Party. Indeed, the more shrewd and insightful among them might conclude that continued high levels of immigration of the sort that we have been experiencing for the last four decades constitute one more excuse for the build up of the administrative state they have come to distrust, if not abhor outright. This is why any narrow focus on the economic or even fiscal impacts of immigrants on specific segments of society misses the deeper resentment felt by large numbers of Americans toward the failure of our political elites to stem the current influx.

Yet those disaffected with the constrained debate over immigration are concerned about something more fundamental. In part, they are asking why our political elites, on a matter of critical concern to *all* Americans, have been taking business interests at their word? Even those who consider themselves, correctly or not, as materially or concretely disadvantaged by prevailing policy are trying to say, however inarticulately, that America is not just a market but a nation—a political community.

This fundamental concern underlies the outrage frequently expressed over the 11 million illegals in our midst. Without a doubt, the anger expressed toward these "criminals" and "lawbreakers" is in part directed at the elites who have allowed this situation to fester, who have benefitted from it, whether politically or economically, and who now seem perfectly willing to overlook the illegality involved.

Nevertheless, while such populist sentiments are understandable, they are also misdirected and short sighted. Indeed, it is precisely because America *is* a political community that we all share some responsibility for this dilemma. However justified the disaffection and anger directed toward our elites, Americans need to remember that we still live in a free and vibrant democracy. We must also remind ourselves that millions of undocumented immigrants have been able to come here and remain because of flaws in our immigration laws that, in most cases, were understood when enacted—but were nevertheless the best that could be achieved at the time. If 11 million illegal immigrants have broken our laws, then so have a commensurate number of employers and other Americans who have either winked at the law by relying on documents very likely to be false, or simply conspired with the undocumented to evade the law.

Furthermore, it is now the case that, with the passage of time and because America is such an open and absorptive society, these 11 million are substantially integrated into our communities. As a result, "we" (including the millions of undocumented) are all in this together. And we cannot extricate ourselves from it without recognizing the complicity in this nettle of American lawmakers, business interests, and, yes, American voters.

However, none of this relieves the undocumented of responsibility for their predicament. Nor does it ignore or deny the legitimate concerns of many Americans about the challenges and burdens posed by their presence. Accordingly, as I have laid out elsewhere,[2] we should grant as many of the undocumented as possible permanent legal status, and do so as expeditiously as possible— that is, with appropriate criminal background checks but otherwise with minimal bureaucratic hurdles and penalties. On the other hand, the one penalty

---

2. Peter Skerry, "Splitting the Difference on Illegal Immigration," *National Affairs* (Winter 2013).

that I believe both political and ethical realism call for is that eligible illegals be granted permanent residency—*but never be eligible for full citizenship* (with exceptions carved out for those undocumented who arrived here as children or minors).

Of course, whatever appeal such a proposal (or some variant of it) might have, it addresses only one aspect of our immigration dilemma. Restriction-ist sentiment now demands that any efforts to address the plight of the un-documented must await "securing the border." In response, immigrant advocates rightly point to the enormous increases in resources and manpower that have been focused on our border with Mexico over the past 25 years. Yet while enor-mous progress has been made in this regard, border security can hardly be limited, especially in this post-9/11 era, merely to stemming surreptitious bor-der crossings or even to identifying those entering legally through our ports of entry. Since anywhere from forty to fifty percent of undocumented aliens are visa over-stayers (including several of the perpetrators of 9/11), we need fi-nally to implement an effective program monitoring the *departure* of visitors. For a variety of reasons—bureaucratic, fiscal, and political—this has proved to be virtually impossible. But effective and meaningful control of our bor-ders requires it.

A related issue already raised by some of the presidential candidates concerns so-called "sanctuary cities," local jurisdictions that have restricted their involve-ment with the enforcement of federal immigration laws. The Department of Homeland Security has reported that as of October 2014, there were over 270 such jurisdictions in the United States—including agencies in Chicago, Miami, New York, Philadelphia, Baltimore, Washington, DC, and San Francisco.

The challenge here surfaced recently in the latter city, where this past sum-mer the Sheriff's Department released a man with five prior deportations and seven felony convictions, even though federal authorities had requested he be kept in custody until they could pick him up. Instead, the Sheriff released Juan Francisco Lopez-Sanchez, who subsequently fired three shots and for no ap-parent reason killed thirty-two-year old Kathryn Steinle at a tourist attraction at the Embarcadero. Such incidents only further arouse Americans already confused and offended by the Supreme Court's 2012 decision in *U.S. v. Ari-zona*, which asserted the supremacy of federal authority in this policy domain while striking down much of that state's effort to control its own borders.

At the same time, we must not allow the on-going debate's narrow and al-most exclusive focus on undocumented immigrants to neglect the broader mi-gration phenomenon confronting us. Even if we manage successfully to address the challenges of undocumented immigration with more secure borders and adequate, sustained interior enforcement, most aspects of the continuing influx that have aroused the anxieties of large numbers of Americans—fiscal costs, burdened schools and social services, labor market competition, social disorder and crime, assimilation and cultural change—will remain. And because immigrant advocates, business interests, and their political allies have routinely addressed concerns about *illegal* immigration with proposals to open the doors wider to *legal* immigration, these strains will almost certainly be exacerbated.

Indeed, the political response to many of our immigration dilemmas has typically been addition: rather than make tough choices among alternatives, we have typically avoiding saying no to anyone and instead afforded various interests some of what they want. The resulting "inflation" fails to address the basic issues, and as a result has meant a steady increase in total levels of legal immigration: more skilled workers, more family members admitted from long waiting lines in places like India or China, more slots for refugees, more agricultural workers, and so on. Such incremental gains have worked for pro-immigrant forces in the past, but now this issue is too heated, and the more aroused segments of the public are not likely to be as pliant as they have been.

Some policy-makers have recognized this problem and sought a path forward with proposals for temporary or guest workers—whether low-skilled agricultural labor or more skilled technical or scientific workers. Yet aside from the almost unavoidable vulnerability of such workers to exploitation by employers, we know from our own experience, as well as that of other nations, that guest workers tend not to remain "guests" and typically end up staying on in the host country, whether legally or illegally. Acknowledging this reality, some have proposed "temporary worker programs" that, after a few years of employment, offer the option of permanent residence and then citizenship. But then of course we're back to increasing overall numbers of permanent immigrants and just playing word games.

However difficult it will prove to be, sooner or later Americans will have to engage in a national discussion about how many immigrants should optimally be admitted each year. This will not be easy, in part because there is no technical, social scientific, or even economic answer to this question. This discussion will have to reflect competing economic and fiscal interests, as well as judgments about the capacities of our communities to absorb newcomers. So, too, however clumsily, concerns about assimilation and integration will inevitably enter into such discussions. These will not be easy conversations but something approaching them will be necessary as an alternative to the heretofore elite-dominated policy debate that evaded deeper concerns in favor of a narrow agenda shaped by business and economic interests, sweetened with lots of money poured into border enforcement.

What we need is a discussion about how America's immigration policy aligns with the national interest. Easy nostrums about our immigrant grandmothers

or the meaning of the Statue of Liberty will no longer do. Nor will mean-spir-
ited vilification of migrants seeking better lives for themselves and their children. If we are truly to entertain "comprehensive immigration reform," such
a national conversation will be crucial. It is even conceivable that this might lead
to a genuine consensus for increased levels of migration, though that would require much more trust in our business and political elites than substantial segments of the American people now exhibit.

Targeting Disease: Musculoskeletal Conditions

Steven R. Goldring, MD[*]

Prepared for the Focusing the Presidential Debates Initiative

Much of the public debate about health care in America has focused on access to care. This is, of course, an important issue. But it is also important that we focus on basic research holding promise for cure or reduction in the burden of disease. This is particularly so for diseases where a substantial percentage of the US population is affected, where the total cost of the disease is high, where existing research funding has been relatively low, and where new biological and medical knowledge offers promise for reduction in the disease burden. Enhanced research in such settings offers promise for cost savings which are potentially an order of magnitude greater than the research costs. Further, greater success in cures or treatments would mean that millions of Americans would no longer be condemned to a lifetime of pain and disability.

Our Nation should consider whether individual groupings of diseases today meet criteria where substantially increased research funding could both return many times the costs, and increase the quality of life for millions of Americans. That is, are we at a point where more rapid advances in biological and medical knowledge suggest that the Nation should embrace a more robust approach to *Targeting Disease?* This paper will recommend that Musculoskeletal Conditions, including osteoarthritis and rheumatoid arthritis, which are the top causes of disability among US adults, should initiate such a national effort.

Musculoskeletal (MS) conditions are among the most disabling and costly conditions affecting the American population. They include a diverse group of disorders that affect the bones, joints, tendons, ligaments and muscles and en-

---

[*] Steven R. Goldring, MD is Chief Scientific Officer Emeritus, Hospital for Special Surgery and Professor of Medicine, Weill Cornell College of Medicine.

compass a broad spectrum of conditions, from those of acute onset and short duration related to injury and/or overuse to chronic disorders that include arthritis, bone diseases and low back and neck pain.

In the 1990s, the World Bank commissioned the first global burden of disease (GBD) study, which resulted in the assessment of disease burden for over 100 diseases and injuries, including musculoskeletal conditions (1-9). This study and a follow-up analysis completed in 2010 (GBD 2010) found that musculoskeletal conditions affected more than 1.7 billion people worldwide. Five major musculoskeletal conditions were studied in detail, including osteoarthritis (OA), rheumatoid arthritis (RA), gout, low back pain (LBP) and neck pain (NP). Data from other musculoskeletal disorders including autoimmune and inflammatory rheumatic diseases such as systemic lupus erythematosus, psoriatic arthritis, ankylosing spondylitis and juvenile inflammatory arthritis were also captured. Globally, all musculoskeletal disorders accounted for 21.3% of the total years lived with disability (YLDs), which was second to mental and behavioral problems (23.2%) (1,9).

In North America, musculoskeletal conditions are responsible for more functional limitations than any other group of disorders and are the major cause of years lived with disability. Data from a representative study in Canada revealed that musculoskeletal conditions accounted for close to 40% of all chronic conditions and 54% of all long-term disability, and 24% of all restricted activity days (10). Importantly, the pain and physical disability associated with musculoskeletal conditions affects social functioning and mental health, further compromising an individuals' quality of life.

In 2010-2012 the CDC analyzed data from the National Health Interview Survey (NHIS), which revealed that 52.5 million (22.7%) of adults aged ≥18 years had self-reported doctor-diagnosed joint symptoms, and 22.7 million (9.8%, or 43.2% of those with arthritis) reported arthritis-attributable activity limitation (AAAL) (11). With the aging of the US population, the prevalence of arthritis is expected to increase so that by the year 2030, an estimated 67 million adults aged 18 years and older will have doctor-diagnosed arthritis. **Figure 1** shows that by 2030, an estimated 25 million adults (37% of adults with arthritis or 9.3% of all US adults) will report arthritis-attributable activity limitations. These estimates may be conservative, as they do not account for the current trends in obesity, which may contribute to future cases of arthritis.

Osteoarthritis (OA) is by far the most common form of arthritis and accounts for a majority of the patient and physician reported cases of arthritis (11). OA is characterized by loss of joint cartilage and alterations in adjacent weight bearing bone tissues that leads to loss of function and progressive disability.

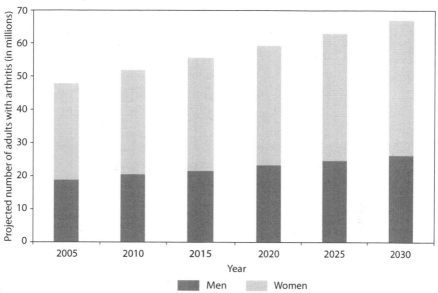

Figure 1. Estimated Number of Adults with Arthritis

http://www.cdc.gov/arthritis/data_statistics/national-statistics.html

Pain is the most prominent symptom in most people with OA (12), and is the most important determinant of disability (13). OA most commonly affects the knees, hips and hands, although all joints can be affected. Close to 10% of men and 18% of women aged >60 years are affected by OA. Age is the strongest predictor of the development and progression of OA, and the predicted increase in life expectancy in this country will result in greater numbers of individuals at risk. The ability to replace joints destroyed by the osteoarthritic process has revolutionized the treatment of patients with end-stage OA, but the projected increase in the number of individuals undergoing joint replacement will place an increasing financial burden on the healthcare system in this country and there is a need for interventions that can slow or even halt the progression of OA.

Rheumatoid arthritis (RA) and gout are inflammatory conditions that characteristically affect multiple joints, leading to acute and chronic inflammation and deformity (2,7). Major research discoveries and the development of new and effective therapeutic agents have dramatically improved the outcomes in patients with RA (14-16). However, even with these new therapeutic advances, over one third of individuals with RA continue to experience symptoms and progressive loss of joint function (16). Similar advances in the development of drug therapies hold the promise of reducing the disease burden of gout, but despite these advances, the incidence of gout and associated joint disease is increasing in the general population (7, 17).

Osteoporosis, is a systemic skeletal disorder that is characterized by low bone mass and deterioration in bone structure and strength. It is a major risk factor for fractures of the hip, spine, and distal forearm (6). Hip fractures are particularly debilitating and may be associated with close to 20% mortality and 50% permanent loss in function (18). Research in the field of bone diseases has led to the development of multiple drug therapies that can improve bone health and substantially reduce the risk of fracture and disability (19, 20). The present therapies have been shown to reduce the rate of bone loss but additional so called anabolic therapies are needed to increase bone mass in individuals who present with fractures and reduced bone mass (20).

Low back and neck pain are the final categories analyzed in the GBD 2010 study (4,5,18). They are the most prevalent of the musculoskeletal conditions, affecting nearly all individuals at some point in their lives and about 4–33% of the population at any given point. Most episodes of low back pain resolve or improve within several weeks, but recurrences are common with further acute episodes affecting 20–44% of working individuals within one year and a lifetime recurrence rate of up to 85%. Low back pain is associated with age, physical fitness, smoking, obesity, and strength of back and abdominal muscles. Occupational factors such as heavy lifting, bending, and twisting are additional risk factors (21, 22).

The rate of musculoskeletal conditions is 76% greater than that of chronic circulatory conditions, which include coronary disease and heart conditions, and nearly twice that of all chronic respiratory conditions (11, 23). On an age-adjusted basis, musculoskeletal conditions are reported by 54 persons per every 100 in the population. This compares to a rate of 31 and 28 persons per every 100 in the population for circulatory and respiratory conditions, respectively. These incidence rates are reflected in the impact of the conditions on disability as shown in **Figure 2** (23).

In the US in 2012, twenty eight million individuals with a musculoskeletal condition between the ages of 18 and 64, reported lost work days in the previous 12 months, totaling more than 216 million days. On average, workers lost nearly 8 days in a 12-month period. This accounts for more than four times as many lost work days as depression, which is the second most common condition associated with lost work days. Chronic circulatory conditions, including high blood pressure and other cardiovascular conditions, accounted for 32.3 million lost work days. Chronic respiratory conditions accounted for 16.5 million lost work days. The impact of musculoskeletal injuries and conditions compared to other major illnesses and disorders is in **Figure 3.**

Figure 2. Top 10 Causes of Disability Among US Adults, 2005 (ref. 11, 23)

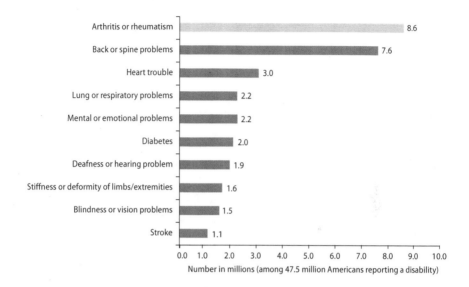

Number in millions (among 47.5 million Americans reporting a disability)

Figure 3. Proportion of Lost Work Days due to Major Health Conditions

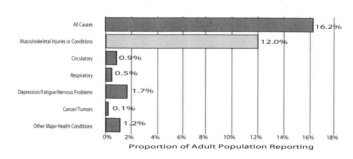

Proportion of Adult Population Reporting

Source: National Health Interview Survey (NHIS), Adult Sample.
www.cdc.goc/nchs/nhis/nhis_2012_data_release.htm July 2, 2013

The annual average proportion of the US population with a musculoskeletal condition requiring medical care now constitutes more than 33% of the population (24). This is an overall rate of increase of 19%. The majority of the growth is in the 45 to 64-year age bracket. The annual estimated direct and indirect cost attributable to persons with a musculoskeletal disease is $213 billion (24). Taking into account all costs for persons with a musculoskeletal disease including other comorbid conditions, the cost of treating these individuals and the direct cost to society is currently estimated to be nearly $874 billion, or 5.73% percent of the U.S. gross national product (24).

In spite of the widespread prevalence of musculoskeletal conditions, they are not among the top ten health conditions receiving research funding (25). In part, this is attributable to the low mortality from musculoskeletal conditions in comparison with other health conditions. However, because musculoskeletal conditions restrict activities of daily living, cause lost work days, and are a source of lifelong pain, the morbidity and cost to society of musculoskeletal conditions is tremendous.

Despite the enormous financial and personal impact of musculoskeletal conditions, research funding to alleviate these major health conditions remains substantially below that of other major health conditions such as cancer, respiratory and cardiovascular diseases. The National Institute of Arthritis and Musculoskeletal and Skin Diseases (NIAMS) was formed in 1987 and is the principle NIH Institute that provides extramural financial support for musculoskeletal research. Research funding for musculoskeletal conditions has declined in relative terms, so that presently less than 2% of the annual NIH budget is appropriated to musculoskeletal disease research. Over the last five years (2009 to 2013), funding for musculoskeletal research from the NIH totaled $7.8 billion, while that of cancers and heart/circulatory disorders totaled $43.5 billion and $25.9 billion, respectively. **Figure 4** illustrates the relative distribution of funding for several major disease categories including musculoskeletal diseases.

In March 2002, President George W. Bush proclaimed the years 2002–2011 as the United States Bone and Joint Decade, providing national recognition to the fact that musculoskeletal disorders and diseases are the leading cause of physical disability in this country. At the end of the decade, the United States Bone and Joint Initiative (USBJI), a part of the Global Alliance for Musculoskeletal Health, was created. The goal of USBJI is to improve the quality of life for people with musculoskeletal conditions and to advance understanding and treatment of these conditions through research, prevention, and education.

The USBJI, conducted a strategic planning process that solicited input from a panel of experts in the fields of musculoskeletal research, education and care to set priorities "beyond the decade." This was accomplished by six task groups (Arthritis, Bone Health and Osteoporosis, Pediatric Musculoskeletal Conditions, Spinal Disorders and Low Back Pain, Trauma and Injury, and Research).

Figure 4. Distribution of NIH Research Support for Major Diseases

Research Funding to NIAMS*

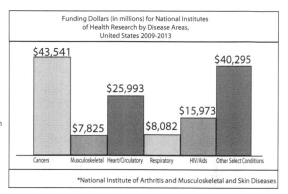

$7.8 billion = Total research funding for years 2009 to 2013.

- Less than 2% of annual National Institutes of Health (NIH) research budget allocated to NIAMS
- Annual average share of funding declining since 2000
- In spite of prevalence and high morbidity, muscoloskeletal diseases research dollars a fraction of allocations for other common conditions

Funding Dollars (in millions) for National Institutes of Health Research by Disease Areas, United States 2009-2013

$43,541 — Cancers
$7,825 — Musculoskeletal
$25,993 — Heart/Circulatory
$8,082 — Respiratory
$15,973 — HIV/Aids
$40,295 — Other Select Conditions

*National Institute of Arthritis and Musculoskeletal and Skin Diseases

Source: National Institutes of Health. Estimates of Funding for Various Research, Condition, and Disease Categories. http://report/nih.gov/categorical_spending.aspx Accessed December 17, 2013.

It is beyond the scope of this review to provide a detailed description of the recommendations of the task force, which were recently published (26), and therefore, only the key points of the recommendations will be highlighted:

Priority Area 1.2: Education of Policy Makers (Government and Non-Government)
Policy makers need to be made aware of the personal and financial impact of musculoskeletal conditions and Federal funding for arthritis-related public health initiatives, as well as for professional training, research, and health-care systems. for arthritis care, should be substantially increased.
Priority Area 1.5: Research
Given the enormous impact of musculoskeletal disorders on individuals and society, funding for arthritis-related research needs to substantially increase across the full spectrum of basic, translational and clinical research, including epidemiology, outcomes, and comparative effectiveness of arthritis treatments.
Priority Area 4.2: Establishment of Infrastructure for Multidisciplinary Collaboration on Research and Education
There are large gaps in our knowledge of the causes of many spinal disorders and low back pain. Multidisciplinary evidence-based guidelines for diagnosis and treatment need to be established and research involving partnership with industry, public health organizations, and government need to be expanded.

Priority Area 6.1: Basic Research

Musculoskeletal conditions are under-researched relative to the burden of disease and the discrepancy between research funding and the prevalence of disease impairs progress in reducing the burden of musculoskeletal disease. The primary goal should be to increase the quantity, quality, and relevance of musculoskeletal research. A secondary goal should be to foster translation of basic results into new prevention measures, risk assessment tools, and therapies.

Priority Area 6.2: Comparative Effectiveness Research

One mechanism to facilitate translation of research to clinical practice is through comparative effectiveness studies that provide data on how to choose among therapeutic strategies. There is a need to define identify and prioritize research needs such as evaluation of treatments for osteoporosis and osteoarthritis, that can allow investigators to assess differences in effectiveness of treatments.

Priority Area 6.3: Clinical Research and Innovative Trial Designs

There is a need for more innovative clinical trial designs than randomized controlled trials, which can be prohibitive because of difficulty attaining an appropriate sample size and because of cost. There is a need to foster more collaborative public private partnerships to allow for the breadth and depth of expertise necessary to design, implement, and analyze clinical data and to provide greater financial support for important trials.

Summary and Conclusion

Musculoskeletal disorders are the major cause of disability in the United States. Given the enormous impact of musculoskeletal disorders on individuals and society, there is a urgent need to substantially increase Federal funding and non-governmental support for arthritis-related public health initiatives, as well as for professional training, research, and optimization of health-care systems. Research funding for musculoskeletal research needs to be increased across the full spectrum of basic, translational and clinical research, and the discoveries and findings translated into new prevention measures, risk assessment tools, and therapies. Research discoveries have profoundly altered and improved the natural history of many musculoskeletal disorders, including for example the development of effective biological and small molecule therapies for rheumatoid arthritis and identification and testing of new drugs for the treatment of osteoporosis. These discoveries highlight the impact that research can have on improving the lives and outcomes of individuals suffering from the disabling effects of musculoskeletal disorders and should stimulate and incent policy makers to allocate more resources to address the unmet needs for these conditions.

References

1. Murray CJ, Vos T, Lozano R, et al. Disability-adjusted life years (DALYs) for 291 diseases and injuries in 21 regions, 1990-2010: a systematic analysis for the Global Burden of Disease Study 2010. Lancet 2013 Dec 15;380(9859):2197e223.

2. Cross M, Smith E, Hoy D, et al. The global burden of rheumatoid arthritis: estimates from the Global Burden of Disease 2010 Study. Ann Rheum Dis 2014;73:1316e22.

3. Cross M, Smith E, Hoy D, et al. The global burden of hip and knee osteoarthritis: estimates from the Global Burden of Disease 2010 Study. Ann Rheum Dis 2014;73:1323e30.

4. Hoy D, March L, Brooks P, et al. The global burden of low back pain: estimates from the Global Burden of Disease 2010 Study. Ann Rheum Dis 2014;73:968e74.

5. Hoy D, March L, Woolf A, et al. The global burden of neck pain: estimates from the Global Burden of Disease 2010 Study. Ann Rheum Dis 2014;73:1309e15.

6. Sanchez-Riera L, Carnahan E, Vos T, et al. Global burden attributable to low bone mineral density. Ann Rheum Dis 2014;73:1635e45.

7. Smith E, Hoy D, Cross M, et al. The global burden of gout: estimates from the Global Burden of Disease 2010 Study. Ann Rheum Dis 2014;73:1470e6.

8. Smith E, Hoy D, Cross M, et al. The global burden of other musculoskeletal disorders: estimates from the Global Burden of Disease 2010 Study. Ann Rheum Dis 2014;73:1462e9.

9. Vos T, Flaxman AD, Naghavi M, et al. Years lived with disability (YLDs) for 1160 sequelae of 289 diseases and injuries 1990-2010: a systematic analysis for the Global Burden of Disease Study 2010. Lancet 2013 Dec 15;380(9859):2163e96.

10. Badley EM, Rasooly I, Webster GK. Relative importance of musculoskeletal disorders as a cause of chronic health problems, disability, and healthcare utilization: findings from the 1990 Ontario Health Survey. Journal of Rheumatology 1994;21:505-14.

11. "http://www.cdc.gov/arthritis/data_statistics/national-statistics.html" http://www.cdc.gov/arthritis/data_statistics/national-statistics.html

12. Kazis LE, Meenan RF, Anderson JJ. Pain in the rheumatic diseases. Investigation of a key health status component. Arthritis and Rheumatism 1983;26:1017-22.

13. van Baar ME, Dekker J, Lemmens JA, Oostendorp RA, Bijlsma JW. Pain and disability in patients with osteoarthritis of hip or knee: the relationship with articular, kinesiological, and psychological characteristics. Journal of Rheumatology 1998;25:125-33.

14. http://directorsblog.nih.gov/2013/01/14/nih-research-leads-to-new-rheumatoid-arthritis-drug/#more-384

15. Meier FM, McInnes IB. Small-molecule therapeutics in rheumatoid arthritis: scientific rationale, efficacy and safety. Best Pract Res Clin Rheumatol. 2014 Aug;28(4):605-24.

16. Burmester GR, Feist E, Dörner T.Emerging cell and cytokine targets in rheumatoid arthritis. Nat Rev Rheumatol. 2014 Feb;10(2):77-88. doi: 10.1038/nrrheum.2013.168

17. Robinson PC, Dalbeth N. Advances in pharmacotherapy for the treatment of gout. Expert Opin Pharmacother. 2015 Mar;16(4):533-46.

18. Anthony D.Woolf, Bruce Pfleger. Burden of major musculoskeletal conditions. Bulletin of the World Health Organization 2003;81:646-656.

19. Reid IR. Short-term and long-term effects of osteoporosis therapies. Nat Rev Endocrinol. 2015 Jul;11(7):418-28.

20. Drake MT, Clarke BL, Lewiecki EM.The Pathophysiology and Treatment of Osteoporosis. Clin Ther. 2015 Aug 1;37(8):1837-50.

21. Felson DT. Does excess weight cause osteoarthritis and, if so, why? Annals of Rheumatic Disease 1996;55:668-70.

22. Andersson GB. Epidemiological features of chronic low-back pain. Lancet 1999;354:581-5.

23. Hootman JM, Brault MW, Helmick CG, Theis KA, Armour BS. Prevalence and Most Common Causes of Disability Among Adults—United States, 2005. Morb Mortal Wkly Rep. 2009; 58(16): 421–426.

24. http://www.boneandjointburden.org/2014-report/i0/big-picture

25. Weinstein S: 2000–2010: The Bone and Joint Decade. J Bone Joint Surg Am 2000;82:1-3.

26. Jacobs JJ1, King TR, YPERLINK"http://www.ncbi.nlm.nih.gov/pubmed/?term=Klippel%20JH%5BAuthor%5D&cauthor=true&cauthor_uid=24005209"Klippel JH, Berven SH, NK"http://www.ncbi.nlm.nih.gov/pubmed/?term=Burr%20DB%5BAuthor%5D&cauthor=true&cauthor_uid=24005209"Burr DB, Caskey PM, Elderkin AL, Esposito PW, Gall EP, Goldring SR, Pollak AN, Sandborg CI, Templeton KJ. Beyond the decade: strategic priorities to reduce the burden of musculoskeletal disease. J Bone Joint Surg Am. 2013 Sep 4;95(17):e1251-6.

Social Security Optionality: Reducing the Wealth Gap

*Peter Ferrara**

Prepared for the Focusing the Presidential Debates Initiative

Executive Summary

The latest Annual Report of the Social Security Board of Trustees warns that Social Security will run short of funds to pay promised benefits by 2033, and quite possibly as soon as 2028, just 13 years from now. Indeed, the disability insurance portion of Social Security will not have sufficient funds to pay promised benefits *next year*.

Once the trust funds run out, under intermediate assumptions, the current total Social Security payroll tax rate of 12.4 percent will have to jump in 2033 by close to 40 percent to start, to about 17 percent. Under so-called pessimistic assumptions, paying all promised benefits in 2030 would require raising the total Social Security payroll tax rate to close to 20 percent, an increase of almost 60 percent. Paying all benefits financed by the payroll tax would require that tax to soar to close to 40 percent, more than double.

All workers across the board, of all income levels and family combinations, would now get much higher benefits saving and investing in the market through personal accounts than the benefits Social Security even promises today, which the program cannot pay. A two earner middle income couple saving and investing over their lifetime in their own personal savings and investment account what would otherwise be paid into Social Security would reach retirement at just standard long term market investment returns with $1,223,602 in today's dollars, after adjusting for inflation.

That fund would be able to pay out of the continuing investment returns alone just about *twice* what Social Security promises to pay them under current law,

---

* Peter Ferrara is Director of the International Center for Law and Economics.

while still allowing them to leave the $1.2 million fund to their children. Or they could use the fund to buy themselves an annuity that would pay them over four times what Social Security currently promises, let alone what it can pay.

A Proposal for Social Security Reform

All workers under 40 would be allowed the freedom to choose such personal accounts for their Social Security retirement benefits. For those that make this choice, taxes will be rebated into their accounts equal to 10% of the first $10,000 they earn each year, and 5% of everything above that, up to the Social Security maximum taxable income. That would be roughly equal to the employee share of the payroll tax. But the rebates would be financed by general revenues, leaving all Social Security payroll tax revenues to continue to flow into Social Security unchanged.

The Treasury Dept. would contract with private fund managers to offer investment funds to workers who exercised the personal account option, invested entirely into index funds for the S&P 500. For those that choose personal accounts, workers of all income levels and family combinations would receive higher total future retirement benefits, rather than lower benefits. Workers would receive the benefits that can be financed by their personal accounts. Plus they would also receive a portion of promised Social Security retirement benefits equal to the portion of lifetime Social Security payroll taxes (OASI) that they had already paid while working, before they made the choice for personal accounts.

Those that choose personal accounts would be backed by a federal guarantee that those funds combined would equal at least what Social Security promises them under current law, or they will be paid a guarantee benefit every month equal to the difference. This would maintain the current Social Security safety net in full.

Social Security survivors and disability benefits would continue to be paid as promised under current law without change. There would be no change in Social Security of any sort for those already retired, or workers 40 and over not eligible for the personal account option. For those that do not choose to make the choice for personal accounts, they would continue to receive Social Security benefits as provided under current law without change as well, with no benefit cuts or tax increases of any sort.

Workers with personal accounts would be free to choose to leave any portion of their funds to their families or children. Those funds and any benefits payable from the personal accounts would be free of any tax.

Workers with personal accounts would be free to choose their own retirement age for benefits from the account, with market incentives to delay it as long as possible, because the longer they wait, the more funds would accumulate in the account, and the higher the benefits it can pay.

Such reform would eliminate all future deficits of Social Security, without any benefit cuts or tax increases, as validated by the Chief Actuary of Social Security. Indeed, ultimately the resulting savings in federal spending from the reform would amount to the biggest reduction in government spending in world history.

The proposed personal accounts for Social Security would do more to address the issue of wealth inequality than everything dreamed up by Elizabeth Warren and Hillary Clinton put together. After the first 15 years under the reform, working people across America would have accumulated $7.8 trillion in today's dollars in their personal accounts. After the first 25 years, workers would have accumulated $16 trillion in today's dollars.

The personal accounts funnel mighty, new rivers of savings and investment into the economy. Higher savings and capital investment mean higher productivity and increased wages for working people. That creates new jobs and new opportunities. The bottom line is increased economic growth.

* * *

The Social Security Financial Crisis

For Social Security, the future the government's actuaries have long warned about is here. The latest Annual Report of the Social Security Board of Trustees warns that Social Security will run short of funds to pay promised benefits by 2034, and quite possibly as soon as 2028.[1] That is no longer sometime in the next century. That is as soon as 13 years from now. Which means it will affect people already retired today.

Indeed, U.S. government reports project that the disability insurance portion of the program will not have sufficient funds to pay promised benefits *next year.*[2]

The root of the financial problem is that Social Security does not have a cushion of real savings and investment that can weather bad times. Social Security does not save the funds workers and their employers are paying in today

---

1. 2015 Annual Report of the Board of Trustees of the Old Age and Survivors Insurance and Disability Insurance Trust Funds, July 22, 2015, Table IV.B4, p. 66.

2. Id., p. 2, Table IV.B4, p. 66

to finance their future benefits. Social Security uses the tax payments coming in today to immediately finance the benefits for today's retirees. Social Security expects the future tax payments of future workers to finance the future benefits for today's workers.

Even when the system was running annual surpluses, close to 90 percent of the money coming in was paid out within the year to pay current benefits. The remaining annual surpluses each year were not saved and invested either. They were lent to the federal government and spent on other government programs, from foreign aid to bridges to nowhere, with the Social Security trust funds receiving only internal federal IOUs promising to pay the money back when it is needed to pay benefits. These internal federal IOUs are all that is held by the so-called Social Security trust funds, now totaling roughly $2.7 trillion.

As a result, Social Security is not a savings and investment system. It is a tax and redistribution system, where the money is taken from one group of people through taxes and just immediately redistributed to other people in benefits and other government spending.

When Social Security runs a deficit, as it is doing today and will do indefinitely into the future until the trust funds are exhausted, Social Security turns some of those trust fund IOUs over to the U.S. Treasury to get money back to continue paying promised benefits. But there is no cash or other savings and investment held in reserve to pay back those IOUs. So where does the U.S. Treasury plan to get the money to pay them back?

From you. Since those IOUs are national debt, not assets of the federal government, they are owed by you, and you will have to pay them back for retirees to continue to receive all their promised Social Security benefits. Paying back the IOUs will be in addition to the hundreds of billions of dollars you and other taxpayers must pay in payroll taxes each year. When Social Security comes to the Treasury turning in trust fund IOUs to get the cash to pay promised benefits, the Treasury will get that cash either by raising your taxes or by borrowing still more and running even bigger deficits. This is why the long-term Social Security financing crisis has already begun.

That financing crisis accelerates in earnest once the trust funds run out. Payroll tax rates will then have to increase sharply to continue paying all the benefits promised by Social Security. Under so-called intermediate assumptions, the current total Social Security payroll tax rate of 12.4 percent will have to jump in 2035 by close to 40 percent to start, to about 17 percent.[3]

---

3. 2015 Trustees Report, Table VI.G2, p. 203.

Under so-called pessimistic assumptions, which may be the most realistic,[4] paying all promised benefits in 2030 would require raising the total Social Security payroll tax rate immediately to close to 19 percent, an increase of about 55 percent.[5] Paying all benefits financed by the payroll tax would ultimately require the total payroll tax rate to soar to 35 percent, more than double, under so-called pessimistic assumptions.[6]

Payroll tax rate increases in these ranges will cause soaring unemployment, which in turn will mean less revenue than expected, which will require still higher tax rates. This gives a bracing new reality to the term "death spiral." The threat of this "death spiral," and the economic burden of such soaring payroll tax rates, does threaten future benefit cuts, which the U.S. Supreme Court has already specifically ruled are not constitutionally guaranteed, or even contractually guaranteed.

Why Personal Accounts Would Provide Better Benefits for Seniors Than Social Security

Even if Social Security could somehow pay all of its promised benefits, those benefits are inadequate, and represent a low, below market return on the Social Security payroll taxes working people and their employers pay throughout their lives. For most working people, even if Social Security could pay all of its promised benefits, those benefits would represent a real rate of return of less than 1% on the Social Security taxes paid throughout their working years.[7]

For many workers, that real return would be negative, meaning less than 0%.[8] That is like depositing money in the bank, but instead of the bank paying you interest, you pay the bank interest for holding the deposit of your money.

---

4. New studies from researchers at Harvard and Dartmouth show that Social Security's actuaries routinely underestimate the program's financial problems. Konstantin Kashin, Gary King, Samir Soneji, Systematic Bias and Nontransparency in U.S. Social Security Administration Finances, *Journal of Economic Perspectives*, Vol. 29, Number 2, Spring, 2015, pp. 239-258; Konstantin Kashin, Gary King, Samir Soneji, Explaining Systematic Bias and Nontransparency in U.S. Social Security Administration Finances, *Political Analysis*, American Economics Association, May 7, 2015.

5. Id., Table IV.G2, p. 204.

6. Id.

7. Peter J. Ferrara and Michael Tanner, *A New Deal for Social Security*, (Washington, DC: Cato Institute, 1998), Chapter 4.

8. Id.

Worst of all, **this is where Social Security is heading for all workers in the future.** For if the government raises taxes or cuts benefits, or does both, to eliminate the long-term deficits of Social Security, then the effective rate of return under Social Security will decline further for all workers across the board. Eventually, virtually all workers under Social Security would be driven down into the range of negative effective real returns.

Why doesn't Social Security pay better benefits? Because Social Security operates as a pure tax and redistribution system, with no real savings and investment anywhere, as discussed above. The tax money paid into the system by today's workers and their employers is not saved and invested for their future retirement. It is immediately paid out to finance benefits to today's retirees.

That means working people lose the compounding real returns they would gain from a lifetime of real savings and investment. Compare the pitiful redistribution Social Security returns above with real, standard, long term investment returns in the financial markets. Jeremy Siegel, in his definitive book *Stocks for the Long Run,* documents that the real annual compound rate of return on corporate stocks in the United States over the 200 year period 1802 to 2001 was 6.9 percent, after inflation.[9] It was the same 6.9 percent over the period 1926 to 2001, which included the Great Depression, World War II, the Korean War, the Vietnam War, and the Great Inflation of the 1970s.[10]

From 1926 to 2013, the real rate of return on Large Cap stocks, representing the larger companies in America, was 8.9 percent. The real rate of return on Small Cap stocks, representing smaller, mid-size firms, was 13.5 percent. A sophisticated, diversified portfolio of 90 percent Large Cap and 10 percent Small Cap stocks earned a 9.36 percent real return over that period. *This period covers the 2008 financial crisis.*[11]

Moreover, over the 50 year period from 1946 to 1996, corporate bonds averaged a real return of 4 percent.[12] Harvard Professor Martin Feldstein, former Chairman of the National Bureau of Economic Research, and his associate

---

9. Jeremy Siegel, *Stocks for the Long Run* (New York: McGraw-Hill, 2002), 3rd ed.

10. Id.; *Stocks, Bonds, Bills, and Inflation 2014 Yearbook* (Chicago: Ibbotson Associates); Jeremy Siegel, *Stocks for the Long Run* (Chicago: Irwin Professional Publishing, 2014).

11. *Stocks, Bonds, Bills, and Inflation 2014 Yearbook.*

12. Edgar K. Browning, "The Anatomy of Social Security and Medicare," *The Independent Review,* Vol. XIII, no. 1, Summer 2008, p. 12. See also, Siegel (the average real return on corporate bonds over the 200 year period from 1802 to 2001 was 5 percent); José Piñera, "Toward a World of Worker Capitalists," Transform the Americas, www.transformamericas.com, April 2000.

Andrew Samwick calculated in 1997 a portfolio of 60 percent stocks and 40 percent bonds would have generated a real return of 5.5 percent over that same 50 years, and the same return over the period going back to 1926.[13]

Compounding the much higher, long-term, standard market investment returns over a lifetime adds up to an enormous difference as compared to the much lower returns offered by Social Security's pay-as-you-go, tax and redistribution system. A two earner middle-income couple saving and investing over their lifetime in their own personal savings and investment account what would otherwise be paid into Social Security would reach retirement at just standard long term market investment returns with $1,223,602 in today's dollars, after adjusting for inflation. That fund would be able to pay out of the continuing investment returns alone just about *twice* what Social Security promises to pay them under current law, *while still allowing them to leave the $1.2 million fund to their children.* Or they could use the fund to buy themselves an annuity that would pay them over four times what Social Security currently promises, let alone what it can pay.[14]

All workers across the board, of all income levels and family combinations, would now get much higher benefits saving and investing in the market through personal accounts than the benefits Social Security even promises today, which the program cannot pay. Two low-income spouses somehow earning little more than the minimum wage over their entire careers would reach retirement with well over half a million in their personal accounts in today's dollars. That fund would be sufficient to pay them more than three times what Social Security promises them but cannot pay.

Across America, hundreds of billions, and ultimately trillions, in new savings and investment each year would flow through the personal accounts, increasing economic growth. The personal accounts over time would transform the payroll tax, the highest tax most working people pay, into a personal family wealth engine. This effective tax relief would further spur the economy. The result would be new jobs and higher wages and family income for working people today.

---

13. Martin Feldstein and Andrew Samwick, "The Economics of Prefunding Social Security and Medicare Benefits," National Bureau of Economic Research Working Paper no. 6055, National Bureau of Economic Research, Cambridge, MA, June, 1997.

14. Ferrara and Tanner, *A New Deal for Social Security*, Chapter 4.

Proven Reforms That Have Already Been Shown to Work in the Real World

Such reforms have already been tried and proven to work spectacularly in the real world. That started with the South American nation of Chile, which enacted such a system of personal accounts for their Social Security system in 1981, which virtually all workers chose in preference to the public system. After more than 30 years of experience with those personal accounts, workers are enjoying multiples of the benefits that were promised but could not be paid under the old system, for about half the required payments, with dramatic gains for the economy as also described above.

Similar reforms have been adopted in other countries in Latin America, and elsewhere around the world. That includes the local government workers in 3 counties in Galveston, Texas right here in the USA, who adopted a similar system when that was allowed for state and local government workers prior to 1983, with similar results as in Chile. Another successful model for such personal accounts has been the Federal employee Thrift Savings Plan adopted 30 years ago.

A Proposal for Social Security Reform

The analysis above should make clear that the only real solution for Social Security is to transform its fundamental means of financing from pay-as-you-go tax and redistribution to fully funded savings and investment in personal accounts for each worker, as most voters thought Social Security originally was. That is what would be achieved through a proposal to empower working people with the freedom to choose personal savings and investment accounts that they each individually own to finance their future Social Security retirement benefits.

Under this plan, all workers under 40 would be allowed the freedom to choose such personal accounts for their Social Security retirement benefits. For those that make this choice, taxes will be rebated into their accounts equal to 10% of the first $10,000 they earn each year, and 5% of everything above that, up to the Social Security maximum taxable income. That would be roughly equal to the employee share of the payroll tax. But the rebates would be financed by general revenues, leaving all Social Security payroll tax revenues to continue to flow into Social Security unchanged. That means that this proposal would only cause the Social Security trust funds to grow to very high levels in the future, the highest in history.

The Treasury Dept. would contract with private fund managers to offer investment funds to workers who exercised the personal account option, as in the Federal Employee Thrift Savings program. These investment funds would be invested entirely into index funds for the S&P 500, a simple, low cost option that would earn high, long term, market investment returns.

For those that choose personal accounts, workers of all income levels and family combinations would receive higher total future retirement benefits, rather than lower benefits. Workers would receive the benefits that can be financed by their personal accounts. Plus they would also receive a portion of promised Social Security retirement benefits equal to the portion of lifetime Social Security payroll taxes (OASI) that they had already paid while working, before they made the choice for personal accounts.

Those that choose personal accounts would be backed by a federal guarantee that those funds combined would equal at least what Social Security promises them under current law, or they will be paid a guarantee benefit every month equal to the difference. This would maintain the current Social Security safety net in full in the personal account framework. Social Security survivors and disability benefits would continue to be paid as promised under current law without change. There would be no change in Social Security of any sort for those already retired, or workers 40 and over not eligible for the personal account option.

For those that do not choose to make the choice for personal accounts, they would continue to receive Social Security benefits as provided under current law without change as well. There would be no benefit cuts or tax increases of any sort for these workers, or anyone else, whether already retired or still working.

Workers with personal accounts would be free to choose to leave any portion of their personal account funds to their families or children, or to any other heir they designate. Those funds and any other benefits payable from the personal accounts would be paid free of any tax. Workers with personal accounts would be free to choose their own retirement age for benefits from the account, with market incentives to delay it as long as possible, because the longer they wait, the more funds would accumulate in the account, and the higher the benefits it can pay.

This proposal would be very similar to the personal accounts legislation proposed by Congressman Paul Ryan (R-WI) and Senator John Sununu (R-NH) in 2004 and 2005. That proposal was scored by the Chief Actuary of Social Security, who concluded that it would eliminate all future deficits of Social Security, without any benefit cuts or tax increases. That is because the reform would shift so much responsibility over time for the financing of retirement benefits to the private financial markets, and off the federal budget altogether. This reform would achieve the same results. Indeed, ultimately the resulting savings in federal spending from the reform would amount to the biggest reduction in government spending in world history.

The Chief Actuary of Social Security also concluded that the personal accounts proposed in the Ryan-Sununu legislation would be so obviously a better deal for workers and their families than Social Security, that he estimated that 100% of workers would choose the personal accounts. That score is still available at the Social Security Administration website at www.ssa.gov. The same would be true for the personal accounts proposed here.

The reform would also sharply reduce the unfunded liabilities of Social Security, currently estimated at about $25 trillion, which is effectively implicit national debt. That is almost 50% larger than the current official national debt. The proposed Social Security personal account reform would sharply reduce that unfunded liability, as the fully funded personal accounts over time take over more and more responsibility for Social Security retirement benefits. With 100% of workers choosing to exercise the personal accounts, the reform would produce the greatest reduction in effective national debt in world history.

Economic Effects: Addressing Inequality and Economic Growth

The proposed personal accounts for Social Security would do more to address the issue of inequality of wealth than everything dreamed up by Elizabeth Warren and Hillary Clinton put together. With such personal accounts, working people at all income levels would hold a substantial ownership stake in America's business and industries. The Chief Actuary's score for the Ryan-Sununu legislation concluded that after the first 15 years with those personal accounts, workers would have accumulated $7.8 trillion in today's dollars, after adjusting for inflation. After the first 25 years, workers would have accumulated $16 trillion, again in today's dollars. The same results would be achieved by the personal accounts for Social Security proposed here. A study by Harvard University Prof. Martin Feldstein indicated that if Social Security were shifted to a fully funded system like personal accounts, the concentration of wealth in the United States would be reduced by half.[15]

---

15. Martin Feldstein, "Social Security and the Distribution of Wealth," *Journal of the American Statistical Association* (December 1976), pp. 90-93.

The personal accounts funnel mighty, new rivers of savings and investment into the economy. Higher savings and capital investment mean higher productivity and increased wages for working people. That creates new jobs and new opportunities. The bottom line is increased economic growth. Such increased capital would finance the practical implementation of our rapidly advancing science, leapfrogging our economy further generations ahead. These would all benefit working people today, soon after the reforms were adopted.

The personal accounts also effectively involve a major tax cut, effectively displacing the employee share of the payroll tax for workers under 40. That would further promote economic growth.

Financing the Transition

Any plan for personal accounts for Social Security involves a transition financing issue. As discussed above, Social Security currently operates on a pay-as-you-go basis; virtually all the money that comes in today goes out immediately to pay current benefits. If part of the money coming in goes for savings and investment in personal accounts instead, additional funds will have to come from somewhere else to continue paying all benefits promised to today's retirees. The need for this transition financing phases out over time as workers who are relying on their personal accounts instead of payroll taxes retire.

This is a cash-flow financing issue, however, not a matter of transition "costs." What the transition is financing is the increased savings and investment involved in shifting from a pay-as-you-go system with no real savings and investment, to a fully funded savings- and investment-based system. The Chief Actuary of Social Security wisely called it the "transition investment issue."

When you save $1,000 in a bank, you don't think that cost you $1,000. It doesn't *cost* you anything, because you still have the money, in your savings account. Of course, because you can't have your cake and eat it too, you can't spend the $1,000 you are saving, or else you wouldn't be saving it. That may create a cash-flow problem for you, depending on your personal finances. But it is not a matter of the savings *costing* you $1,000.

The transition financing for a system of personal retirement accounts is thus a matter of effectively financing the savings going into the personal accounts of working people across the United States, ultimately amounting to trillions and trillions of dollars. That accumulated savings and investment is not a cost to the economy; it is a mighty, productive contributor to the economy. Working people seeing money growing in their own personal accounts would certainly recognize it is not a cost but in fact an asset. The personal accounts are just a politically sophisticated means of shifting from current, completely non-invested, Social Security to a fully funded system based entirely on private savings and investment. That shift should be readily recognized as the complete, responsible, desirable solution to the problems of Social Security.

One simple means for financing this transition is just to borrow the funds. This would not constitute a net drain on private savings and investment, because of all the increased savings and investment going into the personal accounts. At most, this would involve a net wash, just borrowing back the increased savings and investment going into the accounts.

This was really Milton Friedman's vision for Social Security reform. He proposed just recognizing the unfunded liability of Social Security as effectively already federal debt. He consequently favored just formally recognizing the debt by issuing federal bonds to cover it. Working people could then just proceed to save and invest funds in their own personal accounts to finance their own future retirements.[16] That would still involve replacing over time Social Security's tax and redistribution, pay-as-you-go system with a fully funded, savings and investment system, with no unfunded liability.

But there is another way. My latest book, *Power to the People: The New Road to Freedom and Prosperity for the Poor, Seniors, and Those Most In Need of the World's Best Health Care* (Heartland Institute, 2015), discussed how to reform all the major entitlement programs—Medicare, Medicaid, Obamacare, and welfare, besides Social Security. Just as seniors are better off with personal accounts, receiving higher benefits rather than lower benefits, the other reforms leave the dependents on these entitlement programs better off than today as well.

All federal, means-tested welfare programs would be sent back to the states through fixed, finite block grants, just like with the 1996 welfare reforms of just one federal program, the old, New Deal, Aid to Families with Dependent Children program. The reform of that one program was enormously successful, with two-thirds of dependents on the program leaving it to go to work. Studies documented that those who did leave the program for work increased their incomes on average by 25%. But federal taxpayers gained as well, as the program, renamed Temporary Assistance for Needy Families (TANF), cost 50% less than it would have otherwise after 10 years, based on prior trends.

However, there are more than 150 additional federal means-tested welfare programs, all of which can be sent back to the states with fixed, finite block grants, just like AFDC in 1996. The estimated cost of those programs over the next 10

---

16. That savings and investment can be required by law as the alternative to a payroll tax that would have to be paid otherwise.

years alone is more than $10 trillion. States would then be empowered to adopt their own entirely new welfare systems as they choose, including a work based safety net that will assure work for the able-bodied poor, like the original Reagan concept of workfare. That would potentially eliminate poverty entirely nationally. Instead of taxpayers paying the bottom 20% of the income ladder nationally effectively not to work, under this reform private employers would pay them more to work, and contribute to the economy, as a mighty wave of increased labor supply that would match the mighty wave of increased capital coming from the personal accounts. That would create an economic boom overall.

This alone would generate enough savings in government spending to ultimately finance the entire transition to personal accounts. Then there would be the further savings from repealing and replacing Obamacare with free market, Patient Power medicine, and additional savings from positive, populist reform of Medicare, as explained in *Patient Power*. With the transition financed entirely by reduced spending, the personal accounts would produce a massive contribution to national savings and investment, with no offset for increased government borrowing to finance the transition. Altogether, this would amount to the biggest reduction in government spending in world history, with total federal spending as a percent of GDP cut in half from what it would be otherwise.

The workability of this approach was demonstrated by the Ryan Roadmap, the comprehensive legislation introduced in 2010 by the then-House Budget Committee chairman, Paul Ryan, who is now Chairman of the Ways and Means Committee. That proposal included personal accounts for Social Security, fundamental reform of Medicare and Medicaid, general health care reform, tax reform, and other budget reforms. CBO officially scored the Ryan Roadmap as achieving full solvency for Social Security and for Medicare while balancing the federal budget indefinitely into the future, completely eliminating all long-term federal deficits, with no tax increases, and ultimately paying off the national debt entirely. The transition to personal accounts for Social Security was consequently fully paid for, effectively by the spending reductions.

In practice, the transition may be financed by a combination of these two approaches, with some paid for by shorter term federal borrowing, and the rest paid off by long term entitlement reform. This was, in fact, how Chile financed their personal account reforms, through a combination of government borrowing, and reduced government spending.

The net result of all these reforms overall would ultimately be the greatest gain in social welfare in world history.

Controlling the Deficit

Peter Ferrara[*]

The Deficit Has Been Driven By Increases in Spending Not By Decreases in Taxes

America Needs *Higher* Growth and *Lower* Spending; Not *Higher* Taxes

Prepared for the Focusing the Presidential Debates Initiative

Executive Summary

It is well understood that the national debt, standing at over eighteen trillion dollars today (even excluding major pension obligations), is a major national problem that must be brought under control. As the debt accelerates in coming years, primarily under the influence of mandatory entitlement spending, the debt burden will become unsustainable. Interest on the national debt will become a larger and larger share of the federal budget as the debt rises, and bondholders will at some point begin to demand a higher risk premium. If the debt bomb remains unaddressed, ultimately the United States will go through a Greek style crisis, but this time with no European Union bail out. Further, the tilting point for a debt crisis, triggering a demand by debtors for higher and higher interest rates could happen suddenly should debtors become convinced that the United States is not on a sustainable path to resolving its debt problem. Fortunately, the United States still has time to address this problem, but it must move within the next few years toward meaningful reform.

There are only three ways to address this developing crisis, other than the unthinkable path of default or the undesirable path of run-away inflation.

---

[*] Peter Ferrara is Director of the International Center for Law and Economics.

First, substantially increase the growth rate of the United States (likely still requiring some nibbling at the edges of the mandatory entitlement growth), second, reduce expenditures, or third, increase taxes. Of course, there could also be some combination of the above. Since both reducing social expenditures and raising taxes are unpopular, and each is supported by a different part of the political spectrum, there is a tendency to simply ignore this real and developing debt problem. In the alternative, those focusing on the deficit usually suggest that we need to have a "balanced" approach to solving the problem by both reducing expenditures and raising taxes, an approach facing political opposition from all parts of the political spectrum and, as a result, possibly even more difficult politically. This "balanced" approach is also an approach which would likely negatively affect growth, as taxes are raised and incentives are reduced. In turn, the "balanced" approach would make the problem of the deficit even more difficult due to the feedback in reduced economic growth.

It is likely that the better path to getting the deficit under control is to focus on increasing the growth rate, while limiting the growth path of mandatory entitlements and enabling entitlement reform where possible to achieve greater effectiveness at lower cost. An important factor in increasing the National growth rate is to lower taxes on income, investment and capital formation. This would, along with other pro-growth reforms, create a virtuous cycle in which revenues increase faster than expenditures. A parallel paper to this one shows, in turn, how Social Security optionality (offering private accounts to a younger generation forty and under) would both dramatically reduce entitlement spending while ensuring much higher returns to a younger generation and Social Security solvency for all others now under the traditional system. The low hanging fruit of genuine Social Security reform, along with pro-growth policies, is a combination offering both a realistic path to deficit control while enhancing growth and maintaining the social safety net.

But there is yet another reason why a "balanced" approach to deficit reform is not the answer. And that is that the contemporary deficit problem has not been caused by decreases in federal taxation. Rather, it has been driven by a growth in mandatory entitlement spending; an out-of-control growth in spending not present in the previous post-war settings in which the Nation dramatically reduced its wartime debt after each war. We cannot simply forever increase expenditures, and then when the deficit gets too high, call for a "balanced" reduction which would increase taxes.

The deficit is also related to growth and overall wellbeing in America. A deficit which is too large, even short of provoking a debt crisis, serves as a drag on the economy inhibiting economic growth, as scarce resources are diverted to pay carrying cost of the debt, and ultimately the debt itself. In addition, borrowing to cover the deficit drains investment capital from the private sector, which is the foundation of economic growth. There is good evidence to suggest that a national debt beyond 90% of GDP slows growth substantially. Unfortunately, that is where we are today!

Growth, in turn, is of the utmost importance for every woman, man and child in America. A one percent per year increase in the growth rate (increasing growth from 2% to 3%) will in twenty five years make the Nation 27% wealthier than it would otherwise be at the lower growth rate. A two percent per year increase in the growth rate for twenty five years would make the Nation 62% wealthier than it would otherwise be. And a two percent per year increase in the national growth rate continued over a second 25 years would increase the national income by 164% in a generation (50 years). Such an increase in national income would have profound benefits in covering the deficit, enhancing the general welfare, and providing for the national defense.

Throughout American history the deficit has tended to dramatically increase during periods of war. Understandably, the preservation of our national freedom, and that of our allies, remains foremost. This was true in the Civil War, World Wars I & II, and the Korean War. But in the aftermath of those wars the Nation typically made major progress in reducing the debt. Under President Lyndon Johnson's "Great Society," however, not only did the Nation fight a war; the Vietnam War, but it also dramatically increased mandatory entitlement expenditures.

Federal spending as a percent of GDP boomed to record levels during World War II of over 40% of GDP. But it stabilized in the 1950s to around 18% to 20% of GDP, where it stayed over the long term for several decades. This was the long-term, postwar, consensus level of federal spending as a percent of GDP, from the early 1950s until 2008.

Federal spending increased from 16.6% of GDP in 1965[1] to 19.8% in 1968, an increase of almost 20% in the size of the federal government relative to the economy. That reflected Johnson's boom in entitlement spending, with the adoption of Medicare and Medicaid and the War on Poverty in 1965. But total federal spending remained within the postwar consensus of 18% to 20% of GDP thereafter.

The 1980's brought the Reagan tax cuts, a reprise of the Kennedy rate cuts, which again caused the economy to boom. Federal revenues still doubled dur-

---

1. That 16.6% of GDP in 1965 was below the postwar 18% to 20% consensus because the economy was booming in 1965 due to the sweeping Kennedy tax rate cuts, adopted in 1964, which cut federal income tax rates by about 23% across the board. That boom was a sudden surprise to the economy, which temporarily made federal spending smaller as a percent of GDP. Federal spending over the prior 4 years averaged precisely 18% of GDP.

ing the 1970's even with those tax rate cuts, but federal spending grew even more, which caused the rise of much larger federal deficits. Still, *the largest deficit of the Reagan years was only $221 billion* in 1986, and by 1989 the deficit was back down to a normal, postwar consensus range of 2.7 percent of GDP.

By Fiscal 2007, under the last budget left by Congressional Republican majorities that had controlled Congress since 1994, the Federal deficit was $160.7 billion, which was only 1.1 percent of GDP. Federal spending was 19.1% of GDP that year.

The all-time record U.S. deficit before President Obama came into office was at the worst of the financial crisis in 2008, at $458.5 billion, which was 3.1 percent of GDP. Yet, the deficit *every* year since President Obama has been in office has never again been as *low* as that previous all-time record, even as a percent of GDP.

In 2009, President Obama's first year in office, federal spending rocketed to 24.4% of GDP, about one-fourth more than the postwar consensus, higher than in any other year since 1945, at the end of World War II, nearly two-thirds of a century earlier. The 2009 deficit consequently roared to an all-time record $1.413 *trillion* dollars. That was also 9.8% of GDP, an all-time record except for the four years of World War II. That 2009 deficit was *three times the previous highest deficit in American history* of $458 billion, which was at the bottom of the financial crisis. It was *6.5 times the highest deficit during the Reagan years.*

Two years of such extreme federal spending, plus the addition of still another, huge, long term entitlement burden in Obamacare, roused the country in November, 2010 to sweep out the Democrat House majority. Voters replaced it with a decisive, Republican majority, in an historic, New Deal size, 63 seat, landslide gain, which effectively put a fiscal check on the Administration. The resulting government shut-down fight over spending in the fall of 2011 resulted in the sequester, which halted federal spending growth.

The new House majority held to the sequester, which resulted in an actual decline in total nominal federal spending two years in a row, for the first time in 60 years, since the draw down in federal spending after World War II in the 1950s under President Eisenhower. As a result, by 2014, Federal spending as a percent of GDP was restored to near its prior long-term trend, at 20.3 percent.

But that came too late to stop the Obama Administration *from accumulating more national debt than all prior Presidents, from George Washington to George Bush, combined.* Gross Federal Debt is consequently already now more than 100 percent of GDP.

The right measure for President Obama's record is not to compare the recovery to the recession, but to compare Obama's recovery with other recoveries from other recessions under previous Presidents. By that measure, what is clear is that the Obama Administration produced *the worst recovery from a recession since the Great Depression*, worse than what every other President who has faced a recession achieved.

With declining middle class incomes and increasing poverty, inequality has actually gotten worse under President Obama. Only the top 20 percent has gained.

President Obama's Fiscal 2016 budget proposed to spend over $50 trillion over the next 10 years, the highest spending by any government in world history. Obama's own budget projected that by Fiscal 2025 that would increase the gross federal debt to $26.3 trillion, the highest debt by any government in world history.

In sharp contrast, the federal budget adopted by the Republican Congress proposed to spend $7.2 trillion less over the next 10 years. That Republican budget would also balance the budget within 10 years, eliminating the federal deficit entirely.

The Republican budget achieved those results with no tax increases. Indeed, that budget accommodates comprehensive federal tax reform that would sharply lower marginal tax rates, which would substantially boost economic growth and recovery.

President Obama's budget proposes to increase federal spending faster than the economy over the next 10 years, increasing federal spending to 22.2 percent of GDP by 2025. That would consequently break federal spending again out of the long standing, post-World War II consensus of 18% to 20% of GDP. The Republican budget, by contrast, would reduce federal spending to 19% of GDP, restoring the long-term consensus. With federal spending held to that 18% to 20% of GDP postwar consensus, America was able to maintain booming long term economic growth, to become the richest and mightiest nation in world history.

This history shows that the problems of federal deficits and debt can and should be resolved with pro-growth policies and reasonable spending restraint, without any tax increase. Such policies would best help restore traditional, more robust American economic growth.

* * *

Introduction

Some basic parameters of federal fiscal history will help us judge federal taxes, spending, deficits and the federal budget today. Federal spending, deficits and debt of course exploded during World War II, because we had to win that war whatever the cost. But after the war, federal spending wisely tapered down during the 1950s Eisenhower years especially. Federal spending finally settled down for the long term at about 18% to 20% of GDP. It was remarkably stable around that level for more than half a century, until 2009.[2]

The stiff spending restraint during the Eisenhower years caused gross federal debt to decline sharply during those years to 54 percent of GDP by 1960, down from the all-time U.S. record of 118.9% of GDP in 1946, resulting from the war years.[3] The sweeping Kennedy tax rate cuts caused the economy to boom during the 1960s, which caused federal debt as a percent of that booming GDP to decline sharply to 36 percent by 1970.[4]

Federal spending increased from 16.6% of GDP in 1965[5] to 19.8% in 1968, an increase of almost 20% in the size of the federal government relative to the economy. That reflected Johnson's boom in entitlement spending, with the adoption of Medicare and Medicaid and the War on Poverty in 1965. But total federal spending remained within the postwar consensus of 18% to 20% of GDP thereafter. The 1980s brought the Reagan tax cuts, a reprise of the Kennedy rate cuts, which again caused the economy to boom. Federal revenues still doubled during the 1970s even with those tax rate cuts, but federal spending grew even more, which caused the rise of much larger federal deficits. Still, *the largest deficit of the Reagan years was only $221 billion* in 1986,[6] and by 1989 the deficit was back down to a normal, postwar consensus range of 2.7% of GDP.[7]

By Fiscal 2007, under the last budget left by Congressional Republican majorities that had controlled Congress since 1994, the Federal deficit was $160.7 billion,[8] which was only 1.1 percent of GDP.[9] The *all-time record U.S. deficit before President Obama came into office was at the worst of the financial crisis in 2008 under George W. Bush, at $458.5 billion,*[10] *which was 3.1 percent of GDP.*

---

2. The President's Budget, Fiscal Year 2016, Historical Perspectives, Table 1.2.

3. The President's Budget, Fiscal Year 2016, Historical Perspectives, Table 7.1.

4. Id.

5. That 16.6% of GDP in 1965 was below the postwar 18% to 20% consensus because the economy was booming in 1965 due to the sweeping Kennedy tax rate cuts, adopted in 1964, which cut federal income tax rates by about 23% across the board. That boom was a sudden surprise to the economy, which temporarily made federal spending smaller as a percent of GDP. Federal spending over the prior 4 years average precisely 18% of GDP.

6. Id., Table 1.1.

7. Id., Table 1.2.

8. Id., Table 1.1.

9. Id., Table 1.2.

10. Id., Table 1.1.

Yet, the deficit *every* year since President Obama has been in office has never again been as *low* as that previous all-time record.

In 2009, President Obama's first year in office, the deficit rocketed to an all-time record $1.413 *trillion* dollars.[11] That was also 9.8% of GDP,[12] an all-time record except for the four years of World War II, when America was fighting both Nazi Germany and Imperial Japan. That 2009 deficit was *three times the previous highest deficit in American history* of $458 billion. It was *6.5 times the highest deficit during the Reagan years.*

The 2009 deficit was driven by an explosion of federal spending, from 20.2 percent of GDP in 2008, which was still within the long-term, 60-year, postwar, consensus trend line of 18% 20% of GDP, to 24.4 percent of GDP in 2009, higher than in any other year since 1945, nearly two-thirds of a century earlier. Even Franklin Roosevelt was not so blinkered during the Great Depression itself, when the federal deficit was never nearly so high, in any year, and total federal spending never popped much more than a bit over 10 percent of GDP.

That 2009 explosion in federal spending and deficits reflected President Obama's decision to address the financial crisis by returning to the Keynesian economics that President Reagan had left for dead almost 30 years previously in 1981. Keynesian economics is the doctrine that the way to restore booming economic growth is through *increased* federal spending and deficits. It was this policy decision by President Obama, on top of the long term rise in federal entitlement spending, that is the foundation of the contemporary federal deficit and debt problem.

The very next year, 2010, the deficit was $1.294 *trillion*, still nearly *three times* the previous all-time record in American history. That deliberate, chosen deficit, as the supposed road to recovery, was 8.7 percent of GDP.[13]

Those two years of extreme federal overspending, plus the addition of still another, huge, long term entitlement in Obamacare, roused the country in November, 2010 to sweep out the Democrat House majority. Voters replaced it with a decisive, Republican majority, in an historic, New Deal size, 63 seat, landslide gain, which effectively put a new check on the Obama Administra-

---

11. Id.

12. Id., Table 1.2.

13. Some have argued that the booming economy of the Reagan years was caused by the Reagan deficits rather than by the all-time record Reagan tax rate cuts. But Reagan's deficits were negligible compared to Obama's deficits. Those Obama deficits utterly failed to generate *any* serious economic growth, certainly nothing anywhere near the booming economic growth of the Reagan years, which was at least three times any growth that showed up during President Obama's incremental recovery.

tion. That new Republican House majority still only stabilized the deficit the next year, 2011, at $1.3 trillion, driven by a still *all-time record $3.603 trillion in federal spending* that year. But the resulting government shut-down fight that fall over spending resulted in the sequester that squelched federal spending growth, and began to tame the federal spending explosion.

The deficit the next year, 2012, did decline to $1.1 trillion, only the fourth time in U.S. history with a federal deficit over a trillion, all under President Obama. That decline resulted because the new Republican House majority held to the sequester, producing a rare, actual decline in total nominal federal spending.

The next year, the Republican House held to the sequester again, which resulted in another actual decline in total nominal federal spending, the first time that had happened two years in a row in 60 years, since the draw down in federal spending after World War II in the 1950s under President Eisenhower. That persistent spending restraint resulted in a sharp decline in the deficit for 2013 to $680 billion, still nevertheless 50 percent more than the prior record deficit under all prior Presidents of $458 billion.

The House agreed to ease up some on the sequester the next year, 2014, but the result was still another sharp drop in the deficit to $484.6 billion, still above the prior record for all previous Presidents. Federal spending as a percent of GDP was now restored to near its prior long term trend, at 20.3 percent. The federal deficit for 2015 is now projected to come in at $469 billion, which is still higher, *for the seventh straight year under President Obama, than the prior record under all previous U.S. Presidents.*

The increase in Gross Federal Debt under President Obama is now projected under his own budget to total $8.642 trillion by the end of this year, an increase of 87 percent since 2009. *That Gross Federal Debt is already now more than 100 percent of GDP.*[14] An international study for the National Bureau of Economic Research by Kenneth Rogoff of Harvard and Carmen Reinhart of the Peterson Institute for International Economics, covering the experience of sixty-six countries over 800 years, found that economic growth slows substantially when national debt climbs over 90 percent of GDP.[15]

Federal debt held by the public is projected by President Obama's budget to increase this year by $7.7 trillion, to $13.506 trillion, up from $5.803 trillion

---

14. The President's Budget, Fiscal Year 2016, Historical Perspectives, Table 7.1.

15. Carmen M. Reinhart and Kenneth S. Rogoff, Growth in a Time of Debt, National Bureau of Economic Research, Working Paper No. 15639, January, 2010; Carmen M. Reinhart and Kenneth S. Rogoff, *This Time Is Different: Eight Centuries of Financial Folly*, (Princeton, NJ: Princeton University Press, 2009).

in 2008, an increase of 133 percent, well more than doubling. *This means that the Obama Administration has accumulated more national debt than all prior Presidents, from George Washington to George Bush, combined!*

The Worst Recovery Since the Great Depression

President Obama wants his economic policies to be judged by whether the economy is better today than it was at the depth of the recession when he entered office. But recoveries are always better than the recession they are recovering from, by definition. So that is no achievement.

The right measure for Obama's record is not to compare the recovery to the recession, but to compare Obama's recovery with other recoveries from other recessions under previous Presidents. By that measure, what is clear is that Obamanomics produced the *worst* recovery from a recession since the Great Depression; and a record worse than every other American President who has faced a recession.

When President Obama came into office, the recession, which started in December, 2007, was already 12 months old.[16] There have been 11 other recessions since the Great Depression.[17] The average duration of those recessions was 10 months.[18] So the recovery was already overdue when he came into office. All he really had to do was stay out of the way.

The recession did officially finally end in June, 2009, after 18 months, according to the National Bureau of Economic Research (NBER),[19] which is considered the official authority for when recessions begin and when they end. That made it actually the longest recession since the Great Depression. But our experience feels like that was not the end, because the recovery has been so weak in the six years since the recession officially ended.

The American historical record is actually the worse the recession, the stronger the recovery. That is because coming out of a recession, the economy has historically grown faster than normal for a while to catch up to its long term economic growth trend line. So by this metric, the economy should have come out of 2009 in an historic, long term, economic boom. But to this very day, 6 *years* later, that has *still* never happened.

---

16. US Business Cycle Expansions and Contractions, National Bureau of Economic Research, http://www.nber.org/cycles/cyclesmain.html.
17. Id.
18. Id.
19. Id.

In the 11 previous recessions since the Great Depression, prior to the last recession, the economy recovered all jobs lost during the recession after an average of 25 months after the prior jobs peak (when the recession began).[20] So the job effects of prior post-Depression recessions lasted an average of about 2 years. But under President Obama's recovery, the recession's job losses were not recovered until after *76 months*, or more than *6 years!* Today, 90 months after the recession started, under President Obama's recovery the economy has created only 2.5 million more jobs on net overall, during those entire 7.5 years.[21]

That included the longest period since the Great Depression with unemployment above 8%, 43 months, from February, 2009, when Obama's so-called stimulus costing nearly $1 trillion was passed, until August, 2012. It also included the longest period since the Great Depression with unemployment at 9.0% or above, 30 months, from April, 2009, until September, 2011. In fact, apart from the disastrous employment record under President Obama, during the entire *65 years* from January, 1948 to January, 2013, there were no months with unemployment over 9%, except for 18 months during the bitter 1981—1982 recession, which slayed the historic inflation of the 1970s. That is how inconsistent with the prior history of the American economy President Obama's extended unemployment was.

Reagan suffered arguably the most severe recession in post-Depression history, 1981-82, which resulted from the monetary policy that broke the back of the roaring 1970s inflation. But all the job losses from that recession were recovered after 36 months,[22] with the recovery fueled by traditional pro-growth policies. In the Reagan recovery, 76 months after the recession started, the economy had created *12.8 million more jobs*, compared to zero on net at this point in the Obama recovery.[23] After 90 months of the Reagan recovery, the economy had created *17 million more jobs!*[24] That compares again to 2.5 million more jobs on net at this point in the Obama recovery.

The pitiful jobs record of Obamanomics reflects the more basic reality that the economy has not been growing under President Obama. In the 11 previous, post-depression recessions before President Obama, the economy recovered the lost GDP during the recession within an average of 5 quarters after the

---

20. The Recession and Recovery In Perspective, The Federal Reserve Bank of Minneapolis, http://www.minneapolisfed.org/publications_papers/studies/recession_perspective/index.cfm.

21. Id.

22. Id.

23. Id.

24. Id.

recession started.[25] But it took Obama's recovery *14 quarters*, or 3.5 *years*, to reach that point. The Reagan recovery took half that time, 7 quarters, to recover all the lost GDP from the 1981-82 recession. Today, 30 quarters, after the recession started, the economy (real GDP) under the Obama recovery has grown 8.5% above where it was when the recession started.[26] By sharp contrast, after 30 quarters of the Reagan recovery, the economy had boomed by 30.5%, almost one-third.[27]

Some might say Reagan was a different era, not relevant to today. But here is the major real difference between the Reagan era, and the Obama era today. Reagan used pro-growth policies, to address his recession. The results he got are the same as have been experienced with those policies throughout human history. Obama has used anti-growth policies, *raising taxes and pouring on regulation,* to address this last recession. The results are the same as have been experienced with those policies throughout human history.

President Obama's Economic Performance Even Worse Than Presidents Bush and Carter

President Obama's economic performance was much worse than even President George W. Bush's. Jeffrey H. Anderson, a senior fellow at the Pacific Research Institute, wrote in *Investors Business Daily* on January 13, 2013, "Prior to Obama, the second term of President Bush featured the weakest gains in the gross domestic product in some time, with average annual (inflation-adjusted) GDP growth of just 1.9%, [according to the official stats at the Bureau of Economic Analysis (BEA)]" But average annual real GDP growth during Obama's entire first term was less than half as much at a pitiful 0.8%, according to the same official source.

Indeed, not only was economic growth during Bush's awful second term more than twice as much as during Obama's entire first term. Even Jimmy Carter produced 4 times as much economic growth during his one term as Obama did during his entire first term. In fact, as Anderson noted, real GDP growth under Obama's first term was the worst of any President *in the last 60 years!*

---

25. The Recession and Recovery In Perspective, The Federal Reserve Bank of Minneapolis, http://www.minneapolisfed.org/publications_papers/studies/recession_perspective/index.cfm.

26. Id.

27. Id.

But it's even worse than that. Obama's first term real GDP growth was actually less than half as much as the worst of any President in the last 60 years. In other words, even if you doubled actual GDP growth under President Obama, *it would still be the worst record of any President in the last 60 years!*

President Obama's Declining Middle Class and Booming Poverty

The slow growth, and negligible job creation under Obama, in turn caused declining middle class incomes. The Census Bureau's Current Population Survey showed that real median household income declined by more than $4,500 during Obama's first term, about 8%, meaning effectively that the middle class lost annually the equivalent of one month's pay under Obama. Even President Bush again did better during his disastrous second term, when real median household income at least rose by 1.7%, not enough, but still positive rather than negative.

Even if you start from when the recession ended in June, 2009, the decline in median real household income since was greater during Obama's first term than it was during the recession. Three and a half years into the Obama recovery, real median household income had declined nearly 6% as compared to June, 2009. That is more than twice the decline of 2.6% that occurred during the recession from December, 2007 until June, 2009. As the *Wall Street Journal* summarized in its August 25-26, 2012 weekend edition, "For household income, in other words, the Obama recovery has been worse than the Bush recession."

Despite his rhetoric, Obama has failed to deliver for the poor, as well as for the middle class. Indeed, the only thing booming under Obamanomics has been poverty. Poverty soared under Obama, with the number of Americans in poverty increasing to the highest level in the more than 50 years that the Census Bureau has been tracking poverty. During Obama's first term, the number in poverty increased by nearly 31%, to 49.7 million, with the poverty rate climbing by over 30% to 16.1%. This is another natural result of negligible economic growth, paltry job creation, declining real wages, and the worst economic recovery since the Great Depression.

President Obama has tried to make an issue out of inequality. But with declining middle class income and booming poverty under his policies, inequality has actually gotten worse. Only the top 20 percent has gained while he has been President. That is shown by official government data, including the Gini coefficient, the official statistical measure of inequality.

Reversing the Accelerating Downward Spiral

President Obama's Fiscal 2016 budget released in January, 2015 proposed to spend over $50 trillion over the next 10 years, the highest spending by any government in world history.[28] Obama's own budget projected that by Fiscal 2025 that would increase the gross federal debt to $26.3 trillion,[29] the highest debt by any government in world history.

In sharp contrast, the federal budget adopted by the Republican Congress proposed to spend $7.2 trillion less over the next 10 years.[30] That Republican budget would also balance the budget within 10 years, eliminating the federal deficit entirely, as scored by CBO.[31] Indeed, that budget would produce surpluses by 2024, and thereafter, reducing the Gross Federal Debt to below $20 trillion.[32]

The Republican budget achieved those results with no tax increases. Indeed, that budget accommodates comprehensive federal tax reform that would sharply lower marginal tax rates, which would substantially boost economic growth and recovery.

President Obama's budget proposes to increase federal spending faster than the economy over the next 10 years, increasing federal spending to 22.2 percent of GDP by 2025.[33] The Republican budget, by contrast, would reduce federal spending to 19 percent of GDP, restoring the long-term consensus, with federal spending growing slower than the economy. With federal spending held to that 20 percent of GDP consensus, postwar America was able to maintain robust long term economic growth, to become the richest and strongest nation in world history.

This history shows that the problems of federal deficits and debt, which in the United States have been generated by excessive federal spending, can and should be resolved with pro-growth policies and reasonable spending restraint, without any tax increase. Such policies would best help restore traditional higher rates of American economic growth.

---

28. The President's Budget, Fiscal Year 2016, Table S-1.

29. Id., Table S-13.

30. Concurrent Resolution on the Budget, Fiscal Year 2016, 114th Congress, First Session, Report 114-000, Table 1.

31. Id.

32. Id.

33. Id.

What Tax Reform Should Look Like Under the Next President

*Grover Norquist**

Prepared for the Focusing the Presidential Debates Initiative

American families and businesses are overtaxed and Washington spends too much money. Progress has already been made curtailing spending when the Republican-controlled Congress implemented discretionary spending caps through passage of the 2011 Budget Control Act. Because of these caps, overall spending has since declined from 24 to 20 percent of GDP and discretionary spending has decreased from over nine percent of GDP to less than seven percent of GDP.

The next step must be enacting comprehensive, pro-growth reforms to the tax code to help get the economy back on track and increase economic growth. The next president must start by reducing income tax rates across the board so American families are able to spend, save, and invest more of their hard-earned income.

Any changes to the tax code should move toward a consumption base, simplify the system, and ensure that revenue is kept at the historical average of 18 percent of GDP. In addition, any changes must be considered using dynamic scoring, which will provide greater accuracy over macroeconomic effects. Finally, tax reform should be a net tax cut, not a backdoor for increasing the tax burden on Americans.

These principles provide an outline of how to reform the countless problem areas in the tax code to reform.

---

* Grover Norquist is President of Americans for Tax Reform, a former economist at the U.S. Chamber of Commerce, and a former Commissioner on the National Commission on Restructuring the Internal Revenue Service.

First, US business tax rates are some of the highest in the world, not to mention inconsistent. Rates should be lowered and simplified.

Second, tax extenders, the temporary provisions within the code, must be made permanent, or redundant under tax reform to encourage efficiency and clarity.

Third, the tax code must stop discouraging business investment by allowing full expensing.

Fourth, the US must move from a worldwide system of taxation to a territoriality system.

Fifth, it should become easier for taxpayers to use tax advantaged savings accounts.

Sixth, the Death Tax and the AMT should be repealed. Ideally the capital gains tax should be repealed too, or reduced.

Seventh, entitlements should be reformed and Social Security and Medicare payroll taxes should be phased out.

While there are many flawed areas within the tax code that require reform, there are also many proposals that would push the code in the wrong direction by increasing complexity and inefficiency. For one, tax reform must ensure that the IRS is reined in and is kept out of tax preparation business. New taxes, for example those on the internet and online commerce should not be considered. And there is no need to implement a "Buffett Rule," requiring upper income earners to pay a certain minimum percentage of their income. Taxpayers can already pay more if they feel so inclined.

The ideas outlined in this paper should serve as a guide toward improving the tax code to better serve the American people and promote economic growth and prosperity. In general, metrics outlining specific reductions have not been included, as this can vary plan to plan. But by implementing these ideas, the next president has an opportunity to simplify the tax code for families and businesses, remove inconsistencies and inefficiencies, provide certainty, promote stronger growth and create more jobs.

Move Toward a Consumption Tax Base

Any changes to the tax code should be based around moving toward a consumption base: curtailing or eliminating most tax exclusions, adjustments, deductions, and credits and taxing labor at the point of consumption while leaving savings alone.

Moving toward this type of tax base is not only the least demanding on the free market, but also on supply and demand because it leaves the maximum amount of productive income untouched from taxation so that it can increase productivity, grow wages, create jobs, augment nest eggs, etc. Eventually, even this income is consumed and subject to taxation, so there are no loopholes.

As a result, it is the most economically efficient base and promotes stronger economic growth.

Utilize Dynamic Scoring to Analyze Macroeconomic Effects of Tax Cuts

The merits of any change to the tax code should be analyzed through the perspective of dynamic scoring. Currently, all tax legislation is analyzed and "scored" by the Joint Committee on Taxation (JCT), a bureaucracy that does not divulge their full methodology, or make their work available for peer review. For decades, JCT analysis did not incorporate the Laffer Curve in their methodology, which simply states that moving from very high to very low marginal income tax rates increase the incentive of taxpayers to work, save, and invest. Doing the opposite—moving from a very low to a very high marginal income tax rate—has the opposite effect.

Under their outdated methodology, JCT does not take into account "macroeconomic" changes. In other words, they didn't think that large tax changes impact the economy.

Fortunately, the Republican controlled Congress has taken steps to rectify this oversight. Now, JCT scoring of legislation takes into account changes in behavior. This does not mean, as some on the left try to argue, that tax cuts somehow pay for themselves. It simply means that commonsense economic effects are taken into account.

The Congressional Budget Office (CBO) estimates that every 0.1 percentage points in higher GDP growth equates to roughly $59 billion in revenue over ten years. Extrapolating, tax reform that can achieve four percent growth—as opposed to the current anemic two percent—equates to roughly $1.12 trillion more in revenue over ten years. Dynamic scoring allows this kind of growth to be factored into any proposed changes to the tax code.

Maintain Revenues of 18 Percent of GDP or Less

The historical average of tax revenues is 18 percent of GDP, which should serve as a guide for future fiscal policy assumptions and decision-making. Under the current tax system, revenue as a percentage of GDP will continually rise because of real bracket creep (incomes rising faster than inflation-adjusted tax brackets). As a result, Americans will be taxed more and more if lawmakers do nothing.

CBO projects that because of bracket creep, federal tax revenues will rise from $3.2 trillion in 2015 to $5 trillion in 2025. As a percentage of GDP, tax revenues also rise in this period, from 17.7 percent to 18.3 percent of economic output (note that the historical average is just under 18 percent of GDP). Revenues will reach 20 percent of GDP in 2045, 21 percent in 2056, 22 percent in 2068, 23 percent in 2079, and fully 24 percent of GDP by the end of the century.

When politicians seek to increase taxes, they conveniently ignore these numbers. After all, it naturally leads to the conclusion that there is no reason to increase taxes on the American people. And it makes keeping the Taxpayer Protection Pledge, a promise made by a politician to their constituents, a reasonable, common-sense commitment.

Reduce Business Rates so America Can Compete with the Rest of the World

There are two main problems with business taxes under the code today. First, the code treats businesses differently depending on whether they register as corporations or flow-through firms. This means that the choices a business owner makes will result in drastically different and confusing tax, legal, and employment consequences. Removing this discrepancy and treating all businesses equally will level the playing field and help simplify the tax code.

Secondly, American business tax rates are uncompetitive with the rest of the world. This is problematic because corporations have greater choice over which country to be based in, and where to take their jobs. Including state income taxes, the business tax rate stands at 39 percent for corporations and approaching 50 percent for flow-through firms. By comparison, the UK's rate is 20 percent, and Germany and Canada's rate is just 15 percent. In fact, the average rate among developed countries is just under 25 percent. With such high rates, the US simply cannot compete.

For businesses, the equation is simple. If they are going to make an extra billion dollars, they would rather do it in a country where that billion dollars will lose 25 percent in taxes than in a country where it will lose 40 percent in taxes.

Luckily, fixing this problem is relatively simple—lower the rate to a level that competes with other developed nations. This means the federal rate needs to be lower than 25 percent, as states impose their own business tax.

Corporate Tax Rates Across the World	
Country	Corporate Tax Rate
United States	35%
Italy	30.6%
Germany	30%
Mexico	30%
China	25%
Finland	20%
Singapore	17%
Hong Kong	16.5%
Canada	15%
Ireland	12.5%

Reduce Uncertainty in Tax Planning

Every year or two, Congress reauthorizes a set of around 55 tax provisions that are about to expire, or have just expired. These "tax-extenders" include many important provisions including 50-percent business expensing, a research-and-development tax credit, and provisions to prevent double taxation.

The most important extenders, like the three above, should be made permanent. Others can be made permanent, be removed entirely, or made redundant by ironing out inconsistencies in the code. Doing so would reduce uncertainty for taxpayers and small businesses. For policy makers, it would ensure a more stable, fixed understanding of the tax revenue baseline, and will make pro-growth reform easier.

Move from the Current System of Depreciation to Full Business Expensing

Ideally, the tax code should allow full business expensing. When a business invests in new equipment such as computers, automobiles, machines, and furniture they should be able to reduce their taxable income dollar-for-dollar by the amount purchased. This encourages owners to put more of their hard-earned income back into their business, which will help create jobs and stronger economic growth.

Under the current tax code, there is a bias that discourages business owners from making investments. Some business investments are given immediate expensing under the tax code while others are subject to a slow multi-year deduction process known as depreciation.

There is no rhyme or reason to how each item is categorized, or over how many years a certain purchase can be deducted. However, the complex formula under which costs are deducted creates burdens on business owners that ends up discouraging business investment.

Congress currently has a temporary tax extender that allows businesses to deduct a percentage of business purchases (currently 50 percent). The remainder is subject to depreciation.

Ideally, any tax plan should move toward full-cost recovery for business purchases. 100 percent, full business expensing would increase economic growth, create new jobs, and raise wages.

Promoting investment through business expensing has been an issue that has drawn widespread support. President Obama has included bonus depreciation in past proposals, and Democrats proposed full business expensing back in 1981.

Business owners should not be discouraged from investing in new equipment.

Move From Worldwide to Territorial System of Taxation

Most of the world has a territorial tax system. They tax money earned in their country but welcome the return of money earned abroad tax-free. This makes sense because this money is already taxed in the country where it was earned.

The US is different. It is one of only seven OECD countries (with Chile, Greece, Ireland, Israel, South Korea, and Mexico) in the world that has a worldwide tax system, which means that if you are an American, the IRS tries to tax everything you earn regardless of where you earn it. Incidentally, every other country that has a worldwide tax system has lower rates than the US.

Changing to a territorial system will help simplify the tax code, stop the IRS from harassing businesses and taxpayers, and make it easier for the US to compete globally.

Moving forward, one option toward this change is to have optional repatriation of business income stored overseas. Currently, American businesses are sitting on over $2 trillion in after tax earnings overseas and so bringing this money back through repatriation would provide a boost to the economy, create jobs, and increase income.

In fact, there is already a model to follow, when repatriation last occurred in 2005. That year, businesses could bring back income at a rate of 5.25 percent—far below the normal rate the IRS double taxes income.

Switching from the current worldwide tax system, to a territorial system should be a no-brainer. Not only will it make the country more competitive and reduce complexity, but it will also be a massive economic stimulus.

Encourage and Simplify the Use of Tax-Preferred Savings Accounts

Currently, there are about 15 tax-advantaged savings accounts that taxpayers can use to save for retirement, health care, and education. When used correctly these saving accounts drastically reduce the tax burden on families. There is just one problem—the current system is so complex it is enough to make your head spin, and it causes most Americans to under-save. Taxpayers have too many options, which encourages them to make the wrong choice—do nothing and instead consume what could have been saved.

One solution is to roll these fifteen choices into a streamlined system with a few flexible, but defined savings accounts. Back in the mid-2000s, the Treasury Department came up with a proposed three-account system to replace the existing system. Here's how it would work:

Employer Retirement Savings Accounts (ERSAs). This would replace all the employer options that exist. The accounts would work much like Safe-Harbor 401(k) plans do today, where employers make sure that all employees benefit in exchange for a waiver of onerous non-discrimination testing. The current 401(k) elective deferral limit ($18,000 in 2015, plus a $6,000 catch-up for older workers) would apply. Deferrals could be either pre-tax or after-tax, depending on participant wishes.

Retirement Savings Accounts (RSAs). These would replace all the personal IRA-type products that exist today. Anyone could save up to $10,000 per year into an RSA. The money would be deposited after tax, but would grow tax-free if used for retirement after age 55. There would be no income limits on contributions, so they would be very easy to understand.

Lifetime Savings Accounts (LSAs). These would work just like RSAs, but there would be no requirement that the funds be used for retirement. In addition to retirement, they could be used for health-care, education, a first home, to start a small business, etc. Importantly, there would be no earned income requirement, so even the parents of children could make annual LSA contributions on their behalf. LSAs would replace HSAs, FSAs, HRAs, 529s, and Coverdells.

Another option is to create an additional account (not displacing what's already there), but which allows saving in the simplest possible way. These types of accounts already exist in Canada and the United Kingdom, and they are doing very well.

In Canada, the government created "Tax Free Savings Accounts" (TFSAs) in 2009. Any adult can contribute up to $10,000 per year (with rollover of contribution eligibility if you skip or partially skip a year). The money grows tax-free, and can be used for any purpose, including but not limited to retirement. The accounts can be opened at any bank or brokerage firm, online or in person. This is as simple as it gets. The British version is called an "Individual Savings Account" (ISA), and there you can sock away an amazing $23,000 per year with tax-free growth.

Clearly, tax-preferred accounts need to be simplified. While these accounts already exist, the reality is they are far too confusing and complex for most American families. By simplifying these saving accounts, Americans would almost certainly save more than they currently do (and be taxed less).

Repeal the Alternative Minimum Tax

First imposed in 1969, the Alternative Minimum Tax (AMT) was established to prevent certain Americans and corporations from using otherwise available deductions to reduce (and in some cases eliminate) their income tax liability. The AMT sets a certain income threshold and requires individuals whose income exceeds this threshold to calculate both regular tax burden and

AMT and pay the higher amount. The AMT was thus intended to act as a fail-safe mechanism to ensure that a small number of upper income individuals could not abuse deductions.

But as with just about every other tax, the AMT has expanded to hit a far larger percentage of Americans than was ever intended. In 1970, the tax hit just 20,000 taxpayers but by 2011, it had grown to hit 4.3 million including many upper-middle class taxpayers.

Because wages are continuously increasing, the AMT will only continue to hit more and more taxpayers over time.

This tax is an unnecessary complication within the code and no longer meets its intended purpose. It should be repealed.

Reduce Capital Gains Tax Rates

A capital gain is a profit derived from the sale of a stock, bond or other asset and together with dividends are taxed at a lower rate. Currently, the top rate today is 23.8 percent for assets held longer than a year, an unusual number due to the sum of the 20 percent statutory capital gains rate plus the 3.8 percentage point surtax from Obamacare.

In the ideal consumption base model, income derived from investments (as well as income saved) would be not be taxed at all. The capital gains tax hits income that has already been subjected to income taxes and has been reinvested to help create jobs, grow wages, and increase economic growth. This double taxation makes no sense from the perspective of encouraging investment and stronger growth.

Recently, presidential candidates from both parties have proposed taxing "carried interest" capital gains—the portion of investment that the expert investor receives from the transaction—as ordinary income. Essentially, these proposals would hike taxes on expert investors from 23.8 percent to 39.6 percent (assuming no change in the top rate.)

Taxing carried interest capital gains as ordinary income is a proposal that goes in the wrong direction. In fact, every time this has been proposed, it has been quickly shot down by those who realize it is a back door proposal to taxing all capital gains as ordinary income. Lawmakers should be encouraging, not discouraging investment.

As it stands now, Uncle Sam takes a bite every time a transaction is made. A key policy goal should be incremental progress toward a consumption base of taxation and therefore cutting the tax rate on capital gains (and dividends, distributed after-tax corporate earnings) to zero.

Repeal the Death Tax

One of the most intrusive and unfair taxes is the Death Tax, which requires you to tell the IRS about everything you own at the moment of death—your bank accounts, investments, home, value of your business, and more. Perhaps worse, the Death Tax is a tax you pay on savings you have already paid taxes on at least once, and probably more than once. Right now, the tax sits at 35 percent with an exemption threshold of $5.43 million, so grieving families will have to pay millions when hit with this tax.

Not only is the Death Tax unfair, it is easily avoided by the truly rich, who are able to avoid paying the tax with an army of accountants, attorneys, and charitable planners. Because the tax can be avoided by the very wealthy, those who are hit by the Death Tax tend to be those who didn't plan ahead. First and second generation families, with a small business are those hit hardest.

There are clear benefits to repealing this tax. For one, repeal of the Death Tax would cost almost nothing. Right now, the tax makes up less than one percent of federal revenue and that number is dropping. The tax is also unpopular—it has been opposed by 60 to 70 percent of adults, registered voters, and likely voters in poll after poll after poll.

Lastly, repealing the Death Tax is good for the economy. It is estimated that repeal will create 139,000 jobs, increase private business hours by 0.1 percent, and increase wages by 0.7 percent.

Make Social Security and Medicare Payroll Taxes Redundant Through Reform

Even though the Republican controlled Congress has reined in spending, it remains high. In 2015, spending as a percentage of GDP reached at 20.5 percent. The culprit is not day-to-day spending, but entitlement spending on Medicaid, Medicare, food stamps, and Social Security. Social Security and Medicare taxes account for about one-third of all federal taxes collected, so reforming these programs could both rein in spending and reduce taxes.

When Social Security was first enacted in 1935, there were 42 Americans in the workforce for every retiree of age to get Social Security. That ratio has since dropped to 5.04 workers per retiree in 1980 and 4.65 workers per retiree in 2000. By 2050 there will be 2.65 workers per retiree.

The numbers are similarly bleak for the long-term sustainability of Medicare. These programs clearly need reform. Fortunately, the direction to go in is obvious.

Privatizing Social Security and reforming Medicare to make it a defined-contribution 401(k)—style savings program would take these programs off budget and dramatically drop the cost of total government spending while also reducing the tax rates needed to fund the these programs.

Of course, this would have to be a gradual process—allowing those who have paid into the existing system to continue using it, while slowly phasing it out and allowing younger workers to use a more efficient private system.

Reforming these programs in this direction will not only strengthen and protect entitlements for future generations, it will also drastically lessen the tax burden on American families and business.

Stop Internet Taxes and Taxation Without Representation

While the most obvious check on taxation without representation is our republican form of government, a critical check has also been established in states through the concept of "physical nexus." This means that a person or business has to have some kind of physical presence—employees, own or lease property—within a state in order to be subject to the taxation authority of a state.

As the digital and physical world meld together, the physical nexus is being threatened. In many cases, states are using the expansion of digital commerce to expand their tax base by assessing business, income, franchise, and sales taxes across borders on businesses that have customers, but no property or employees in the taxing state.

Appropriate boundaries need to be set on taxation authority to withstand regulatory overreach. But rather than restrain this behavior, some in Washington want to encourage it. Misleadingly named legislation like the "Marketplace Fairness Act" and "Remote Transactions Parity Act" give states cross-border tax authority over businesses located outside their jurisdiction.

These bills are a perfect example of what not to do. In reality, they have nothing to do with "fairness" or "parity," but instead open the door to taxation without representation and inhibit the innovation that the internet provides.

Shifting the cost of government to non-residents poses a direct threat to the principle of republican governance by the people. It also violates the "benefits principle" by pushing the tax burden onto those that receive no direct benefit from the state.

Physical presence must be maintained not only in order to prevent state tax base expansion, but also to prevent states from exporting their lawsuits, tax liens, and other policing to non-residents.

People Who Feel They Are Undertaxed Can Already Do Something About It

Taxpayers so inclined can already pay more taxes through a "tax me more account." Any American may make a donation today simply by writing a check to the Treasury, to a fund known as "Gifts to the United States." In addition, at least eight states have a "tax me more fund" that allows those who feel they are not paying enough in taxes to contribute to their state's treasury.

Warren Buffett has famously complained that his average effective tax rate was too low compared to his secretary. Over the years, the "Buffett Rule"—the idea that the wealthy should pay a higher tax rate than middle class families—has been brought up by time and time again by some on the left. These same people continue to ignore the fact that they can already pay more in taxes if they so wish.

While extreme examples undoubtedly exist, the tax code is already steeply progressive. The top one percent of households pay an average income tax rate of over 20 percent, and a total tax rate of 29 percent. By comparison, the middle quintile of households pays an average income tax rate of 2.4 percent and a total tax rate of over 11 percent.

A Buffett Rule is clearly nothing more than a talking point of the left. If anything, implementing it would result in AMT style bracket creep, and this new tax would soon expand beyond its initial intent to hit millions of taxpayers.

Keep the IRS Reined In and Out of the Tax Preparation Business

Some argue that the IRS needs more resources to better do its job and expand its reach. In reality, the opposite is true. Even after adjusting for inflation, the IRS has far more funding than it had 30 years ago.

One annual suggestion is that the agency should expand to tax preparation. After all, the IRS has all this information on you anyway, so wouldn't it just be easier and better if they simply prepared your taxes for you?

For one, it's a giant conflict of interest for the IRS to determine your tax liability, and then to be able to seize your wages and assets in order to collect that tax liability. And even without this conflict of interest, this idea makes no sense. There already exists "free file" tax preparation software that can be easily used by taxpayers across the country.

The IRS has completely failed to serve taxpayers in recent years, from its targeting of political non-profits, to its bumbling implementation of Obamacare, to its recent failure to protect the personal information of hundreds of thousands of taxpayers. The agency clearly needs reform and greater efficiency, not to be made bigger. Through simplifying and removing inconsistencies in the tax code, the ability of the agency to abuse its power will be curtailed.

Freedom and Authority: "Right-Sizing" Government

John Norton Moore[1]

Prepared for the Focusing the Presidential Debates Initiative[2]

How do we "right-size" government? Even today, when discussing the proper size of government, we tend to use the vague terms "left" and "right," terms inherited from the French Revolution of 1789, when supporters of the King sat

---

1. Professor of Law, the University of Virginia. Formerly the Chairman of the Board of the United States Institute of Peace, a United States Ambassador, Chairman of the National Security Council Interagency Task Force on the Law of the Sea (coordinating eighteen federal agencies), and Deputy Special Representative of the President for the Law of the Sea Negotiations, among six presidential appointments. Professor Moore also served as Co-Chairman with the Deputy Attorney General of the United States of the first talks between the United States and the USSR on the Rule of Law (Moscow and Leningrad, 1990), Consultant to the Arms Control and Disarmament Agency (1987-91), Chairman of the American Bar Association Standing Committee on Law and National Security (1982-86), Counselor on International Law to the Department of State (1972-73), and Chairman of the Governance & Ethics Committee of Freedom house, among other governmental and private sector assignments. He is the initiator and original draftsman for Freedom House of what subsequently became the Community of Democracies. He is also the 2013 recipient of the American Bar Association's Morris I. Liebman Award in National Security Law. Most recently, he won Bronze as a member of the United States Masters Bench Press team in the 2015 World Championships.

Professor Moore cautions that he is not a professional economist, though he was an undergraduate major in economics. The ideas in this paper, largely borrowed from far better economists, were developed in a unique seminar he taught at the University of Virginia entitled "The Rule of Law: Controlling Government," in which the Nobel Prize winning economist James M. Buchanan was a regular speaker.

The views expressed in this paper are solely those of Professor Moore, and this project is not associated with the University of Virginia or any governmental or other organization with which he is or has been affiliated.

2. The papers, and videos of the press conferences, associated with this initiative will be posted on an initiative website at: www.FocusingThePresidentialDebates.com.

on the right of the National Assembly and supporters of the Revolution sat on the left. The near vacuous nature of these terms can be quickly illustrated by looking at aggregations of groups said to be "on the left" and "on the right." The left includes not just progressives, but also anarchists, socialists, and communists. And the right includes not just conservatives, but also monarchists and neo-liberals. It is time to retire a vocabulary so lacking in real meaning. But how do we at least ask the right questions about "right-sizing" government? Surely this is a relevant question as we select a presidential candidate to lead the Nation.

As a starting point, we know today that democratic governments perform much better in the aggregate than totalitarian or authoritarian governments. The evidence is striking across many indicators. Freedom House calculated that 24 percent of the world population living in "free" and "partly free" nations produced 86 percent of the world economic product, and the 66 percent of the world population living in "mostly not free" and "not free" nations produced only 13 percent of the world product.[3] While the past decade of rapid economic growth in China is an outlier,[4] democratic nations as a whole continue to strongly outperform economically. Democracies rarely, if ever, engage in major wars with other democracies. When engaged in war, democracies win at a higher rate than non-democracies. Democracies have far better records on human rights; in contrast totalitarian regimes have slaughtered their own and neighboring populations in the millions, as we see with the Holocaust under the Nazis, Mao's starvation of millions of Chinese, or Pol Pot's slaughter of over 20% of the population of Cambodia. Democracies do not themselves experience famines, which we now know to be a product of non-democratic governments, as in North Korea today, or colonialism, as under British rule in India and Ireland. Democracies even have better environmental records.[5] Most importantly, full or "liberal" democracies not only elect their leaders through free and regular elections, but protect important human freedoms: religious liberty, freedom of speech and association, freedom of the press, freedom to petition the government for redress of grievances, due process of law, equal

---

3. *See generally, World Survey of Economic Freedom, 1995-1996,* at 9 (Richard E. Messick, ed., 1996). Freedom House each year publishes *Freedom in the World,* a survey of freedom for every nation in the world, across many indicators. The percentages of governments in the four categories, of course, have changed over those used in this 1995-96 survey of *Economic Freedom.* For the 2015 *Freedom in the World* survey *see*: https://freedomhouse.org/report/freedom-world/freedom-world-2015#.VpVfG1LW_aU.

4. And strains in the Chinese economy are much in the news today.

5. For a fuller discussion of the superiority of "liberal" democracies to authoritarian and totalitarian regimes *see* John Norton Moore, *Solving the War Puzzle,* 2-7 (2004).

protection under the law, property rights, and the right to a fair and speedy trial. But while living in a "liberal" democracy (not just an electoral democracy which has elections but only curtailed freedoms)[6] is one of the greatest blessings an individual can enjoy, democracies too have government failure—just an order of magnitude less failure than totalitarian and authoritarian regimes. Today, thanks to the work of Professor James M. Buchanan on "Public Choice Theory,"[7] which won the Nobel Prize in economics for him, and which I refer to also as "Government Failure Theory," we know a great deal about the causes of government failure.

The starting point for "right-sizing government" must be to ask what is the alternative to government? While the family, the church, and many volunteer organizations carry out essential functions,[8] for the most part the alternative to government we think of is individual exchange, or markets. If that is our focus, then we have a readily available basis for answering many of the questions about "right-sizing" government. Economic theory, particularly "welfare economics," tells us a great deal about the strengths and weaknesses of markets. And, "government failure theory" tells us a great deal about the strengths and weaknesses of government. Many of the answers then, about "right-sizing" government are simply to be found at the intersection of these important fields of knowledge.

This paper will seek to clarify that intersection of important theories by first examining the strengths and weaknesses of markets. Second, it will provide a beginning analysis of government functions in relation to market needs and market failure. Third, it will review some of the mechanisms causing government failure. Fourth, it will develop a theoretical analysis of categories of government failure. Avoidance by government of those categories of government failure will then point the way to a "right-sized" government. Caution is in order,

---

6. The spectrum from best form of government to worst runs from liberal democracy, through electoral democracy, through authoritarian regimes, to totalitarian regimes. The United States, the United Kingdom and Switzerland are examples of liberal democracies; Nazi Germany, Stalin's Soviet Union, Mao's China, and Kim Il Sung and his successor's North Korea, are examples of totalitarian regimes. Russia today is an "electoral democracy," but its curtailment of freedoms under Putin suggests that it may be better characterized as an authoritarian government.

7. For an overview of Professor Buchanan's work *see*, W. Shughart II, "Public Choice" *Concise Encyclopedia of Economics*, available at http://www.econlib.org/library/Enc/Public-Choice.html.

8. There is, I believe, a strong argument for strengthening the family as one of the antidotes to an overly large government. Yet many of our tax and welfare policies seem to create incentives, whether intentional or not, which diminish the family.

however, in not assuming that this analysis generates mechanical "cookie cut-ter" answers for the profoundly difficult issues in "right-sizing" government. There will always remain important differing value choices as to the appropriate size and composition of the "safety net" for individuals, and a myriad of other choices as to assessment of costs and benefits in particular governmental pro-grams. Hopefully, however, a categorization of government failure will at least lead to asking the right questions. Finally, this paper will canvas a few cate-gories of mechanisms designed to reduce government failure and more effec-tively lead to a "right-sized" government.[9]

There is a popular conception that markets are about "greed" and govern-ment about "the greatest good for the greatest number." But this popular con-ception is a myth for both markets and government. Both have strengths and weaknesses and an important role to play. And both need checks where they fail. The magic is in understanding the strengths and weaknesses of each— and in implementing appropriate checks on both.

1. The Strengths and Weaknesses of Markets

Properly functioning markets, or informed free exchanges, have some re-markable qualities. First, a transaction would not take place unless those on both sides of the transaction believe that they will be better off from the trans-action, based upon their own value choices. So, the transaction is a "win-win" for both parties, as well as a "win" for both as assessed by their own values, not the values of some other party. These remarkable starting quali-ties of markets are not accurately described as "greed." Second, markets have low "transaction costs," that is, low costs associated with a simple exchange or transaction. Finally, markets, in society as a whole, are remarkably con-textual (taking place daily with millions and millions of transactions) and, as such, characteristically have reasonably good information available to the participants.

Markets, however, have their needs and problems. First, we need govern-ment to create stable property rights, contracts, and a host of laws to facilitate

---

9. For the United States, a federal structure, there is yet another important set of issues not dealt with in this paper. That is, at what level, state or federal, should a particular gov-ernmental activity be carried out? Clear federal responsibility certainly includes foreign af-fairs, defense and certain central bank functions. On the other side of the scale, one advantage of leaving an issue for the fifty states is the potential for real-world comparison and com-petition.

stable expectations, enable efficient exchange, prevent theft and crime, and maintain macroeconomic stability. Second, markets can generate "market failure" where a transaction imposes costs on non-parties to a transaction (or society as a whole). This is the classic "negative externality." An example would be generating environmental costs when a factory making "widgets" pollutes the water or the atmosphere in its manufacturing process. There can also be a reverse market problem of "positive externalities" when markets will not produce enough because the stream of benefits cannot be fully captured in exchange. This is why we create intellectual property and why government has a role in funding basic research in health and science. There can also be settings in which information is lacking for one of the participants in ways which distort efficient functioning. Finally, there are a host of functional areas where markets will not function optimally alone. These include "insurance failure" (where those presenting high risks will be unable to obtain insurance), "monopoly" (where prices will be distorted by a single supplier), "public goods" (areas such as defense spending generating "free rider" problems of those not opting in if they believe others will bear the cost), and a critical problem for any caring democracy—an appropriate "safety net" for those in society, who because of illness, injury, or otherwise, are not able to work.

2. Government Functions Related to Proper Functioning of Markets

In many respects, understanding the needs and problems of markets leads to an understanding of government functions needed for a proper functioning of markets, as well as government functions needed to meet societal requirements in certain areas where markets simply will not function efficiently. These include:

- A constitutional structure which provides a check on arbitrary power and is capable of maintaining its own structure as a "liberal democracy," including maintaining free elections, a free press, equal protection, and the rule of law;
- A legal system providing stable expectations for exchange and human creativity;
- A legal system protecting "minimum order" that is preventing theft and fraud and protecting individual integrity;
- A legal system regulating "monopolies" and dealing efficiently with "insurance failure" and "public goods." This includes providing public education, insurance regulation, and national defense and security;

- Providing macroeconomic stability;
- Controlling "negative externalities." This includes protection of the environment and public safety;
- Serving unmet needs in settings of "positive externalities," such as funding for basic research in science and health;
- Providing and protecting the truthfulness of information; and
- Meeting a wide range of "safety net" issues for the ill, the unemployed, and other disadvantaged members of society.

The bottom line is that the anarchists who believed government was unnecessary were, of course, badly wrong. A properly functioning market economy needs a properly functioning government, whether to meet market needs for stable expectations or to deal with areas of market failure.

3. Mechanisms Causing Government Failure

Most of the above concepts are likely well understood by the well-educated citizen. But what follows, much of which traces to "Public Choice Theory" which won the Nobel Prize in economics for Professor Buchanan, is not nearly as well understood. Indeed, while there is general understanding of "market failure," as well as a generalized angst about the performance of government, there is far less understanding as to why we have "government failure."

Before we get to the principal mechanisms underlying "government failure" it is important to note that when governments act they do so with certain important disadvantages to properly functioning markets. First, government actions are not "win-win," but instead (even when good) will simply generate greater aggregate costs than benefits (this means certain groups will likely be negatively affected), and that the values advanced through the government action will be some governmental value choice, not necessarily that of the individuals affected. Second, government action is not characterized by low "transaction costs." When government acts it must engage in collective law making, publicize the laws, and then enforce violations. Frequently, there are also not just costs known to those enacting such laws, but a variety of unanticipated costs. Rent control is a good example. In seeking to assist low income needs through holding rents down, unanticipated and unwelcome costs may appear in the form of reduction in maintenance of the facilities, and a reduction in supply of new rental housing. Price controls, with vast unanticipated consequences, as with President Nixon's effort to hold down inflation by mandating price controls, provide well known examples. Transaction costs in governmental actions more fully include: creating and enacting rules and regulations, enforcement of the rules and regulations, inefficiencies in regulatory mode chosen, effect on incentives of taxes and transfer payments, and unwelcome unintended consequences. Finally, government does not act with the same "contextuality" as markets. Rather, government may operate on a "five year plan," or some overall decision process far removed from the myriad of instances affected in day to day life. This may mean that compared to an aggregate of decentralized transactions, government may operate with an information deficit.

These inherent limitations on government action mean that where markets work it is markets that should be the choice for action rather than government. Markets, however, require government action to provide stable expectations in exchange, and to deal with areas of market failure as discussed above. To complicate matters, government action, like market action, is subject to failure for many reasons we understand generally today. It is not enough, then, to simply understand that an area requires government action. Rather, we need to engage in the needed government action while seeking to structure it to lessen the causes of "government failure." The principal causes underlying government failure in a democracy[10] include:

- **Rational ignorance.** That is, government carries out thousands of decisions each day. It simply is not rational for each of us to pay attention to all of these, as doing so would leave no time to live our lives. As such, interest groups form which selectively pay attention to individual issues. Government then tends to respond to the demands of these interest groups as though they represented the entire electorate. Moreover, these special interest groups, benefitting from government actions and expenditures, have more incentive to organize than the marginally affected general taxpayer. This inevitably leads to government support of special interests;
- **Electoral preferences.** Elected officials will understandably tend to support the preferences of those who they believe might vote for them. This means that costs may be more likely to be imposed on minority groups (ethnic, economic or other), unborn generations, and those not of voting age (through deficit spending), and other groups not actively involved in the electoral process;

---

10. Totalitarian, authoritarian, and other non-democratic governments have more profound modalities generating their massive government failure, particularly the ability of the absolute rulers or "vanguard party" to do whatever they like, and externalize costs on the rest of the population.

- **Concealing costs while trumpeting benefits**; thus discouraging real cost/benefit discipline in the minds of the electorate. For example, federal unfunded mandates imposing costs on the states, imposing costs off-budget through regulation of the private sector, and use of rhetoric such as "single-payer," concealing who pays in health care debates. Closely related, government taxes work in innumerable ways to conceal their true costs: impose an estate tax to take assets after the owner is dead and can no longer object; deduct taxes from each paycheck so a large tax bill will not be due at tax time (and government may even generously provide a "refund"); impose federal taxes on your phone bill which you believe you are paying to the phone company, and so on;
- **The time horizon problem.** Since benefits generate support and costs reduce support government officials may seek to reap the benefits of public actions prior to the next election but postpone the costs as long as possible, and certainly until after the election. This may, for example, lead to the United States renting all of its embassies abroad rather than purchasing them, even if the long run savings from purchase would make purchase the better choice;
- **Supply by government agency.** Each agency, and its bureaucracy, believes that its program is the most important and thus each will likely fight for a larger slice of the pie. This thinking is no stranger to congressional entities either. But whether Executive or Congressional, the resulting bureaucratic fight for turf and budget may distort a more efficient overall allocation;
- **Overly risk averse behavior.** Government officials understand that taking an action may be personally riskier than not taking action. This is a classic problem in drug approval. An official responsible for approving a disastrous drug like Thalidomide is gone. Fewer notice a non-approval for a new drug which might have been an effective cure;
- **The tax at a federal level—spend at a state level distortion.** Federal taxes are imposed on the citizens of all the states. But the Senators and Representatives of each state, whether from New York, California, West Virginia or Alaska, want to get back in federal expenditures for their state at least what the citizens of the state paid to the federal government in taxes. This leads to support for wasteful expenditures, simply to get the expenditures in their home state. It also leads to massive national distortions when powerful politicians such as Senator Bobby Byrd of West Virginia (the "paving of West Virginia with government facilities"), or Senator Ted Stevens of Alaska (the "bridge to nowhere") become entrenched as the Chair of the Senate Appropriations Committee;

- **Atherosclerosis of government or "regulatory inflation."** This is simply a growing world of special-interest rules and regulations on top of special-interest rules and regulations, and an inability to break free of the growing inefficiencies. In turn, "rule upon rule" leads to regulations unknown to the average citizen, and undermines the rule of law itself;
- **Limited legal accountability.** Typically, a breach of obligation in markets is subject to legal recourse. But there is only limited ability to bring legal recourse against government failings;[11] and
- **Corpulent government.** This is when government gets so large that its actions, taxes, and/or debts inhibit economic growth. There is considerable evidence, for example, that when the national debt of a country exceeds 90% of its gross domestic product, as is currently the case in America, growth will be significantly affected. Japan and Greece provide all too concerning examples. Similarly, it is even clearer that an excessive regulatory or tax burden will also reduce growth. And in a federal system, at some level of federal tax burden the remaining tax base for the states will be too curtailed for a healthy federalism. The points at which government gets too large through its tax, regulatory, and debt burdens are crucial issues which we know matter, but about which we know too little. The current high debt, tax, and regulatory burdens in America, however, may well be a major cause of our current anemic "new normal" growth rate.

4. Categories of Government Failure

Taken together, the above observations lead to the following categorizations of government failure within democratic governments.[12] Again, this is not some mechanical slot machine for "right-sizing" government, but rather a useful check list for asking questions about a particular government program or action. The principal categories of "government failure" are:

- **Government loses its checks on arbitrary power and becomes simply an "electoral democracy," an authoritarian regime, or worse.** The break-

---

11. There is a limited ability to sue the United States Government for certain torts, for takings in contravention of the Constitution, and for certain administrative and civil rights violations. Suits against foreign governments are even more limited—with "sovereign immunity," a doctrine stemming from old thinking that "the King can do no wrong," still largely dominant over a genuine rule of law.

12. Totalitarian, authoritarian, and other non-democratic forms of government may have additional categories of government failure.

down of Russian democracy under Putin, or Venezuelan democracy under Chavez, are examples;[13]

- **Government fails to act in a setting of market failure.** The pre-1970s failure to address environmental problems caused by market externalities provides an example. A continuing example is the likely failure of government to more robustly fund basic biological and health care research, a classic "positive externality" in market failure—research which could potentially lead to a cure or dramatic reduction in disease burdens saving much more than the costs of the research, and end or reduce the pain and disabilities of millions of Americans;
- **Government acts where markets work better.** If there is no reason why an activity cannot be carried out privately without "market failure," it is likely that government running of the activity will be more costly. An example might be municipalities running their own trash collection;
- **Government acts, but in doing so generates greater costs than benefits.** For example, some of the regulations discussed by Judge Stephen Breyer, now Supreme Court Justice Breyer, in his classic book Breaking the Vicious Circle: Toward Effective Risk Regulation.[14] Showing that foreign affairs are not exempt from government failure, I believe that the decision to invade Iraq for the purpose of replacing Saddam Hussein has generated far greater costs than benefits for America, in each of the human, economic, security and foreign policy realms;[15]
- **Government acts, likely generating greater benefits than costs, but better options are available with better cost/benefit ratios.** The existing Social Security system in the United States is an example. The system provides an important retirement safety net for senior citizens. It fails as a retirement system in not providing a reasonable return on investment, and in not realizing its potential in reducing the wealth gap for American workers;
- **Government acts appropriately, and optimally, but performs poorly in doing so.** For example, the failure some years ago of District of Colum-

---

13. While this category of government failure is not what this paper is about, one can hardly categorize "government failure" without including this ultimate failure, which in turn creates other mechanisms for government failure, including direct and massive externalization of costs by regime elites.

14. Stephen Breyer, *Breaking the Vicious Circle: Toward Effective Risk Regulation* (1992). Some of the real-world examples used by Judge Breyer, from cases which had come before him as a Court of Appeals Judge on the Fifth Circuit Court of Appeals, were outrageous in generating massive costs for only minimal risk reduction.

15. See my discussion of this conclusion in my "Introduction & Overview" paper for this initiative.

bia school system officials to provide textbooks to the students in a timely manner.[16] That poor performance by government remains endemic can be seen in comparing this two decade old example with the 2011 shortage school supplies for students in Madison, WI,[17] and the 2015 shortage of basic supplies, including copy paper, soap, and toilet paper in Philadelphia public schools;[18]

- **Abuse of law.** Government acts ostensibly for one purpose, but actually is motivated by another. Examples include municipal speed traps ostensibly designed to prevent accidents, but which are actually being used to raise revenue and externalize costs on those who do not vote in that municipality, and inappropriate civil forfeitures, ostensibly used to reduce crime but which are actually being used to fund police departments;
- **Abuse of power/crime by government.** This is where government, or government officials, act in contravention of law. The beating of Rodney King in Los Angeles, or corrupt officials taking bribes, are examples; and
- **Government grows too large for sustained growth, or, in a federal system, for healthy federalism.** This is perhaps the most important of all categories of government failure, whether the triggering mechanism is that the debt is too large, the taxes are too high, or the regulatory burden too great. The consequences are severe, possibly eventually even disastrous, and go on and on like the Energizer bunny.

5. Mechanisms for Reducing Government Failure

We need government. But we don't just need government; we need good government. So what might be done to reduce government failure and encourage good governance. Some possibilities include:

- **Enhanced citizenship education in our public schools,** particularly education about the strengths and weaknesses of markets, the causes of

---

16. "What goes on these days in the District of Columbia school system borders on child neglect. Here it is, three months into the school year, and as *Post* staff writer DeNeen Brown reported yesterday, hundreds of students are trying to learn without books. That is an outrage. It is rivaled in absurdity only by the alibis being served up by school officials. A \$500 million school system that fails to supply students with textbooks is misnamed. An educational disgrace is more like it." "No Place for Learning," *Washington Post*, cols. 1-2, page A20 (Dec. 2, 1995).

17. *See* http://www.nbc15.com/home/headlines/School_Supply_Shortage_126297343.html.

18. *See* http://watchdog.org/203938/philadelphia-schools-flush-shortages/.

government failure, and the reasons supporting a culture of lawfulness. If our citizens believe reflexively in markets, or in government, the Nation will lose its ability to achieve an efficient balance and promote good governance. The magic of good governance lies in checks and balances;

- **Enhanced transparency in government programs.** For example, we should consider establishing a small agency charged with publicizing to the American people the most costly and inefficient government regulations;
- **Constitutional, politically imposed (adopted by one or both principal parties), or legislatively imposed structural limits.** These might take the form of balanced budget amendments, limits on taxation, limits on regulatory overreach, measures to reduce the national debt, or measures to return certain federal programs to the states;
- **Fully applying equal protection of the laws.** This is a classic solution offered by economists. It would mean, for example, reducing and controlling progressivity in income taxes, perhaps through a flat tax. Out of control progressivity serves to concentrate the pain of taxes on an ever smaller group of the electorate, and thus largely removes electoral incentives to control tax and spending;
- **Expanding legal recourse.** We might want to review the potential for expanding legal recourse against additional categories of government failure; including excessive "regulatory takings." Expanding legal recourse is particularly needed against intentional actions of foreign governments, and their responsible officials, in supporting terrorism against Americans;
- **Altering incentives for elected and government officials,** such as through imposition of term limits; and
- **Altering incentives for voters to impose costs on others by providing them a greater stake in the economy.** A side-benefit of Social Security optionality, building up substantial stakes in individually owned retirement accounts for American workers, provides an example.

Conclusion

Government is a necessary part of our lives. But when government gets too profligate, as we are witnessing in the unfolding tragedy of Greece, it literally destroys the lives and hopes of its people. Short of the Greek level of collapse, "government failure" imposes unnecessary costs on all of us. Today we know something of the causes of such "government failure." As such, it is the responsibility of our national leaders to work to reduce that failure. There is no magic here. Differences over appropriate "safety nets" and how we assess costs and benefits will remain large. But hopefully a framework which better identifies "government failure" may prove useful in thinking about the problems and ultimately in right-sizing our government.

Part Two:
Foreign and Defense Policy

Introduction — Foreign and Defense Policy

John Norton Moore

Once again this Great Nation has embarked on a journey to elect a new President. The candidates have come forward and the debates are under way. It is in the interest of all Americans that the candidates and their debates seriously address the grave national challenges and opportunities now before the Nation. We cannot afford politics as usual, with candidates vying to be the most immoderate in their Party. The challenges are unforgiving and the opportunities fleeting.

The experts participating in this initiative are deeply concerned about the problems facing this Great Nation and have come together to present suggestions and raise questions for the Presidential candidates; Democrat and Republican alike. The papers being distributed to the Press today are being sent to each of the declared candidates in both parties. The campaign organization of each candidate, as well as the Democratic National Committee and the Republican National Committee, have also been notified of this initiative and invited to send a representative to the press conferences.

Each paper reflects the view of the presenter. There has been no effort to coordinate views; nor is any presenter responsible for the views expressed by other presenters. Some of these papers may appeal more to Democratic candidates and some may appeal more to Republican candidates. The subjects, however, have been chosen for their national importance, and the presenters for their recognized expertise.

It is hoped that as the debates progress in and between both parties that the candidates, and the Nation more broadly, will reflect on the range of serious problems and will consider the questions and/or specific recommendations presented in these papers. We are not able to individually participate in the debates, but we hope to be heard by the candidates and the American people through the great institution of America's free press.

All of the expert papers on each of the subjects under discussion are online at the Initiative website which is www.focusingthepresidentialdebates.com. Videos of all the presentations at the National Press Club are also available there.

Priority Issues in Foreign & Defense Policy

America today has numerous foreign and defense policy challenges; a rogue Russia under Putin's leadership waging unconventional war on Ukraine, bombing to support a genocidal regime in Syria, and threatening elsewhere; an Iran seeking to become a nuclear power and continuing its support for terrorism, destabilization of the Arab Middle East, and implacable hostility to Israel; an intransigent Israeli/Palestinian dispute; an unstable nuclear North Korea continuing to add to its nuclear arsenal; a China doubling down on assertiveness of its oceans claims against Japan in the East China Sea and its ASEAN neighbors in the South China Sea; an out-of-control series of cyberattacks against the West aimed largely at theft of both security and commercial information; a radical Islamist movement (ISIL) currently controlling large swaths of Iraq and Syria, dedicated to a new "Caliphate" setting aside national borders, and seeking to inspire terrorism in North Africa, Europe and America; and finally competing radical Islamist terrorist groups such as Al Qaeda supporting global terror, among more localized violent movements.

As though this panoply of threats is not enough, American credibility (and resulting ability to deter) has eroded through both Republican and Democratic Administrations. It is today clear that the War in Iraq was a serious miscalculation, and a subsequent Administration has compounded the problem by walking away from a red line for Syria not to use chemical weapons in its civil war and failing to develop a timely Syria strategy, not intervening in a timely manner in Iraq to prevent the virtual explosion of ISIL, failing to deter Putin in Ukraine, and concluding an arms agreement with Iraq opposed by a majority of the Congress and by both our Israeli and Arab allies in the Middle East. No one believes these decisions were easy, or that they were not taken in the belief that they were the right decision for the Nation at the time.

But whatever the rationale for these recent American actions, collectively they and other actions have eroded American prestige and credibility around the World. At the same time, budgetary constraints have harmed the readiness of the United States military while problematic actors, such as China and Russia, have continued to increase their military. Other problems in meeting these challenges have included repeated failures, from the Vietnam War, through the War in Afghanistan and the Iraq War, to the war against ISIL, to follow professional military advice for any necessary war fighting; an embrace during the George W. Bush Administration of a "torture-lite" policy which alienated America's allies and damaged the intelligence community; reduced effectiveness of the critical National Security Council system for coordinating United States policy on an interagency basis; absence of an effective structure to engender lasting and meaningful democratic governance in post-conflict settings such as Afghanistan and Iraq; and massive leaks in classified materials undercutting our ability to obtain crucial intelligence information and angering our allies.

A Partial List of Critical Foreign and Defense Policy Issues for the Next President

A partial list of critical foreign and defense policy issues for the next President include:

- Restoring the United States military and defense communities to robust strength; a strength commensurate with the serious and multi-dimensional challenges facing America today. Readiness, following years of conflict in Afghanistan and Iraq, has significantly eroded while the threat has increased. According to the National Defense Panel, commissioned by Congress to review the 2014 Quadrennial Defense Review, our military faces "major readiness shortfalls that will, absent a decisive reversal of course, create the possibility of a hollow force.... ;"
- Russia, a major nuclear power, must be an early and important focus. Putin must be deterred from further escalating the crises in the Ukraine, Syria, or elsewhere;
- ISIL is destabilizing the Arab Middle East and parts of Africa, is carrying out in areas it controls genocide against Christians, Jews and Muslims of different beliefs, is breeding a global terrorist threat, and is working at generating violence in America and Europe. While ISIL likely could have been more easily stopped in its formative period, the challenge today is formidable. An early priority for the new President will be to explore the potential for a global or regional coalition, effective military options, and effective political options to defeat ISIL;
- The conflict in Syria amounts to an ongoing genocide, is generating a massive refugee crisis, threatens a wider conflict, and serves as a base for Putin and Iranian adventurism, and an incubator for ISIL. The United States must explore the potential for a global or regional coalition to address the Syria problem;

- Iran is one of the largest supporters of terrorism in the world today including its support for Hamas, Hezbollah, militias in Iraq, the Houthi rebels in Yemen, the Bashar al-Assad regime in Syria, and at least past attacks directly against United States military in Lebanon and Iraq. Iran must cease its terrorism, and its threats of aggression against Israel and neighboring countries, and the United States must leverage the recent, and flawed, Iran Nuclear Agreement to ensure that Iran never obtains a nuclear bomb;
- China's provocative actions in the South and East China Seas must be firmly addressed. The United States has a direct interest in protecting navigational freedom in the area and has important mutual defense treaties with Japan and the Philippines. Every effort should be made to have China understand that its own interest lies, not in aggressive actions toward its neighbors, but in cooperative efforts with Japan and the ASEAN nations to peacefully resolve these island and oceans boundary disputes;
- Effective engagement for peace in the Israeli/Palestinian conflict. America has in the past played an important role in efforts at peace in this lingering conflict. America should seek to create diplomatic openings offering promise while continuing to support Israel against aggression and terrorism;
- The conflict in Afghanistan is far from over and likely will require American leadership and commitment for a considerable period. The effort must be to create an effective Afghan Army and a more stable political system able to resist a resurgent Taliban and an ambitious ISIL;
- Similarly, the conflict in Iraq is far from over, with ISIL now controlling large swaths of the Nation and Iraq politically tilting as much, or more, toward Iran as toward the United States. The root of the problem is a substantial loss of Sunni support for a sectarian Government, strong Iranian intervention exacerbating the Sunni loss of support, and a failed Army following American withdrawal. Defeating ISIL in Iraq is a core beginning in achieving political stabilization;
- Libya, following the overthrow of Qaddafi, is unstable and a breeding ground for ISIL and for destabilizing Northern Africa. Restoring stability will be a challenge;
- Effective engagement with the United Nations. The United Nations has serious problems, including its blatant discrimination against Israel. But the failure of more effective American engagement has only made matters worse and empowered our enemies. We need a tougher policy of engagement with the United Nations to support American foreign policy and

American values, and those of our allies. In this connection, we should examine "collective security" generally with a view to greater before-the-fact deterrence, explore the Canadian initiative for a more effective stability force as an alternative to unilateral American action, engage more vigorously in diplomatic lobbying in capitals on UN issues, seek to end the Israel bashing which cripples the UN in any Middle East peace process, work to enhance a "democracy caucus" in the UN, and press for more effective UN engagement on promoting democracy and the rule of law;

- Effective engagement in climate change negotiations to ensure that the principal polluting nations, such as China and India, are carrying their fair share of the effort, and that agreed solutions are cost-benefit effective;
- Continuing engagement in promoting freer trade through appropriate agreements which can contribute to American and global growth;
- Prompt Senate advice and consent to the Law of the Sea Convention. This Convention expands United States resource jurisdiction in the oceans off our coasts in an area roughly equivalent to the entire land mass of the Nation, meets all of the security goals sought by the Joint Chiefs, and is supported by all American industry and environmental groups. United States non-adherence to date, in the face of overwhelming international acceptance of the Convention, has greatly weakened the United States ability to engage in critical issues affecting the Arctic Ocean and the South China Sea, and has already lost for the United States two of the four deep seabed mine sites obtained in the negotiations, with strategic mineral deposits of an estimated value of half a trillion dollars, while China and Russia move aggressively to lock up strategic deep seabed sites in America's absence. The scandalous non-adherence to this Convention to date is a classic example as to why listening to the siren song of isolationism is a formula for decline;
- North Korea continues to ramp up its nuclear program and its threats against South Korean. The United States, in conjunction with the United Nations Security Council, which still guarantees South Korea against North Korean aggression, should send a clear deterrent message to the leadership of North Korea;
- The United States should work more actively and effectively on promoting democracy, human rights and the rule of law;
- Cyber-attacks against America and American industry are out of control and must be deterred;
- America should deploy an effective anti-ballistic missile system, whether land-based or mobile sea-based, to protect against rogue nation ballistic missile threats; and

- The National foreign and defense policy apparatus must be strengthened and modernized. This includes ensuring more effective interagency coordination through a strengthened National Security Council system, a better funded diplomatic corps, more effective ideological engagement against totalitarian ideologies such as those of ISIL, a more effective national capacity to build stable governments in conflict zones and failed states, and, where necessary, more effective war-fighting by ensuring that professional military advice is effectively presented to the President as the constitutional Commander-in-Chief. The Nation should never engage in foreign wars lightly, but once engaged, the Nation must fight to win, and win decisively.

*Let us remember that America is, and must always remain, a land of opportunity for all, regardless of ethnicity, gender, color, or religion, a leader in the struggle for peace and justice, a beacon of hope to the world, and the home of the free. We must never forget that America's true greatness lies, **not** in its wonderful "spacious skies ... amber waves of grain ... and purple mountain majesties," but **in its national values and its unquenchable spirit**.*

Defense and Security Policy: Time for a Strategic Approach

Dennis C. Blair

Prepared for the Focusing the Presidential Debates Initiative[1]

A new administration taking office in 2017 faces a diverse set of national security challenges. It would do the nation an incalculable service by articulating an actual strategy—a coherent statement describing the kind of world the United States wants, the role of the United States in that world, and a game plan for achieving it.

The four administrations since the end of the Cold War in 1990 have all grappled with a range of issues and crises with varying degrees of success. None has been able to develop and follow a consistent strategy that identifies enduring American interests in a complicated world; sets priorities for protecting or achieving them; takes timely, forehanded action and balances policies across the diplomatic, economic, and military components of American power and influence.

Some ask whether an overarching strategy is even possible in a post-Cold War world, where so many threats emanate from cyberspace and non-state actors; where we see in real-time widespread suffering of people in their own countries or fleeing them; where we face worldwide crises like climate change and pandemics. Is it possible—indeed, can we afford—to deal with all of it?

We cannot afford not to. In the absence of strategy, American national security policy has become increasingly short-term, crisis driven, expensive and not notably successful. The fundamental national security challenge of the new administration is to restore a publicly supported, bipartisan, and enduring approach to America's responsibilities around the world.

What might a real strategy look like? It would be a statement that avoids laundry lists, and sets forth organized, national security goals to ensure U.S.

---

1. This paper was written by Dennis C. Blair, former Director of National Intelligence and Commander in Chief, US Pacific Command. He is currently Chairman and CEO of the Sasakawa Peace Foundation, USA.

national survival and prosperity. Having, and living by, a strategy is critical for keeping us on course, and does not hogtie us when it comes to responding to inevitable, unforeseen manmade and natural crises.

The International Security Environment: Do Fewer Things Better

One of the most important, early tasks of a new administration is to assess the complicated international security environment and identify the top priorities.

Three national security challenges stand out: the rise of China, the breakdown of stability in the Middle East, and the emergence of Muslim violent extremist groups. While there will be many issues and crises in the next four years, these three will have the greatest, long-term importance for American security. Current American policies for dealing with them are neither adequate nor successful.

China

The only serious rival to the United States is China. As China's economic strength and military power have grown it has more forcibly and aggressively sought to expand its influence. It is pursuing mercantilist policies that unfairly favor its own companies in its domestic market and abroad at the expense of American and other international companies. It is pushing extravagant territorial claims in the East and South China Seas. In cyberspace, it continues to steal American intellectual property. It is rejecting the American model of freedom, democracy and free markets.

Some important aspects of China's rapid development have been beneficial. It has raised hundreds of millions of its citizens out of poverty, it has become an engine of global economic growth, provided inexpensive goods to consumer in other countries, and in important areas it has cooperated with the United States and other countries to deal with regional problems like Iran and North Korea. Moreover, China faces problems that undercut its ambitions. Its economic growth is slowing as it attempts to shift from export and infrastructure investment to consumption and market mechanisms. It faces a massive environmental challenge resulting from its unconstrained recent growth. Its workforce has peaked—its working age population has been falling since 2011—and it has another several hundred million people living in poverty.

The authoritarian Chinese political model has little attraction for countries in the region, and its ambitions frighten them.

An improved American strategy to deal with China is not simply "getting tough," and it is not simply coaching and coaxing China into the US-led economic and security system. China has grown too big for that approach. The United States needs to identify what it wants from China and what it is willing to defend from China, communicate these objectives and limits clearly and both cooperate or compete across the full range of issues.

An improved American strategy for dealing with China needs to be based on strengthened relations with allies and partners in the region—Japan, South Korea, the Philippines, Australia, New Zealand, Taiwan, Thailand, Singapore, and Vietnam. The United States needs to continue to build its military power in East Asia to offset rapidly increasing Chinese capability. While preserving mutually beneficial business relations with China, and encouraging China's continued and beneficial participation in the world economic system, the United States needs to find ways to check its abuses of the system. Using penalties as well as jaw-boning and incentives, United States needs to confront the theft of intellectual property and other government-sponsored policies penalizing American and other international companies in favor of Chinese competitors. The U.S. needs to limit Chinese aggression in the South China Sea, while preserving Chinese cooperation on other regional interests from the Middle East to North Korea.

Middle East

American Middle East policy since the end of the Cold War has been neither consistent nor effective. Granted, there is nothing simple about developing a consistent strategy, or even a set of strategic principles, for dealing with the Middle East. American interests—protection of the world economy's swing producers of oil along the southern Persian Gulf coast, safeguarding the security of Israel, limiting the proliferation of nuclear technology, combatting Muslim violent extremist groups, and supporting the development of good governance—often conflict. Short-term interests, such as cooperation against extremist groups, conflict with longer term interests, such as promoting democratic governance and human rights.

Since the 1970s, the American approach to the region has become heavily militarized. Military campaigns have failed to produce decisive results, despite great expenditures of blood and treasure, yet in the Middle East, diplomacy without the credible threat of force is generally not effective.

The elements of an effective, long-term strategy for the region, however, are straightforward. They include several strategic principles and objectives:

- First, improving American energy security through domestic measures to lessen the strategic importance of Saudi Arabia and other low-cost-oil producing states.
- Second, without sacrificing American political leadership, involving other countries from Europe and Asia, including India and China, in maintaining a regional balance of power that checks the ambitions of Iran or any other country seeking a dominant position in the region.
- Third, shifting much of the campaign against Muslim violent extremist groups in fragile countries, such as Yemen and Afghanistan, from direct military and intelligence action to support for better governance and effective host-nation security capacity.
- Fourth, sustained support for long-term, peaceful democratic change.
- Fifth, greater and earlier use of military measures, short of committing major combat units, such as providing appropriate equipment and sustained training.

There will be constant, individual crises in the region requiring short-term responses, but the United States needs to be able to make progress on these strategic principles and objectives as it works its way through the crisis of the moment.

Violent Extremism

Finally, we need a better approach to violent extremist Islamist organizations that threaten fragile states and are capable of isolated attacks within the United States. Since 9/11, the United States has learned a great deal more about these organizations and the threat they pose, even as their names and locations have changed. We have gained the experience to forge a successful strategy.

An improved counterterrorism strategy should include the following principles and objectives:

- First, maintain the FBI-led campaign to identify and prosecute terror plots originating within the United States, while explaining and building public support for the legal investigative methods necessary to keep the public safe. It has been the FBI and other domestic law enforcement agencies that have thwarted the great majority of intended terrorist attacks on the United States in recent years.
- Second, continue to improve the Department of Homeland Security-led campaign to prevent members of violent extremist Islamic groups from entering the country. There is still a great deal of work to be done to

merge all of the information and intelligence available to identify those who pose a threat.

- Third, strike a better balance between conducting direct American military or intelligence action against terrorist organizations and building the capacity of host governments to provide better governance and security for their citizens.
- Fourth, over the long run, support peaceful democratic development in authoritarian countries that support violent extremist Islamist groups in order to build positive alternative political forces.
- Fifth, and probably most important, promote U.S. national resilience. Explain to the American people that they can never be totally protected from terror attacks unless they are willing to give up treasured rights and freedoms, and that the threat of these attacks should not make us a fearful people living in an intrusive state. The citizens of Boston set a fine example of resilience following the horrific attack at the Boston Marathon. They have proudly upheld the continuity of this iconic, public event, while heeding stringent (albeit controversial) new security measures.

There are many second-tier national security challenges that a new administration will also inherit: dealing with Vladimir Putin's Russia, halting the spread of nuclear weapons, dealing with global climate change, engaging India as a partner in addressing common challenges. These issues, too, require consistent and successful strategies, and the investment of resources and attention.

The National Security System: Time for a Reboot

In addition to understanding the international security environment, identifying American interests, and setting priorities, a new administration needs to overhaul the basic structure of how American security is formulated and carried out. As the Project on National Security Reform (PNSR), a distinguished group of national security scholars and practitioners, stated back in 2008:

> The legacy structures and processes of a national security system that is now more than 60 years old no longer help American leaders to formulate coherent national strategy. They do not enable them to integrate America's hard and soft power to achieve policy goals. They prevent them from matching resources to objectives, and from planning rationally and effectively for future contingencies. As presently con-

stituted, too, these structures and processes lack means to detect and remedy their own deficiencies. [2]

The legislative framework and heritage of the current system favor strong departmental capabilities over integrative functions. As the report states:

> [t]he basic deficiency of the current national security system is that parochial departmental and agency interests, reinforced by Congress, paralyze interagency cooperation even as the variety, speed, and complexity of emerging security issues prevent the White House from effectively controlling the system.

PNSR recommended a set of structural improvements through legislation and executive order that would improve budgeting for national security, make the Office of the President a more strategic and forehanded directing body, improve the flow of knowledge and information across the national security system, and improve the execution of integrated policies in the field.

It is difficult at the beginning of a new administration, with all the demands of recruiting personnel, establishing new policies, handling crises, and answering the inbox, to carve out the time and attention for structural reform. However, unless an administration can make these improvements to the current system, the current trends will continue: short-sighted and crisis-driven policy, White House micromanagement of a few issues and neglect of others, and uncoordinated actions in the field.

In case this sounds like an impossibly daunting or idealistic task, we already have models of integration on which to build. The Goldwater-Nichols Act of 1986 brought an end to crippling rivalries and confusion within the Department of Defense. The Office of the Director of National Intelligence has been integrating the vast, diffuse U.S. Intelligence Community—from technology to personnel policies to operational procedures—since its post-9/11 birth in 2005.

The Armed Forces: Air, Sea, Land, Space, Ether

With the international security situation as complicated as it is, the armed forces of the United States needs to be flexible and multipurpose. As outlined earlier, the United States, at a minimum, needs the military capability to deal with China, an unstable Middle East, and violent extremist Islamic groups, while maintaining a reserve of capability for unexpected crises and challenges.

---

2. *Project on National Security Reform* February 2008, available at http://www.pnsr.org/

The fundamental, standing military task is to deter cross-border aggression against allies or other friendly countries, from members of NATO to South Korea and Japan. This mission involves maintaining ready, conventional force units strong enough, in combination with the armed forces of allies and treaty partners, to convince potential aggressors that cross-border military attacks would not succeed.

The other major American military mission is to deal with violence within states, from insurgencies to civil wars, when that violence is causing wide-scale suffering, or when adversary countries are exploiting local conditions to increase their power and influence. It will always be a fine judgment choosing the time and place of American intervention. It will depend on the degree of threat to US or allied interests, the scale of human suffering, and what is going on elsewhere in the world. However the armed forces need to have the ready capability to take action when the decision is made. Current examples run from the Ukraine to Yemen. American military support in these cases can be for a government defending its authority (Iraq, Ukraine, and Yemen), or it can be for insurgents challenging the government (Syria). This military support will generally take the form of equipment, advisors, air strikes, and logistic support, although there may be times when American combat units are committed.

Finally, specialized military forces are required for operations in a small number of fragile states that are home to violent extremist Islamic organizations that threaten the United States and our friends and allies—Afghanistan, Iraq, Yemen, Somalia, Nigeria, Libya, and Syria, to cite current examples. The mission is to cooperate with local specialized forces to capture or kill leaders of these violent groups, and to otherwise disrupt their operations.

There are three additional sets of functional force requirements—nuclear modernization, cyber defense, and space defense.

In the next twenty years, virtually the entire current nuclear triad—land based missiles, submarine-launched missiles, and long-range bombers—will need to be replaced. An important question is whether the United States needs to replace all three legs of the triad, or if it can be secure with a two-legged dyad.

In the cyber aspects of conflict, even an opponent like North Korea or Iran can pose a formidable threat to American military networks. Both China and Russia devote large resources and skilled personnel to offensive cyber units. To secure its networks, the Department of Defense needs a continuing, major investment in technology, highly qualified personnel, and continuous training and exercises.

The technology for attacking satellites in orbit, their ground stations, and the networked systems that control them is becoming less expensive and more widespread. With all of its likely military theaters far from its shores, the United

States depends heavily on space-based intelligence and communications to support military operations. Survivability of satellite systems can be improved by design features, operational maneuvers, and other techniques. It will become necessary in the near future for the United States to spend more resources on its space systems to ensure that they can be effective against attacks from even medium-level threats.

Defense Budget Choices: Get Real

The currently planned armed forces do not jibe with the military challenges of the future. The projected funding for nuclear modernization, cyber security, and space defense are inadequate. If more funds are budgeted to them, and budgets remain constrained, there will be fewer resources for the regular forces.

The Navy and Air Force require steady increases of funding to pace growing Chinese military capabilities. Special Forces Command needs continued budget increases both to deal with violent extremist Islamic organizations and to train allies and partners. The Army, and, to a lesser extent, the Marine Corps, need to maintain conventional units for alliance commitments in NATO and in South Korea, while increasing their capability to provide military training and other forms of assistance to countries the United States decides to assist or oppose in the Middle East and elsewhere.

Even without a detailed analysis, it is clear that these essential capabilities of the armed forces cannot be maintained with sequestration ceilings or even the relative straight-line projections of the current administration budget. It is also clear that, under realistic budgets, there have to be changes in the traditional, proportional budget shares of the services and their fundamental structures. While maintaining the ability to expand quickly in the case of major threats arising, the Army and the Marine Corps should be reduced in end strength. Navy and Air Force inventories of manned aircraft can be reduced, in favor of unmanned aircraft for several missions, and sea- or ground-based missile systems for air defense.

A new administration will have to make hard choices on the size and shape of its armed forces to support its strategy, and will require skill and persistence to gain approval and funding from the Congress.

Foreign Policy

Chester A. Crocker[1]

Questions on Foreign Policy for the 2016 Candidates

Prepared for the Focusing the Presidential Debates Initiative

Overall Vision and Strategy for the Country

Most experts agree that the US remains the pre-eminent global power—while also acknowledging that power relationships are in flux as power inevitably devolves to some extent to rising states such as India and China. Americans appear to be wary of new military engagements after the inconclusive wars in Iraq and Afghanistan and the continuing, open-ended campaign to degrade terrorist movements such as Al Qaeda and ISIS. Moreover, partisan deadlock at home directly undercuts US standing as a global player and hampers the Nation's ability to address important budgetary needs—e.g., to remedy our decaying infrastructure and to adequately resource the requirements of defense and foreign policy under the so-called budget 'sequester'.

---

1. Chester A. Crocker is the James R. Schlesinger Professor of Strategic Studies at Georgetown University's Walsh School of Foreign Service. He served as chairman of the board of the United States Institute of Peace (1992-2004), and as a member of its board through 2011. From 1981-1989, he was U.S. assistant secretary of state for African affairs and mediated the prolonged negotiations among Angola, Cuba, and South Africa that led to Namibia's transition to independence, and to the withdrawal of Cuban forces from Angola. He serves on the boards of various companies and NGOs, including G3 Good Governance Group Ltd, a business intelligence advisory service, the London-based Global Leadership Foundation, and the International Peace and Security Institute. He is a distinguished fellow at Canada's Centre for International Governance Innovation, and is the author and editor of numerous articles, monographs and books on mediation and conflict management.

The gridlock has a direct impact on the capacity of the Executive Branch of government—under any president—to lead and conduct the Nation's business. It makes it almost impossible for the Executive and Congress to shape a plan for bringing our resources into balance with our many, far-flung commitments. For example, the partisan gridlock explains to some degree the way in which negotiations on the Iranian nuclear challenge have been conducted. Another striking example is the inability of the United States to join virtually everyone else in ratifying the 1982 Law of the Sea Treaty (despite the strong support of the US defense department and a host of former senior US national security officials and favorable votes in the Senate's foreign relations committee); the net result of this is to disable America's ability to assert and defend its global maritime interests in places such as the Arctic and South China Sea. Gridlock hampers any realistic solution to the situation we face with detainees at the Guantanamo facility. These are just a few examples of the *foreign policy costs* of domestic American dysfunction and gridlock. In this context it is especially difficult for an American president to develop and conduct a coherent foreign policy based on a careful reading of our opportunities and the challenges we face in a turbulent world.

- What is your overall vision as a foreign policy leader? Do you think we are overcommitted overseas, not doing enough to assert global leadership, or is the current level of US foreign policy effort about right? What commitments would you reassess? Where should we be doing more?
- As a global power with important alliance commitments and other international responsibilities, the US has far flung interests. As you look at the world situation today, are there regions where we are doing too much or not enough?
  - Would you provide arms to Ukraine?
  - More troops to Iraq?
  - Confront China over cyber issues?
  - Could we do anything about the criminal violence that threatens a number of Central American states?
  - The Pentagon has ramped up US initiatives—training and special forces operations—in Africa. Should we be doing more, or less, to chase 'bad guys' around the Sahel region, North Africa and the Horn of Africa?
  - Has the time come for a negotiated end of the conflict in Afghanistan, and should we be helping there? Should we keep US troops there?
  - Do you believe that the Obama administration has paid enough attention to Europe and NATO where key allies face multiple challenges?

Relations with Russia/European Policy

Some observers and candidates have described Russia under Putin as our greatest national security challenge, pointing to its violation of internationally recognized borders (Ukraine and Georgia), its threatening and provocative aerial maneuvers on the periphery of other European states including both NATO and EU member states. Russian official rhetoric has become increasingly shrill and antagonistic toward Western policies, while at the same time Putin has attempted to insinuate Russia as a champion of left and right-wing opposition political parties in such countries as Greece, Macedonia, Hungary, Germany and France. Russia's decision to welcome Edward Snowden—whatever one thinks of his NSA revelations—clearly signaled Putin's finger-in-your-eye hostility toward the West.

Western sanctions and the oil price collapse have imposed a serious price on the Russian economy and helped to dry up foreign investment there. But there is little evidence that Russia's illegal and bellicose behavior (including the use of hybrid warfare by its troops and security services) is changing or that Russia will in fact respect the Minsk deals aimed at restoring security in Ukraine. At the same time, it is undeniable that the US and Russia share some common interests on such issues as countering jihadi terrorism and the Iranian nuclear negotiations. Russia's role in the UN Security Council can either facilitate or block concerted international action on a host of other issues such as UN peacekeeping, dealing with the Syrian conflict, or supporting a negotiated endgame in Afghanistan. Finally, it is clear that a number of our problems with Russia are really European security challenges, and the US needs European cooperation, support, and coherence in dealing with them.

- Is it possible for the US to be effective in pressuring Russia to end its belligerent conduct and to respect Europe's borders while also seeking Russian cooperation and support for other US priorities?
- What further diplomatic moves and actions would you suggest to get Putin to revise his policies? Arms to Ukraine?
- Should we escalate pressures on Russia (even if our allies won't)? Are we prepared for the consequences if Putin escalates, say in Estonia?
- What can be done to reduce Europe's worrisome dependence on Russian oil and gas, a factor that appears to inhibit a more robust European response to Russia's actions?
- How can the US best persuade our European partners to face up to the need for increased defense efforts at a time when Europe is still recovering from the financial crisis and faces a dramatic refugee crisis?

US Role in the Middle East

Despite the much discussed 'rebalancing' toward Asia, American foreign policy remains to a substantial degree mired in Middle East engagements. US global policy is severely constrained by the extent of these commitments and engagements in a turbulent region that is going through the equivalent of the Reformation in Europe five centuries ago. The challenges facing us there are many, and they have a tendency to overlap and spill into each other: (a) defense of Israel and support for the Israeli-Palestinian peace process; (b) coping with a near nuclear Iran as a regional power; (c) dealing with the Assad problem in Syria; (d) degrading and defeating ISIS in Iraq and Syria while preventing Salafist terrorism from gaining ground; (e) sustaining positive relations with key regional allies Saudi Arabia and Egypt (as well as Jordan and Morocco) while encouraging their positive domestic evolution; (f) helping the only 'success story' of the Arab awakening (Tunisia) while limiting the damage from chaos in Libya and Yemen.

- On Iran, we have worked closely with European partners as well as Russia and China. Is this is a good model for other issues or would you prefer a more unilateral approach?
- Since the problems appear so intractable and our need for Middle Eastern oil has declined substantially, should we be trying to lower our profile and downgrade our level of involvement in the region?
- Could the US play its cards more strategically in the region by pushing its major states toward establishing some framework for regional security cooperation, instead of getting sucked into their bellicose games?
- Should we care if our leading Arab partners are deeply authoritarian regimes that oppress their people?
- What do you think of Netanyahu coming to Washington to lobby Congress against American policy on the Iran nuclear challenge ?
- Would you drop the Iran deal and cease de facto cooperation with Iran in the fight against ISIS?

Containment and Engagement with China

Despite its current economic woes, there is little doubt that a rising China represents a major challenge for US policymakers. That challenge is unfolding in the military-naval balance in East Asia and the Pacific and is reflected in concerns about Chinese efforts to build artificial islands in the South China

Sea, to establish 'air defense identification zones' in the East China Sea, to build expanded military capabilities that could challenge American access to China's maritime periphery and American capacity to come to the assistance of treaty allies and friends in the region. The China challenge also is visible in contrasting views between the US and China on a number of global security issues and governance issues that arise in the UN context and elsewhere. It is generally agreed that China is the source of a large share of the cyber attacks being launched against US businesses and government agencies. At the same time, the US and Chinese economies are interdependent in a number of ways. American consumers and American investors arguably gain from these economic relationships. American and Chinese military and naval officers engage in frequent consultations aimed at reducing the risks of accidental incidents and exploring differences over maritime security and sovereignty claims. The Chinese government and the Obama Administration have developed reciprocal commitments on carbon emissions in an effort to address climate change.

- Against this backdrop, what is the best approach for balancing and guiding the US-China relationship?
- Would you continue the Obama's administration's efforts in this area? What would you change? Is China a friend, partner, rival, or enemy?
- Do you favor the idea of reviewing or revising the US defense posture in East Asia in an effort to reduce the likelihood of dangerous clashes between US and Chinese naval and air forces? How could we do this without sending the 'wrong message' to Beijing?
- Is it possible in your view to negotiate some kind of security understandings or a regional security framework in the area?
- How can we best manage our close relationships with key regional allies and partners such as Australia, Japan, South Korea, Taiwan, the Philippines?
- What would you do if North Korea starts to collapse?

Immigration

Much attention has been given to the issue of immigration in the primary debates. It is noteworthy that this is a global challenge, not an exclusively American one. In Europe there is talk of some 800,000 people seeking entry into EU member countries this year as asylum seekers or economic refugees. Many have died in the attempt to do so, and debate continues in a number of European countries about the correct response and how to share the burden of receiving these immigrants. Migration is also an issue in a number of Asian states. In the US, attention has focused on whether or not to offer undocumented immigrants a path to citizenship, on the status of their American-born children, the best policy for controlling the immigrant pressure on US borders and for treating those people who are already here.

- What is your policy on these issues?
- Do you believe immigrants from Latin America are taking away jobs from American workers or do they mainly take up jobs American citizens don't want?
- What policy toward immigrants is most consistent with American history, American values and American interests?
- Do you support confronting the Mexican government, building a high and costly wall, and sending millions of US residents back south of the border necessitating a huge immigrant roundup operation in the US?

Climate Change

As the Paris meeting of the UN-sponsored climate change process approaches in December of this year, opinion is divided on several aspects of this long standing effort to negotiate a universal and legally binding successor to the 1997 Kyoto Protocol. Leaving aside those who basically deny the validity of the science concerning the sources and gravity of climate change, there is general agreement that this is a serious global problem with significant economic, humanitarian, political and national security implications. Senior officers of the US military establishment warn of its implications for international security and for the operating environment for US armed forces. President Obama has elevated the issue of curbing carbon emissions to a prominent place in his agenda, and has taken some controversial steps using executive action to place limits on emissions from US coal-fired power plants, among other measures.

Some observers favor a continued international effort to negotiate a UN agreement with legally binding effect to succeed the Kyoto protocol, arguing that the problem is global and that all countries—the major emitters as well as those countries likely to be most seriously affected—should be part of the process. Others point out that a massive UN-based negotiation with 193 other states is inevitably unwieldy, prone to unhelpful coalition politicking, and likely to pit developing nations against developed.

However, this is not necessarily and either/or situation. In their Joint Announcement on Climate Change in November 2014, Obama and China's Xi Jinping announced several national targets reducing or capping growth of carbon emissions and committed to work jointly and with other states toward the goal of adopting a successor climate protocol or other form of universal and legally binding accord at the Paris conference of the parties in December under the 1992 UN Convention on Climate Change. Indications are that we will see UN-based negotiation, bilateral commitments such as these and climate talks in more limited multilateral forums such as the G20 which comprises the world's major economies.

- In light of the likelihood of gridlock in Congress on US domestic legislation, do you believe that president Obama is doing all he can to address these issues?
- How do you come down on the trade-off between coal mining jobs and addressing climate change?
- Is he doing too much, and should the US focus instead on pressuring other countries to up their game on climate?
- Do you believe it is important for the US to be a global leader in this field and how should it lead?

The Opening to Cuba

The Obama Administration moved to terminate the isolation and non-recognition of the Cuban government in 2015, a potentially historic move that was widely welcomed in Latin America and among many in this country and in Cuba itself. A policy of embargoes and sanctions has been ended. A small but proud nation less than 100 miles off our shores remains under the one-party rule of the Marxist regime established by Fidel Castro and now dominated by his brother Raul. Critics of this initiative argue that it risks handing a life jacket to a failing Marxist regime and breaking the morale of long-suffering Cuban opposition voices.

- Do you support the gradual normalization process that has started and would you intend to continue it?
- Have US sanctions against the Havana regime 'worked' and could they have continued to work? Do you support lifting the embargo or should we be trying to get a tougher deal?
- What are the best tools for bringing about genuine democratic change in Cuba—should we ramp up American presence, goods and social media activity?

Trade

Since the collapse of the WTO's Doha round of multilateral trade negotiations over eight years ago, countries in the Pacific region (as well as the Atlantic Community) have looked for alternative ways to liberalize the regional and global trading systems through a growing number of proposed trade agreements at the multilateral, regional, and bilateral level. Continuing an initiative begun by President Bush (43), President Obama has considered that the Trans-Pacific Partnership process was good trade policy and a central pillar of the US strategy of 'rebalancing' toward Asia. The 12 current TPP countries account for close to half of world trade.

A TPP pact would be a major milestone in the modern history of trade negotiation, a signal accomplishment for the Administration and a striking example of bipartisan coordination on an issue that tends to unify Republicans and divide Democrats over a range of labor and environmental issues. Seeking to overcome opposition in his own party, the Obama Administration promises that this will be the most progressive trade agreement in history. In June of this year Congress granted the Administration 'fast track' negotiating authority on the TPP. But the goal of completing a 12-nation agreement remains elusive due to electoral timetables and a host of national concerns about opening markets in agriculture and dairy products, autos, pharma, intellectual property, investment and services, to name just a few key sticking points. Should the TPP process stall, the question will be whether progress can be made in smaller groupings or in other forums.

- What is your stance on these trade issues which appear to be one area of potential non-partisan policymaking? Is Obama on the right track here, and would you continue these efforts in the TPP context and other regions?
- Opponents of the TPP claim that the 'fast track' authority is a major victory for big money and major corporations who seek to use these negotiations to further liberalize—i.e., deregulate—trade regimes, impose US domestic standards on other countries, and weaken worker and environmental protections. What is your answer to those charges?

Supporting Democracy, Human Rights and Rule of Law

David J. Kramer[1]

Prepared for the Focusing the Presidential Debates Initiative

Why Promoting Democracy Is Important

Most of the problems facing the world today originate from countries with non-democratic systems of government and/or from extremist non-state actors that seek to blunt the advance of democracy. They view the spread of freedom and systems rooted in rule of law as threats to their own hold on/grab for power. From Russia's invasion of Ukraine (including the first annexation of one European country's territory by another since World War II) and now its military move into Syria, China's muscle-flexing in the South China Sea and cyber-attacks against the U.S., and the danger of a nuclear-weapons capable Iran to terrorism from the Islamic State or Al Qaeda, we face significant threats to our interests and to our values.

Russia, China and Iran are corrupt, authoritarian regimes that show no respect for their own people's human rights. How a regime treats its own people is often indicative of how it will behave in foreign policy. Thus, we should not be surprised when Vladimir Putin violates the sovereignty and territorial integrity of his neighbors, whether Georgia in 2008 or Ukraine in 2014 to the

---

1. This paper is adapted from work done by the Democracy & Human Rights Working Group, a nonpartisan initiative bringing together academic and think tank experts and practitioners from NGOs and previous Democratic and Republican administrations, seeking to elevate the importance of democracy and human rights issues in U.S. foreign policy. That group is convened by Arizona State University's McCain Institute for International Leadership, and David Kramer is co-chair of the group.

present, in light of the worst crackdown on human rights inside Russia since the break-up of the Soviet Union. Nor should we be shocked by threats from the Iranian regime to destroy the state of Israel or its support for the Assad regime in Syria, given that Iranians are subject to the whims of the mullahs. And under President Xi Jinping, China has increased use of the death penalty and gone after bloggers, lawyers and others amid a deteriorating human rights situation while simultaneously throwing its weight around in the Asia-Pacific region.

By contrast, we have few problems—certainly none comparable to those with authoritarian regimes—with countries that are democratic, respect human rights and observe rule of law. Accordingly, it is in U.S. national interests to advance the cause of democracy, human rights and rule of law around the world. After all, the United States is safer and more prosperous in a more democratic world and should take the lead in advancing this cause. Getting other governments to respect universal values and promote democratic development advances the cause of freedom and also mitigates the challenges we face. Free nations are also more economically successful, stable, reliable partners, and democratic societies are less likely to produce terrorists, proliferate weapons of mass destruction, or engage in aggression and war. This means that the advance of democracy benefits not just the U.S., but order and peace around the globe.

For nine straight years, freedom has been in decline, according to Freedom House's *Freedom in the World 2015* report. "More aggressive tactics by authoritarian regimes and an upsurge in terrorist attacks contributed to a disturbing decline in global freedom in 2014," Freedom House argues. According to the International Center for Not-for-Profit Law (ICNL), between 2004 and 2010, more than 50 countries considered or enacted measures restricting civil society. This overall decline in freedom means a more dangerous and unstable world.

And yet despite recent disturbing developments and trends, it is important to understand that the state of democracy in the world has improved over the past several decades. In 1972, according to Freedom House, there were 44 countries rated as "free." Today, there are 89 countries in that category. The establishment of democracy is not a short-term proposition. It takes time and commitment by those fighting for it, and the process is not necessarily a linear one. The United States has had democracy for nearly 250 years, and we are still perfecting it, so we cannot expect other countries, especially those without democratic traditions or history, to get it right the first time. Ask the citizens of Mongolia, Tunisia, Poland, or Serbia whether the United States has helped them in their path toward democracy, and the answer is likely to be a resounding yes.

America's Unique Role

For decades, the United States has supported democracy, human rights and rule of law around the world. The United States was founded on the principles of life, liberty and the pursuit of happiness, and Americans believe that all people should enjoy these rights. We do not seek to impose the American model on other countries; each country, if given the opportunity, will develop in its own unique way. But we stand with and support those forces in countries around the globe who seek to build democratic societies that allow people to live in freedom, lead to greater economic success, better protect intellectual property rights, and provide a more stable investment environment. Given the option, most people around the world would choose to live in free societies. According to the most recent World Values Survey, more than 82% of respondents believe having a democratic system of government is a good thing.

Democracy advocates and human rights defenders look to the U.S. for moral, financial, and political leadership and support, making American leadership indispensable. Remaining silent or reducing the profile of these issues abandons people who, in many cases, sacrifice their liberty and lives struggling for a more democratic society.

We need to elevate democracy promotion, human rights and rule of law to a prominent place on the American foreign policy agenda by supporting indigenous forces and helping create space for them to work within their own country. We should seek to promote universal values — freedoms of expression, assembly, association, and religion — and partner with other democracies, both those with a history of freedom and those who have more recently transitioned, to strengthen efforts to spread these universal values. The Universal Declaration of Human Rights, adopted by the United Nations General Assembly in 1948, defined the terms "fundamental freedoms" and "human rights." These include rights and freedoms of association, religion, speech, and assembly — many of which are still lacking or limited in many other countries.

Thus, we should support:

- Rule of law and accountability
- Separation of powers, an independent judiciary, and checks-and-balances,
- Free, fair, and competitive elections and political party development,
- Respect for women's rights,
- A diverse and independent media, including internet freedom,
- A vibrant civil society,

- Democratic governance and representative, functional institutions,
- Respect and tolerance for minority groups and for religious freedom, and
- Protection of property rights.

Promoting these universal values, rights and rule of law involves training, building capacity, helping to establish systems of democratic governance, and fostering dialogue, both in countries that are struggling to establish democracy and those that are led by opponents of democracy. Supporting democratic forces, however, is only part of the equation, albeit a large part. We also should push back against the authoritarian challenge by imposing consequences on those involved in serious human rights abuses. Unless authoritarian leaders incur costs for their antidemocratic actions, they will see no reason to change their behavior. The United States government has many tools at its disposal both to assist those who are struggling for freedom and to pressure antidemocratic forces to change their behavior. These tools exist across many areas of U.S. foreign policy, from diplomatic tools and military assistance to trade agreements and economic partnerships. As much as possible, these tools should be leveraged in a coordinated manner with like-minded democracies to support those fighting for democratic change in countries around the world.

Recent Disappointments

After finding no weapons of mass destruction in Iraq following the invasion of that country in 2003, the Bush administration sought to bring democracy to Iraq, an effort that has largely failed. The freedom agenda of President Bush, while admirable in its rhetoric and aspiration, was troubled by inconsistent implementation. Influenced by that experience, Barack Obama told the *Washington Post* editorial board five days before his inauguration as president in January 2009 that he did not support promoting democracy "through the barrel of a gun."

His implicit criticism of the Bush administration's efforts to promote democracy in Iraq and Afghanistan has evolved into a broader reluctance over the past nearly seven years to promote democracy and human rights around the world—see, for example, his administration's reaction to and handling of the Green Movement in Iran in June 2009, the Arab Spring in 2011 and the Egypt coup of 2013, and the reluctance to meet with the Dalai Lama for fear of offending Beijing. He rarely meets with human rights and civil society activists either in Washington or during travel overseas.

The Obama administration's public and repeated rejection of the notion of linkage with Russia—in which it made clear that Putin's crackdown internally would have no implications on the bilateral relationship—gave the Russian leader a green light to go after his critics and opponents without worrying about paying any price for doing so. Its opposition in 2012 to the Sergei Magnitksy legislation, which passed with huge bipartisan support and imposes sanctions on Russian officials engaged in gross human rights abuses, similarly sent the wrong signal to Moscow and to Russia liberals who strongly supported such measures. In the recent nuclear accord nuclear with Iran, that country's abysmal human rights situation never factored into the negotiations. The resumption of diplomatic relations with Cuba has largely downplayed the repression in that country as well.

Taking on the Skeptics/Realists

The Obama administration's aversion to promoting democracy and human rights is shared by some on both the left and right of the political spectrum. These "doubters" set up false choices in which policymakers would be pressured to choose promoting either our values or our interests. In fact, promoting our (or universally recognized) values advances U.S. interests, for the two really are inseparable. Supporting democracy, human rights and rule of law need not be mutually exclusive to pursuing economic and/or security interests. Indeed, we can enhance our overall interests by ensuring that democracy and human rights feature prominently in our relations with other countries.

Some will argue that it is not America's role or responsibility to tell other countries what kind of political system is in their interest, to impose our system on others, or to criticize other governments for human rights abuses, especially when we ourselves are not perfect.

In fact, it *is* our business—and in our interest—to promote freedom around the world; indeed, the United States has a special obligation to help those fighting to live in freedom and those with a limited voice in their society often look to us to play that role. We do not insist that others follow the American model, and recognize that we also make mistakes, but we should urge governments to respect universal human rights and democratic principles, even while developing their own character, consistent with international covenants and agreements that they have signed. Rather than attempting to dictate the directions countries take, we are instead refusing to remain silent when peaceful political activity is crushed or made illegal.

Similarly, we hear the argument that the U.S. should focus on problems at home before going around the world lecturing others. And yet the world simply will not wait for the United States to "get our own house in order." In fact, voids in leadership would likely be filled by governments or movements that not only do not share our interests, but fight actively against them. We have to be able to do both: address our own shortcomings while supporting democracy movements and showing solidarity with human rights activists elsewhere.

What democracy promotion really means is regime change through the use of force, the critics argue. The American people do not want to devote any more resources to toppling dictators—these countries need to deal with their own problems, they add. To be clear, the wars in Iraq and Afghanistan were begun for reasons of national security, not to impose democracy. Once the regimes fell, the U.S. implemented its decades-old policy of supporting democratic activists internally to help them rebuild their governments; indeed, we had a responsibility to do so, for the alternative was chaos (as we've seen in Libya). Regime change must be separated from the U.S. policy—implemented for the past 30 years through the National Endowment for Democracy and associated NGOs—of helping democratic activists establish the building blocks of democracy such as the rule of law, free elections, an effective civil society, and freedom of the press. We recognize that support for democracy can result in regime change by virtue of helping citizens find their political voice, even if that is not the primary purpose of such assistance.

Others will say that democracy is not necessary for a country to be successful—look at China or Singapore. While China and Singapore are the rare examples of countries that are doing well economically without allowing political freedom (although the bloom is off the Chinese economic rose these days), in the majority of cases, such as in Japan, South Korea, and Taiwan, it has only been after the establishment of democracy, or alongside it, that countries have flourished economically. China (which is experiencing both significant challenges to the Party's monopoly on power and a disconcerting crackdown under President Xi) and Singapore are not the right models to look to—rather it is the vast majority of countries that have pursued both democracy and economic development and have succeeded.

In addition, skeptics of democracy promotion argue that attempted democratic transitions in the Arab World have only led to chaos and violence, strengthening ISIS and other terrorist groups. Some countries are simply not ready—and may never be ready—for democracy and need authoritarian leaders to maintain stability, they claim. It's important to get cause and effect straight: the chaos and violence are not due to democracy promotion efforts but rather to the legacy of decades of dictatorship, oppression, and lack of opportunity. Without democratic traditions to fall back on, it is more challenging and takes more time for certain nations to establish themselves as stable democracies. Rather than shying away from supporting these efforts, we should be more engaged, providing much-needed training and examples from not only the United States, but preferably from countries that have been through democratic transitions far more recently like Poland or the Czech Republic and, one hopes, Tunisia.

There are always going to be skeptics when it comes to promoting democracy, fundamental human rights and rule of law around the world. The bottom line, however, is that supporting these causes is both morally the right thing to do and in the United States' best interests–economically and with regard to our national security.

As President Ronald Reagan said in his address to Members of the British Parliament on June 8, 1982 "We must be staunch in our conviction that freedom is not the sole prerogative of a lucky few, but the inalienable and universal right of all human beings."

Part Three:
Criminal Justice
System Issues

Introduction—Criminal Justice System Issues

John Norton Moore

Once again this Great Nation has embarked on a journey to elect a new President. The candidates have come forward and the debates are under way. It is in the interest of all Americans that the candidates and their debates seriously address the grave national challenges and opportunities now before the Nation. We cannot afford politics as usual, with candidates vying to be the most immoderate in their Party. The challenges are unforgiving and the opportunities fleeting.

The experts participating in this initiative are deeply concerned about the problems facing this Great Nation and have come together to present suggestions and raise questions for the Presidential candidates; Democrat and Republican alike. The papers being distributed to the Press today are being sent to each of the declared candidates in both parties. The campaign organization of each candidate, as well as the Democratic National Committee and the Republican National Committee, have also been notified of this initiative and invited to send a representative to the press conferences.

Each paper reflects the view of the presenter. There has been no effort to coordinate views; nor is any presenter responsible for the views expressed by other presenters. Some of these papers may appeal more to Democratic candidates and some may appeal more to Republican candidates. The subjects, however, have been chosen for their national importance, and the presenters for their recognized expertise.

It is hoped that as the debates progress in and between both parties that the candidates, and the Nation more broadly, will reflect on the range of serious problems and will consider the questions and/or specific recommendations presented in these papers. We are not able to individually participate in the debates, but we hope to be heard by the candidates and the American people through the great institution of America's free press.

All of the expert papers on each of the subjects under discussion are online at the Initiative website which is www.focusingthepresidentialdebates.com Videos of all of the presentations are also available on the website.

Priority Issues in Criminal Justice Reform and Reducing Crime

Too Many People in Jails and Prisons

The Nation's prison and jail population has more than quadrupled since 1980. With less than 5% of the world's population the United States has nearly a quarter of the World's prison and jail population. According to a recent Washington Post article, approximately 1 in 100 adults in America are behind bars. The cost is great to house this many prisoners, but even greater in the loss of potential earnings power, higher unemployment rates, and damage to the families of the incarcerated. Moreover, we are using jails to house too many of our mentally ill, rather than providing effective medical treatment and care. For the world's leading democracy this silent blight of over incarceration is not just wrong, but a national scandal.

We have come to this sad state in part because of a genuinely difficult war on drugs, in part because of sentencing reforms aimed at encouraging uniform sentencing, in part because we have tended to criminalize every infraction whether or not violent, and in part because politics supports a message of "tough on crime;" thus supporting tougher and tougher criminal laws and sentencing. But what is really needed are more effective policies in preventing crime. We are also much overdue for a National Commission to review the sentencing guidelines for non-violent offenses to make sentences more appropriate for the crime. But the problem goes beyond sentencing and more effective crime prevention. We have made one non-violent offense after another subject to criminal penalties. Literally, we have piled law upon law, and embellished them with criminal sanctions and prison terms. This excessive criminalization too should be reviewed in light of penalties other than incarceration, and sanctioning approaches other than criminalization. Did the Nation really benefit from putting Martha Stewart in jail at enormous cost to the taxpayer rather than simply levying a large fine against her? Did the criminal charge against the accounting firm Arthur Andersen, a corporation rather than a person, serve the national interest when it destroyed one of the big five American accounting firms in 2002, putting over 80,000 innocent employees out of work for the asserted abuse by a few in their accounting for the bankrupt Enron

Corporation? Would a substantial fine, or license suspension of the individuals involved, as opposed to a corporate criminal sanction, have been more in the national interest? Have we applied criminal sanctions too broadly to the business world?

Further, Texas and other states, along with many other countries in the World, are exploring alternatives to lengthy incarceration. Some of these approaches seem to be working well. A national criminal justice review should be looking carefully at all of these issues, more effective policies in preventing crime, sentencing reform, over criminalization, better alternatives for those needing psychiatric care, and alternatives to lengthy jail sentences.

Importantly, however, as we seek to reduce prison populations our reform should not generate greater problems than it solves. Particularly, it is important that in dealing with repeat non-violent offenders we not lose the option of their being required to do jail time. We do not want to make committing non-violent crimes, however repeat, a get out of jail card.

Although not addressed here, there are many other areas of the criminal justice system in need of reform. These include dealing with an out of control civil forfeiture system, enhancing the availability of public defenders, and addressing the issues we know are the culprits in the too frequent conviction of the innocent, including junk science, witness misidentification (particularly through poorly constructed "line ups" and the use of corrupt jail house "snitches"), prosecutorial misconduct and incompetent representation.

The paper by Harry R. Marshall, Jr., a former Senior Legal Adviser in the Criminal Division of the United States Justice Department, explores a range of these issues with a focus on reducing prison populations.

Reducing Crime and Enhancing Community/Police Relations

Despite previously unprecedented levels of incarceration, the Nation still has a serious crime problem, a problem particularly acute in victimizing minority communities in major cities. This blends with too few resources for police departments, too little community understanding of the difficulties faced by the police, and sometimes inadequate police training, to generate the witches' brew of disorders and reduced trust between the police and the residents they serve—a toxic brew seen recently in Ferguson, New York, Baltimore, and other cities. This too is a major national problem, and a complex one, which must be addressed. Quite possibly we must enact even tougher laws for repeat violent offenders or firearm homicides. But the problem will not be solved simply by increasing incarceration rates.

Two of the papers being presented in this initiative address these intertwined problems of enhancing police and community relations. Collectively, these papers address likely the most effective avenues to crime prevention; much more effective anti-crime pro rule-of-law education of our youth, and "community" or "relational policing," much more effectively engaging the police and the community they serve. The paper by Dr. Roy S. Godson is on "Education against Crime: Fostering Culture Supportive of the Rule of Law."

If we were able to better instill an anti-crime message in our public schools, a message rooted in powerful information about the costs to the perpetrator, the victim, the city, minority communities, and society in general, we would be reaching the most important point for crime control—that is, the belief system of the individual. Dr. Godson has pioneered the teaching of these innovative programs around the world. They deserve a trial in America.

The paper by Chief Timothy J. Longo, Sr., the nationally respected Chief of Police of Charlottesville, Virginia, addresses "Relational Policing," a title the Chief believes better addresses needed engagement than "Community Policing." Chief Longo's paper addresses how greater police involvement directly with residents in a community can both assist the police and lead to safer communities. More effective policing will likely require higher police budgets for more old-fashioned "walking the beat," a police presence contributing to direct deterrence of crime as well as better police/community relations, more police, better salaries for police, community youth programs run by the police, greater police training (particularly in settings involving potential use of deadly force), and other modalities of engendering greater interaction and greater trust between the police and the community which they protect, as well as greater visible deterrence against crime. But the reduction in crime, and enhanced respect for the police and the rule-of-law more broadly just might make it a bargain. While such programs are not new in America, their adoption on a larger scale could make a difference. This enhanced "Relational Policing," too, deserves a try.

Strengthening the Judiciary

The courts are a crucial fundament of our rule-of-law democracy. We rightly believe that America has a criminal justice system rooted in fundamental protections for the accused. For the most part that is the case. Recent investigations, however, many triggered by newer DNA science, have demonstrated too many times where the innocent have been convicted. A review of these cases shows that most relate to issues of witness identification (frequently involving poor line-up or other witness identification missteps), junk science, incompetent representation, or over-zealous prosecution at the trial level. All of these issues, as well as that of the substantial national percentage increase in prosecutors deciding to charge, can and should be addressed in a careful review by new Justice Department leadership (and the equivalent in all fifty states) to ensure that American courts remain the bastion of a free peoples. We must also ensure adequate public defenders to make our adversary system work as it was designed.

The Supreme Court of the United States has traditionally come under fire by those who disagree with its decisions. But the Supreme Court is a core institution of our great democracy. It is not designed to reflect the will of the majority, which is a principal role of the Congress, but rather to implement the rule-of-law in interpreting statutes and applying the Constitution of the United States (including the Bill of Rights) and its system of checks and balances. Some discourse about the Court seems to assume that its task is to clear the way for congressional action. A more Madisonian way of thinking about the Court, however, is that it is the principal bulwark in protecting the multiple protections for our freedoms which are built into the Constitution.

The Court protects the separation of powers between the legislative and executive branches. It protects states' rights in our federal system. It protects the integrity of the electoral process. And it protects individual freedom as guaranteed in the Bill of Rights, including freedom of speech and the press as a crucial "fourth estate" so necessary for effective governance. The Court does all of the above by applying the Constitution of the United States as the highest law of the land. As a human institution the Court may sometimes get it wrong, and given its role in protecting minority freedoms, it will frequently be criticized by the public. But the alternative to the Court is a Westminster style democracy without the checks and balances which remain the genius of our Constitution.

*As we conclude, let us remember that America is, and must always remain, a land of opportunity for all, regardless of ethnicity, gender, color, or religion, a leader in the struggle for peace and justice, a beacon of hope to the world, and the home of the free. We must never forget that America's true greatness lies, **not** in its wonderful "spacious skies … amber waves of grain … and purple mountain majesties," but **in its national values and its unquenchable spirit.***

Reducing Prison Populations: One of Many Needed Criminal Justice Reforms

Harry R. Marshall, Jr.[1]

Prepared for the Focusing the Presidential Debates Initiative

Nature of the Problem

Fundamentally, prisons in the United States are significantly overcrowded. Addressing this issue is one of a number of needed criminal justice reforms. With less than 5% of the world's population, the United States, at federal and state levels, has presently incarcerated about 25% of the persons imprisoned worldwide. One widely cited study (see below) has concluded that this comparatively high level of incarceration does not have any substantial positive effect on the crime rate. Further the expense of maintaining correctional facilities and related criminal justice agencies in the United States amounts to approximately $260 billion annually. The average cost per year to incarcerate a federal prisoner is $26,359 and consumes one-third of the budget of the Department of Justice; funds needed on an annual basis to maintain a prisoner in a state prison are between two to three times the amounts allocated in such state for each elementary school student. Many other criminal justice issues abound: e.g., dealing with conviction of innocent individuals and over criminalization.[2]

---

1. Mr. Marshall is an Adjunct Professor of Law at the University of Virginia School of Law. Previously he served as a Senior Legal Advisor in the Criminal Division of the Department of Justice and as a Principal Deputy Assistant Secretary of State.

2. This paper is focused on addressing prison overpopulation. Reducing convictions of innocent persons can be addressed by improving public defender programs, lessening erroneous eye witness testimony, reducing prosecutorial misconduct, and judicial intervention when warranted. De-criminalization of activities not being viewed as posing a significant challenge to public health or safety is another area for needed reform.

Meaningful efforts to reduce prison populations may best be initiated now by the creation of a high-level commission as discussed below.

Establish by Executive Order is

A Presidentially-appointed and well-funded bipartisan commission with a mandate to take all appropriate action to:

- Establish priorities for the commutation and other reductions of imposed sentences for federal offenses and to streamline the process for executing such determinations on a fast track basis;
- Recommend to the United States Sentencing Commission that it accelerate further efforts to adopt lower minimum sentencing guidelines for non-violent offenses;
- Encourage prompt enactment by Congress of legislation reducing statutory mandatory minimum sentences for narcotics offenses and other non-violent crimes;
- Study and take into account how European nations have managed prison terms, resulting in significantly smaller prison populations; and, following European models, develop proposals to significantly reduce sentencing (except in the most serious of cases) for narcotics and other non-violent crimes, and to utilize alternative non-custodial sanctions;
- Recommend that federal criminal justice funding for states be restricted to only those states which achieve significant reductions in numbers of incarcerated persons and which remove onerous and unnecessary constraints on job hiring of former inmates;
- Recommend increased spending for training of inmates and treatment for drug abuse and mental impairments; and
- Include officials from state authorities in the deliberations of the Commission with a view to encouraging similar action on the part of state governments.

Background

Current Impetus and Bipartisan Support. As widely reported,[3] in the wake of announcing commutations of sentences for 46 drug offenders, the President expressed his intention to take steps this year to revamp the criminal justice system, including sentencing guidelines and to call on Congress to act. In the October 7, 2015 edition of *The Washington Post*, it was reported that the

---

3. E.g., "Obama Issues Reductions of Sentences in Drug Cases," *The New York Times*, A1 (July 14, 2015).

Justice Department is preparing to release some 6,000 inmates from federal custody beginning at the end of the month. This action is attributed to reduction in minimum sentencing guidelines for many non-violent crimes which can be applied retroactively. A prisoner who is affected can apply to a federal judge to reassess and reduce his or her sentence.[4]

As reported in *The New York Times,*[5] the Justice Department set criteria last year for incarcerated persons who might qualify for commutation: generally, non-violent inmates who have served more than 10 years and would not have received as lengthy a sentence under current sentencing rules.[6] The *Times* article also points out that overhauling the criminal justice system has become a bipartisan venture as candidates seeking a 2016 Presidential nomination have focused on the issue and lawmakers from both parties are collaborating on legislation.

Bills (S.502 and H.R. 920) seeking enactment of "The Smarter Sentencing Act of 2015 have been introduced and reported to committee in both Houses. Similar bills were introduced in the prior Congress. According to Families against Mandatory Minimums ("FAMM"), the proposed legislation would reduce certain 20-year, 10-year, and 5-year mandatory minimum drug sentences to 10, 5 and 2 years respectfully. The bills would permit some 8,800 federal prisoners who are imprisoned for crack cocaine crimes to seek fairer sentencing in line with the Fair Sentencing Act which reduced, prospectively, the disparity between crack and powder cocaine offenses. The Department of Justice estimates that such enactment will lead to saving $24 billion over 20 years, and remove the need for construction of more than a dozen prisons and the hiring of thousands of new correctional officers.[7] As reported by MSNBC, the Smarter Sentencing Act bills have not proceeded due to lack of sufficient committee support. However, a new bill, titled "The Sentencing Reform and Corrections Act of 2015," was announced by and with the support of the Senate Committee on the Judiciary on October 1, 2015 which encompasses the essential elements of the Smarter Sentencing Act and other measures.[8] A simi-

---

4. Sari Horwitz, "6,000 to leave prison early," *The Washington Post,* p. A1 (Oct. 7, 2015). See also Michael s. Schmidt, "US to Begin Freeing 6,000 from Prison," *The New York Times,* p. A1 (Oct. 7, 2015). 18 USC Sec. 3582(c) provides statutory authority for action by federal judges to reduce sentences if certain conditions are met.

5. *Ibid.*

6. Other conditions also apply, *see* New Clemency Initiative, www.justice.gov/pardon (discussed *infra*).

7. www.famm.org/s-502-the-smarter-sentencing-act.

8. Senators Announce Bipartisan Sentencing Reform and Corrections Act,www.judiciary.senate.gov/ (Oct. 1, 2015); www.msnbc.com/msnbc/bipartisan-breakthrough-criminal-justice-reform.

lar House bill is to be introduced on October 8, 2015 by the House Judiciary Committee Chairman and Ranking Member on October 8, 2015.[9]

A study by the Brennan Center for Justice at New York University School of Law (the "Brennan Center") states that dealing with mass incarceration is now "one of the few issues on which the left and right are coming to agree, [and] notably, Republicans are leading the charge."[10] As reported in *The Washington Post* in August 2015, Charles Koch, the conservative billionaire, has become an advocate of sentencing reform.[11]

In Congressional testimony in July 2015,[12] John Malcolm, a senior official with the Heritage Foundation, notes that Congress is considering a number of reform proposals such as reducing federal mandatory minimum laws, which Malcolm observed ultimately swept more broadly than Congress originally intended. Malcolm also addresses a concern that reducing mandatory minimum laws will reduce incentives of low-level drug dealers to cooperate in an effort to indict and convict organizers of such activity. He contends that even if mandatory minimum laws were revised "there would still be plenty of incentives for defendants to cooperate against 'bigger fish.'" To bolster his contention, Malcolm notes that over 30 states have rolled back mandatory sentences, and he points to a recent report by The Pew Charitable Trusts, that over the period 2008-10, ten states that cut their imprisonment rates experienced greater drops in crime than ten states that increased such rates.[13]

Statistics. As mentioned above, a widely cited statistic found in studies regarding incarceration is that with less than 5% of the world's population, the United States, at federal and state levels, has presently incarcerated about 25% of the persons imprisoned world-wide.[14] As pointed out in the Economist Article, the Brennan Study concludes that this comparatively high level of incarceration does not have any substantial positive effect on the crime

---

9. www.judiciary.house.gov/index.

10. Imimai Chettiar *et al* (editors) "Solutions: American Leaders Speak Out on Criminal Justice," 124 (April 27, 2015) (the "Brennan Study"). See also generally, Eli Lehrer, "Responsible Prison Reform," *National Affairs* (Summer 2013)

11. "Unlikely Allies," *The Washington Post*, A1 (Aug. 16, 2015)

12. John G. Malcolm, Testimony, House Committee on Oversight and Government Reform (July 24, 2015) ("Malcolm Testimony") (Mr. Malcolm is a Heritage Foundation Director and Senior Legal Fellow and former Justice Department Deputy Assistant Attorney General). See also, Natalie Johnson, "'A Matter of Life or Death': Senators, Obama Unite on Push for Criminal Justice Reform," Natalie Johnson, dailysignal.com (Jul. 14, 2015) (report on criminal justice reform bills being finalized by the Senate Judiciary Committee).

13. *Ibid.*

14. The Economist 11 (Jun. 20, 2015) ("Economist Article").

rate.[15] As of October 1, 2015, 205,795 persons are in federal or related custody.[16] As of December 31, 2014, in the United States 1,561,500 persons are incarcerated in state and federal systems.[17] The US incarceration rate has helped drive down crime, though there is a debate as to how much.[18]

Costs and Effect on Educational Funding. A July 28, 2015 Brennan Center piece, points out, as mentioned above, that the cost of maintaining correctional facilities and related criminal justice agencies in the United States amounts to approximately $260 billion annually.[19] Funds needed on an annual basis to maintain a prisoner in a state prison are between two to three times the amount allocated in such state for each elementary school student; e.g. in New York: $18,000 per student vs. $58,000 per inmate.[20] The Malcolm Testimony notes that the cost per year to incarcerate a federal prisoner is $30,620.[21] On September 30, 2015, Education Secretary Arne Duncan asked states and cities to dramatically reduce incarceration terms for nonviolent crimes and to use the estimated $15 billion in savings to substantially raise teacher pay in high poverty schools.[22]

Another commentator on this issue, Steven Hawkins, points out that "more money must go to schools than to prisons before high-crime neighborhoods can truly be reformed." He points out that while states continue to spend more on education that incarceration, the percentage of funds used for the latter is increasing meaning that funds for the former is decreasing. Mr. Hawkins cites the example of Los Angeles where over $1 billion is spent annually to incarcerate people from communities with high crime rates, but the Los Angeles Unified School budget was projecting a deficit of $640 million for 2010-11.[23]

---

15. *Ibid.*

16. www.bop.gov/about/statistics

17. www.bjs.gov/index

18. *The New York Times*, Apr. 23, 2008. Relatedly, since the mid-1970s, prison populations have increased sevenfold while the general population has increased by only 50%. Stephanos Bibas, "Prisoners without Prisons," *National Review* 27 (Sept. 21, 2015).

19. Inimai Chettiar, "Mr. President, Lead on Prisons: Obama Can Force More Criminal Justice Reform," www.brennancenter.org, (Jul. 28, 2015).

20. www.money.cnn.com. Virginia Governor McAuliffe has established the Commission on Parole Review to evaluate the Virginia Corrections System, which costs $1.1 billion per year to operate. See Terry McAuliffe, "A Closer Look at Virginia's Prisons and Parole," *The Washington Post* C4 (Aug. 30, 2015).

21. John G. Malcolm, Testimony, House Committee on Oversight and Government Reform (July 24, 2015)

22. "Education secretary: Reduce incarceration," *The Washington Post*, A# (Oct. 1, 2015)

23. Steven Hawkins, "Education vs. Incarceration," prospect.org (Dec. 6, 2010).

Besides funding federal prison operations and construction, the US Government subsidizes state and local criminal justice costs in the amount of approximately $3.8 billion annually. The Brennan Study recommends that such spending should be provided only to such states that reduce crime and prison populations.[24]

Violent Offenders. The Obama Administration has as a goal the reduction of prisoner incarceration, and recently, the President, in a well-publicized event, commuted the sentences of 46 federal prisoners convicted of drug offenses.[25] However, Fordham Law Professor John Pfaff maintains that the President is wrong in his approach to focus on dealing only with the incarceration of persons convicted for non-violent acts.[26]

Professor Pfaff points out that while nearly half of all federal inmates were convicted for drug offenses, only about 14% of all persons incarcerated in the United States are in the federal corrections system. Professor Pfaff notes that more than half of state prisoners are serving time for violent offenses, and since 1990, 60% of the growth in state prison populations has come from incarcerating violent offenders. So Professor Pfaff points out the realism, and also a "political third rail," that governments will need to reduce the prison terms that violent offenders face if the "breathtaking prison population" is to be reduced. Professor Pfaff urges that the President needs to explain that "extremely long sentences, even for violent offenders, are generally counter-productive by pointing to studies that show that such punishments do not really deter crime and that offenders pose less risk of recidivism as they enter their 30s and 40s."[27] University of Pennsylvania law professor Stephanos Bibas agrees with this analysis, stating that President Obama's narrative "does not fit the facts," as "prison growth has been driven mainly by violent and property crimes, not drugs."[28] Professor Bibas is referring to state

---

24. Imimai Chettiar et al (editors) "Solutions: American Leaders Speak Out on Criminal Justice," 128 (April 27, 2015).

25. *The New York Times*, "Obama Issues Reductions of Sentences in Drug Cases," p. A11, July 14, 2015.

26. John Pfaff, "The wrong path to penal reform," *The Washington Post* A15 (Jul. 27, 2015); see also Susan Grigsby, "Why Dropping Federal Mandatory Minimum Sentences Will Not Solve all of our Prison Problems," www.dailykos.com/story2015/08/16 (Aug. 16, 2015)(The majority of state prisoners are incarcerated for violent crime convictions).

27. *Ibid.* Professor Pfaff also blames the over-population on more aggressive prosecutors in bringing increasing numbers of felony chargers. See also, David Brooks, "The Prison Problem," *The New York Times* Sect A p.27 (Sept. 29, 2015)(Pfaff is "wonderfully objective, nonideological and data-driven.")

28. Stephanos Bibas, "Prisoners without Prisons," *National Review* 27 (Issue dated Sept. 21, 2015).

incarcerations which make up 88% of the total prison population in the United States.[29]

Ill-effects of Long Term Sentences. Professor Bibas argues that more thought needs to be given about ways to hold wrongdoers accountable while minimizing the damage done to families. Crime needs to be punished and condemned "unequivocally," but to do so in ways which reinforce rather than undercut family values. He makes an interesting analogy to punishment for crime committed in colonial America, when few guilty person faced long term separation but were subjected to brief (although sometimes brutal) punishment.[30] The Economist Article notes the ineffectiveness of detaining persons with fifty year sentences which does not deter crime five times as much as a ten year sentence, though it costs more than five times as much.[31] Of course certain very long sentences are justified in circumstances where a death sentence or life imprisonment without possibility of parole might have been appropriate, such as conviction of a person in a position of trust who has engaged in espionage which has gravely injured US national security or cost the lives of US persons.

United States Sentencing Commission ("USSC"). Most federal criminal laws, not including narcotics offenses, carry only maximum sentences.[32] The USSC since 1984 has promulgated sentencing guidelines which include minimum periods of incarceration and are to be used by the federal judiciary in imposing sentences. The guidelines and amendments thereto, as adopted by the USSC, take effect unless Congress objects. A number of current proposals are to take effect in November 2015. The USSC Chair testified in 2014 before a House committee task force regarding USSC priorities which include the reduction of federal mandatory minimum penalties, particularly relating to narcotics offenses.[33] The USSC has identified as a priority reducing the cost of federal incarceration which now exceeds well over $6 billion per year. As indicated in the testimony, the USSC unanimously recommended that Congress

---

29. Email exchange with Professor Bibas (Sept. 16,2015).

30. Stephanos Bibas, "Prisoners without Prisons," *National Review* 27 (Issue dated Sept. 21, 2015). The harmful effect of long term incarceration on families was a major subject of the September 27, 2015 HBO production, VICE Special Report: Fixing the System.

31. *The Economist* 11 (June 20, 2015) ("Economist Article").

32. In addition to narcotics offenses, federal law provides mandatory minimum sentences for certain firearms, immigration, identity theft, sexual activity involving children, explosives, aircraft hijacking, murder, kidnapping, bank robbery, white collar, piracy and miscellaneous offenses. See, "Federal Mandatory Minimums," Families against Mandatory Minimums, www.famm.or (Aug. 6, 2012).

33. Patti Saris, Testimony, House Judiciary Committee Task Force on Over-Criminalization (Jul. 11, 2014) (USSC Chair).

(1) reduce the statutory mandatory minimum penalties for drug trafficking; (2) make the Fair Sentencing Act of 2010 retroactive regarding disparity in penal treatment of crack and powered cocaine; and (3) allow sentences below mandatory minimum penalties for additional non-violent drug offenses.[34]

Commutation. As mentioned above, this summer the President commuted sentences of 46 drug offenders.[35] Similar action could be taken with respect to a significant additional number of non-violent offenses such as the approximate 5000 federal inmates currently serving long sentence related to crack cocaine. The Brennan Center reports that currently there are approximately 100,000 inmates in federal prisons for low-level drug crimes.[36] Last year the Department of Justice established a new clemency initiative intended to prioritize clemency applications for inmates meeting six criteria.[37] Further action should be taken to commute federal the sentences of offenders whose convictions related to crack cocaine to the minimum sentence for powdered cocaine offenses and, as appropriate, persons convicted of other non-violent crimes who demonstrate a habitual non-violent nature.

Also Families against Mandatory Sentencing ("FAMM"), as set forth on its website, led an effort to have the sentencing guidelines for crack cocaine violations applied retroactively in 2007 making 20,000 prisoners eligible for sentence reductions. In 2014, FAMM worked to have the USSC reduce the guidelines for terms of drug sentences. As a result more than 40,000 inmates serving time for drug offenses are eligible to have their sentences recalculated and released early.[38] FAMM has been in the forefront of seeking to have Congress take action on reducing mandatory minimum sentences.

The Pardon Attorney. The Office of the Pardon Attorney within the Department of Justice[39] reviews requests for pardons and commutations of fed-

---

34. *Ibid.*

35. E.g., "Obama Issues Reductions of Sentences in Drug Cases," *The New York Times*, A1 (July 14, 2015).

36. Imimai Chettiar et al (editors) "Solutions: American Leaders Speak Out on Criminal Justice," 124 et seq. (April 27, 2015). See also generally, Eli Lehrer, "Responsible Prison Reform," *National Affairs* (Summer 2013)

37. New Clemency Initiative, www.justice.gov/pardon (Apr. 23, 2014)(Initiative sets forth the following conditions an inmate must meet for clemency action: (1) serving a sentence which would likely have been substantially lower currently; (2) considered a non-violent low-level offender without ties to large scale criminal organizations or gangs; (3) served at least ten years; (4) no significant criminal history; (5) demonstrated good conduct in prison; and (6) no history of violence).

38. famm.org/about/board-and-staff/julie-stewart.

39. www.justice.gov/pardon.

eral convictions and makes recommendations for action by the President pursuant to his Constitutional clemency power.[40] During the Obama Administration some 17,761 requests for clemency have been received. 89 have been granted as of August 31, 2015 including the 46 announced by the President this past summer.[41]

Presidential Commission. In the Brennan Study, former Senator James Webb concluded:

> Now is the time to revive the push for a national commission to address the overall issue of mass incarceration. A national commission is needed to conduct a top to bottom review of our nation's entire justice system.[42]

As Senator Webb elaborates, he initiated such an effort with proposed legislation in 2009 which was not enacted. His article identifies many of the complex issues relating to mass incarceration and spells out how such a commission should be organized. Given the many entities which must be involved in a successful effort to effectively reduce the size of US prison populations, the creation of such a high-level and well-funded commission is an important step in bringing about solutions to the problem.

Bills to create such a commission have been introduced in Congress with little success. The President could create an effective commission by executive order without having to pursue a lengthy and possibly unsuccessful congressional route. Historically it is interesting to note that in 1967, President Lyndon Johnson, in responding to urban riots which had occurred across the nation, appointed the 11-member Kerner Commission which produced a widely-read report proposing a series of reforms to deal with conditions which led to the riots.[43]

European Approaches and Adoption of Alternatives to Imprisonment for Routine Non-Serious Offenses. A 2013 opinion article in *The New York Times* points out that based on a "new" report, the Federal Republic of Germany ("FRG") and the Netherlands incarcerate persons at about one-tenth the rate

40. The President "shall have Power to grant Reprieves and Pardons for Offenses against the United States, ..." Constitution, Article II, Section 2, clause 1.

41. www.justice.gov/pardon.

42. Imimai Chettiar *et al* (editors) "Solutions: American Leaders Speak Out on Criminal Justice," 117 (April 27, 2015).

43. Imimai M. Chettiar, "Why President Obama must act on mass incarceration," msnbc.com/Obama-mass-incarceration-commission (Apr. 24, 2014). President Gerald Ford established a Clemency Board for the sole purpose of recommending clemency for certain violators of US military service laws. Executive Order 11803 (Sept. 16, 1974)

of the United States and under conditions geared toward social reintegration.[44] The article notes that American and European systems differ in every imaginable way and points to the FRG belief that public safety is ensured not simply by imprisonment but by successfully reintegrating prisoners into society. Non-serious offenses carry penalties of fines, probation and community service, and where incarceration is imposed a very high percentage of sentences are 12 months or less. While the article does not identify the report, it may have been: "Sentencing and Prison Practices in Germany and the Netherlands: Implications for the United States.[45] This article points out that officials from Colorado, Georgia and Pennsylvania have begun to apply some European practices in their jurisdictions such as expanding prosecutorial discretion to divert offenders, including higher risk persons and those charged with more serious offenses; and using community-based sanctions rather than incarceration.

Relatedly one of the conclusions in the Brennan Study is that criminal laws should be changed to remove prison as an option for most low level non-serious offenses except in extraordinary circumstances. Another conclusion is to mandate effective treatment for persons with mental health and addiction issues (one-half of persons incarcerated in the United States suffer from such issues) which for non-serious crimes may serve as an alternative to incarceration.[46] The establishment of a "health court" is proposed for Montgomery County Maryland, which would channel into community-based programs some non-violent offenders charged with such offenses as trespassing, public urination or vandalism.[47] Also Fairfax County, Virginia is launching a program to reduce the number of mentally ill inmates by diverting nonviolent offenders into treatment in lieu of incarceration.[48]

---

44. Editorial Board, "Lessons from European Prisons," *The New York Times* (Nov. 7, 2013).

45. Ram Subramanian and Alison Shames, "Sentencing and Prison Practices in Germany and the Netherlands: Implications for the United States," Vera Institute of Justice (2013).

46. Imimai Chettiar et al (editors) "Solutions: American Leaders Speak Out on Criminal Justice," 124 (Apr. 27, 2015). See also generally, Eli Lehrer, "Responsible Prison Reform," *National Affairs* (Summer 2013)

47. "Treatment, not jail time," *The Washington Post*, (Jul. 26, 2015).

48. Justin Jouvenal, "A push for aid instead of jail, "*The Washington Post*, C1 (Aug. 9, 2015).

Conclusion

Regarding the topic of criminal justice reform, clearly much is being uttered by commentators and political leaders in the United States from which can be drawn at least one conclusion: the prison populations at federal and state levels are way too large resulting in diverting substantial government funds from other important programs and not serving any useful purpose with respect to a number of prisoners serving long terms for non-violent, and possibly some violent, crimes. Addressing this problem will take much more than rhetoric but White House prioritization and high level effort, such as the establishment of a Presidential Commission as discussed above, to further analyze the existing situation and take concrete action based on such analysis to reduce the populations though two basis approaches:

(1) Releasing, by means of commutation, persons now incarcerated who are deemed not to constitute any reasonable threat to public safety, and

(2) Reducing the number of persons sentenced to incarceration with long sentences for non-violent and possibly some violent acts.

Such actions to achieve these goals can be undertaken through executive, congressional and judicial initiatives.

Relational Policing

Timothy J. Longo, Sr. [*]

Prepared for the Focusing the Presidential Debates Initiative

Introduction

For the past 34 years, I have had the great honor and privilege of being a police officer. During that time, I have watched my profession evolve. The evolution of policing in America has impacted our strategies to reduce crime, maintain safe and healthy communities, and improve our relationships with those whom we are sworn to serve.

One important aspect of this evolution that has profoundly impacted policing in America is the broader concept of what has been termed "Community Policing" and within it, the notion of problem solving, and how both police departments and their communities contribute to the development of positive-long term relationships and a collaborative effort to identify solutions to the on-going problems that communities face each day.

From my perspective, community policing is about engaging police and citizens in a relationship that is aimed at addressing community needs and problems, reducing crime and the fear of crime, the implementation of long term and sustainable strategies that result in safer communities, and an overall improvement in the quality of an individual's life and the lives of their family. Indeed, community policing has been a guiding force for American policing for decades. Yet, events that have occurred across our nation over the past year have caused some to question whether the underlying principles of community policing and the importance of police-citizen relationships remain a priority in how police officers and their agencies go about their important work.

---

[*] Timothy J. Longo is the Chief of Police of the City of Charlottesville, Virginia.

It is neither my purpose, nor my intent, to confirm or dispel whether the police have fallen short as to the relationship they share with those whom they serve. Rather, I wish to underscore the importance of what I have branded as "relational policing" and how it intersects with the broader concept of police legitimacy; a concept that has been at the forefront of policing for the past several years and one that is critical to restoring the public's trust and confidence where those crucial elements have been compromised.

At 21, I walked the streets of west Baltimore, patrolled the stairwells, hallways, and courtyards of the George Murphy and Lexington Terrace public housing projects, and somehow found a way to recognize the importance of engaging people, developing relationships, and getting to really know those people who made up the place where I came to work each and every day. For me, those *"relationships"* were as important to my work as the technical skills I had been taught and the various tools that occupied both my gun belt and the accessories I had at my disposal within the cock pit of a police car. Community policing was real and its benefits were obvious to me.

Many years later, I have come to believe that there has emerged an ever growing fracture in the relationship between the police and the communities that they serve. I say this not as a criticism aimed at either of the parties, but rather as a firm belief that the tragedies that have occurred across our nation that were the result from police and citizen interactions gone bad, and the manner in which people have reacted to those tragedies, have threatened both the quality of relationships and police legitimacy.

Support for my belief can be found in countless media reports, civil rights claims, and Department of Justice investigations which have resulted in Memorandums of Agreement and Consent judgments aimed at reforming police policy, practice, training, supervision, and the investigation of both force and misconduct. Further evidence can be found in my own experiences as a police practices expert and trainer. It is in that regard that I share the following story.

A few years ago, I was reviewing images taken from an "in-car" video camera system that was related to a civil rights claim filed by the family member of a man who had been shot by a police officer. I had been retained by Plaintiff's counsel to offer an opinion as to whether the actions taken by the officer were contrary to generally accepted law enforcement practice or practices at the time of the incident. In the moments that followed the officer's decision to fire their weapon, large numbers of people rushed to the outer perimeters that had been established by the officers on the scene. Within minutes of the shooting, the crowd grew larger and became increasingly more disruptive and threatening to the many officers who had been dispatched there. As I continued to watch and listen to the chaos that had erupted in a matter of minutes, I could not help but question whether the reaction of this hostile crowd was less about this specific tragic and life-changing event, and more about the absence of police legitimacy and the systemic breakdown of police and community relations in that community, and perhaps in the broader context of that city.

As America watched civil disobedience and violence unfold in Ferguson, Missouri last fall, I once again found myself asking the question of when and under what circumstances the relationship between the police and those who called Ferguson their home began to deteriorate. When did the fracture occur and why wasn't it detected by those with both the authority and the obligation to mend it so that trust, communication, and relationship would not diminish into non-existence?

Undoubtedly, Ferguson is just one example of what can happen when division occurs between the police and their constituents. It is, however, an example that played out not only in Ferguson but in other communities across America that too began to experience the consequences of what may occur when police and community relationships become fractured.

Not a single day passed during those destructive days that citizens in my own community didn't ask the question of whether the events unfolding in Ferguson could happen in our city. The answer, I suppose, is largely dependent upon the strength and value of the relationships that are the foundation of community policing. In my opinion, the concept of community policing will not remain a part of the fabric of American law enforcement unless relationship is restored, and trust and communication finds their way back into those places where they diminished and became non-existent.

The question is how do we get there, and how can those relationships be sustained.

A Road-Map to Restoring Trust

This past May, the President's Task Force on 21st Century Policing published their findings and recommendations that were largely prompted by the events in Ferguson, Missouri. And while those tragic events may have served as a contributing force behind the work of the President's Task Force, I also believe that the need to heal broken relationships between police and citizens that have emerged over time in communities large and small across America also served as a catalyst behind the efforts of the Task Force.

While I don't believe it does much good to place blame for the circumstances that led to unrest, unrest that in some cases became violent and destructive, I do believe that it is important that law enforcement leaders re-commit to examining the policies and practices that impact the manner in which we go about our work to improve police and community relationships, while at the same time sustaining safe and healthy communities. To that end, each and every policy, practice, and operational strategy must be examined and a determination must be made as to how those policies and practices impact our ability to create and sustain a safe community, and at the same time keep the elements of communication, trust, and transparency intact.

In an effort to illustrate how a particular policing strategy may have the unintended consequence of creating mistrust within a community without serving any real value to public safety, I offer the following only as example.

From time to time, police officers have *consensual* encounters with citizens that do not trigger constitutional protections. Some of these encounters may be instrumental in confirming or dispelling a suspicion of crime, the facts of which may fall below the legal standards of reasonable suspicion or probable cause. During the course of these encounters officers may seek, and oftentimes receive, permission to conduct searches of citizens and their property. Sometimes those searches result in the recovery of evidence or contraband, yet oftentimes these intrusions result in nothing and the interaction ends with a citizen questioning whether they had been treated fairly. Not only does the strategy that I have described yield a very small return on investment (and even then rarely) it may well have the effect of alienating members of the community whose trust police are so desperately seeking to regain.

To be clear, I am not calling into question the legality of such a practice, nor am I advocating that law enforcement agencies abandon strategies that are constitutionally permissible. I am, however, suggesting that we begin to view the constitution as the floor and not the ceiling as we review these practices. While a policing strategy may be constitutionally permissible, it may not be the most productive strategy to deploy when balanced against the needs and expectations of the community, particularly when the relationship between police and the community is troubled.

The idea of "building trust" is necessary to restoring life to community policing. Restoring trust where it has diminished, or even disappeared, requires a commitment to examine the manner in which policing services are provided to a community. Evaluating existing policies and policing strategies against evidence based best practices, coupled with the collection and examination of relevant data are important first steps in achieving what is envisioned by the 21st Century Task Force report. Yet, both require fiscal and human capacity that is complimented by both robust data systems and the technical assistance and expertise to examine practices and interpret the data.

The President's Task Force report and recommendations provide a substantive road-map as we move forward in an effort to make procedural justice part of each and every practice that we undertake while at the same time taking steps to restore legitimacy in the communities that we serve. It will be the obligation of our next President to affirmatively assist law enforcement leadership in implementing the recommendations set out in the 21st century policing report. This requires a commitment that encompasses both funding and technical assistance in the area of policy development, data analysis, and training. It also requires a commitment to adequately staff and fund agencies within the federal government that have the resources that can assist local law enforcement agencies in the evaluation and adoption of best practices.

Managing Police Reform and Achieving a Relational Policing Environment

I have previously referenced the Department of Justice and their role in police reform in America Today. A brief history as to how that role has developed may be helpful in understanding the complexity of reform and the resources that are required to bring about change.

In addition to state law claims and federal statutes that provide remedies for police misconduct that may result in the midst of reform efforts, Section 14141 of the Violent Crime Control and Law Enforcement Act of 1994 authorizes the Attorney General of the United States to bring a civil action against a municipality and its police department to *obtain appropriate equitable and declaratory relief to eliminate the pattern or practice.*[1]

The United States Department of Justice has entered into "Consent Decrees" and/or "Memorandums of Agreement" with a host of law enforcement agencies across the country. These agreements have arisen either as a result of litigation, or due to the presence patterns, practices, and customs of unconstitutional conduct on the part of a municipality, its police department, or the officers who serve on behalf of the department and the municipality. Each of these agreements set out a number of terms and conditions that are monitored throughout their duration. Perhaps the most instructive aspects of those agreements focus on areas of policy, training, supervision and the investigation of misconduct and the use of force. All of these broad areas directly im-

---

1. Id.

pact procedural justice and legitimacy, and effect police and community relationships.

In a broad sense, the ultimate goal of these settlement agreements is to *"provide for the expeditious implementation of remedial measures, to promote the use of the best available practices and procedures for police management, and to resolve the United States' claims without resorting to adversarial litigation."*[2]

I believe the elements of these collaborative agreements, coupled with the substantive road map that is provided by the Presidents 21st Century Policing Report, can be invaluable to bringing about the reform that is necessary to heal fractured relationships and restore public trust and legitimacy in communities where it has been lost. There are several federal agencies that have the ability to assist local law enforcement agencies with the technical assistance necessary to replicate the best practices set out in the settlement agreements and that have assisted many localities in the area of police reform and community collaboration.

Perhaps the most obvious resource within the Department of Justice that has played, and will continue to play an important role in assisting local law enforcement in the development and implementation of best policing practices, is the Office of Community Oriented Policing. Since its creation, the COPS office has been a critical partner that has provided local law enforcement with both the funding and the technical assistance necessary to carry out important law enforcement initiatives aimed at ensuring safer communities and stronger police and community relationships. In my opinion there has never been a time when the expertise of the COPS office has been so greatly needed at a local level.

In addition to the traditional services offered by the COPS office, those provided by the Department of Justice Community Relations Service are especially useful to local law enforcement.

Title 42, USC, Section 2000g-1 establishes the functions of the United States Department of Justice Community Relations Service:

> *It shall be the function of the Service to provide assistance to communities and persons therein in resolving disputes, disagreements, or difficulties relating to discriminatory practices based on race, color, or national origin which impair the rights of persons in such communities under the Constitution or laws of the United States or which affect or may affect interstate commerce. The Service may offer its services in cases of such disputes, disagreements, or difficulties whenever, in its judgment, peaceful*

---

2. Id., quoting United States of America v. City of Los Angeles, Consent Decree (2001).

relations among the citizens of the community involved are threatened
thereby, and it may offer its services either upon its own motion or upon
the request of an appropriate State or local official or other interested
person.

This service has been an invaluable resource to communities and police departments both in the aftermath of events that have resulted in large scale unrest, as well as to those that have taken proactive steps to strengthen police and community relationships. The skills and technical assistance provided by the service is of tremendous value to law enforcement and community leaders and has been instrumental in bringing parties who are at odds together with the goal or restoring order and relationship and fostering a collaborative spirit aimed towards long term, positive, and sustainable police and community relationships. Thus, it is imperative that this important asset to both law enforcement and the community have the appropriate capacity to adequately assist police departments in developing strategies around *building trust and legitimacy* as well as to assist in the implementation of those strategies and to measure their outcomes.

This raises an important question for our next President who will inherit both the substance and the spirit of the work undertaken by the 21st Century Policing Task Force; what commitment will be made to ensure that federal agencies tasked with providing technical assistance, funding, and logistical support will have the capacity to deliver the services necessary to localities in order that they may implement these important pillars? In short, will the task force recommendations remain a national priority and will that priority be supported at the highest positions of our federal government?

The effectiveness of a police agency is oftentimes measured not only by the quality of persons who are recruited into their ranks, but by the quality of the *training and education* that those officers receive. Much emphasis has been placed on training officers in the area of enhanced communications skills, to include, among other things using verbal skills to de-escalate situations that may arise on the street and oftentimes result in the use of force.

In addition to enhanced communications skills, there has been a focus on training that pertains to *impartial policing, bias awareness, situational decision making, and the appropriate use of force.*[3] Having served in municipal law enforcement for over thirty-four years, twenty of which were in a command level capacity, I can attest to the fact that during times of fiscal crisis departmental training budgets are often diminished to meet emergent operational needs. To

---

3. See, Virginia Attorney General Mark R. Herring's "white paper" on the 21st Century Policing Initiative.

ensure that the task force recommendations are fully implemented adequate funds must be available to localities to ensure that they can obtain the best possible training in the areas such as impartial policing, implicit bias, effective communication skills, and the reasonable and appropriate application of force.

In years past, the COPS office along with other federal partners, have made available funds to support such training initiatives. In order to ensure that the recommendations of the 21st Century Task Force take root in agencies nationwide and that the principles behind those recommendations are embedded in police culture the assets must be in place and easily accessible to localities to support this important initiative. These assets include, but are not limited to, adequate funding to support the cost of such training, and standardized curriculum based on evidence based practices.

The Role of Training and Supervision in Relational Policing

Both the vision and mission of a police agency is articulated through the manner in which officers go about their work. That work is first and foremost guided by Constitutional principles and other applicable laws. However, an officer's work is also guided by both departmental *policy and oversight.* Policies are the mechanism by which an officer knows how their duties are to be performed. Yet, it is not enough that a police agency have comprehensive and responsive policies to guide an officer's work, there must be mechanisms in place that ensure that those policies are being administered in a fair and impartial manner, and certainly in a manner that is consistent with our Constitution. When those policies are set aside, ignored, or otherwise compromised, unconstitutional patterns and practices begin to evolve and police legitimacy is threatened.

The mechanism that is typically administered to ensure consistent application of good police policy and practice is the concept of supervision. In fact, supervision is the most practical and immediate of management tools to determine whether the policies and practices of the department are being administered in a manner that is fair and impartial and consistent with law. Therefore, it is critical that front line supervisors have adequate training and access to resources in order that they may properly perform their duties and ensure that the officers under the watch are honoring the commitment that they have made when they assumed their important public duties.

An important technology based resource that can be used to compliment effective supervision in monitoring the performance of officers (as well as to detect emerging trends that may prove problematic for both the officer and agency and threaten legitimacy and positive police and community relationships) is the Early Intervention System. Since the early 1980s, many large police departments across the United States began to establish tracking systems that systematically identify patterns of behavior of individual officers.[4] However, if all the system does is track data without analysis or action it cannot be effective at preventing future misconduct and ensuring that departmental policies and practices are being carried out in accordance with the expectations of the community.[5]

Many of the settlement agreements previously mentioned include requirements concerning the collection of data related to high risk critical tasks. Oftentimes, this data is captured within Early Intervention Systems or other records management systems. The collection and analysis of this important data can be useful to supervisors and policy makers, but it can also be useful in reporting information back out to the community about issues of public concern; issues related to citizen complaints, uses of force, vehicle pursuits, and a host of other areas.[6] Balancing the release of such information between a police department's interest in protecting it and the community's interest in receiving it is an important public policy discussion for law enforcement leadership. Data collection, integration, analysis, and dissemination will undoubtedly be a part of how police agencies define strategies, deploy resources, develop policies, and construct ways in which to be more transparent, and thus more accountable, to the people that they serve.

While systems, processes, and strategies are necessary elements to reforming policing practices in America, people will always remain our greatest asset toward reform. It is the police officer interacting with those whom they serve, building trust, breaking down barriers to communication, and collaboratively figuring out the best way in which to make neighborhoods safer so that broader communities become healthier places to live, work, and visit. The answer to how we place more officers in neighbors in order to build trust and form collaborative partnerships, while at the same time preserving order and ensuring a safe and healthy environment, is not necessarily complicated but does require a willingness to rethink how police resources are deployed, acknowl-

---

4. See, *Early Intervention Systems for Law Enforcement,* by Steve Rothlein, PATC, LLRMI, 2006.

5. Id.

6. The manner in which this information is released, as well as the content of such information, may be subject to state law provisions pertaining to Public Disclosure and Freedom of Information Acts.

edging that this may require increased staffing which in turn may require increased funding. It also requires a good understanding of how differential police response model can improve the efficiency of police services while keeping officers on the street and engaged with the citizens they serve.

I believe that one of the principle goals of implementing differential police response is to reduce dispatched calls for service thus creating discretionary time for officers to engage citizens, identify problems in the places they work, and collaborate to develop long term and sustainable problem-solving strategies that meet the community's expectations and effectively address the problems that they helped to identify.

Some common examples of differential police response methods include, but are certainly not limited to, use of on-line and telephone methods to report certain property crimes that don't require the processing or recovery of evidence, and minor incidents which have historically resulted in the dispatch of an officer. In October of 1996, the Baltimore Police Department in partnership with the COPS office, and AT&T implemented the nation's first three-digit non-emergency number, 3-1-1. This alternative method by which to report urgent but non-emergent events reduced calls from the departments heavily overloaded emergency communications system.

3-1-1 was a progressive step towards differential police response that eventually caused local governments to re-think how they captured, tracked, and assigned citizen complaints and referrals, not just for the police, but for a host of government service providers. From a law enforcement perspective, it was a progressive step in acknowledging that we need to be more thoughtful and creative in finding ways to get more officers away from chasing calls and back out in the neighborhoods interfacing with people and doing true relational policing.

There has never been a time when this is more important for our nation.

Conclusion

Not so long ago I invited Retired Raleigh-Durham Police Chief Harry Dolan to speak to my officers about the importance of communication in the way police officers interact with the community they serve. During his visit, the chief had occasion to have dinner with a young police sergeant in my agency who has committed his life to public service. In the midst of their talk, Harry said something to the young man that caught him by surprise but has forever changed the way he will think about his future and the future of policing in our country; "*Bobby*", he said, "*We've never been stronger as a profession.*"

The challenges facing cities across America, the fractured relationships between police and citizens, and the focused attempts to reform the manner in which police agencies and police officers go about their important work present tremendous opportunities for our officers and our communities. What one may characterize as conflict has the potential of leading us to restoration; restoration of trust, confidence, hope, and ultimately relationship. Firmly rooted within a plan for such restoration is the reality that relationships are, in fact, the very essence of community policing, and the most necessary of components to make the 21st Century Task Force recommendations a reality that will make communities safer and forge a greater, long term, and more sustainable relationship between the police and the communities they serve.

Education Against Crime: Fostering Culture Supportive of the Rule of Law

*Roy Godson**

Prepared for the Focusing the Presidential Debates Initiative

ONE OF THE outstanding problems facing our country, its quality of life, and America's global reputation is the lack of a strong culture of lawfulness. A significant portion of our fellow citizens have grown up believing that the rule of law does not benefit them, in whole or in part.[1] Hence they have lit-

---

* Dr. Roy S. Godson is Professor of Government Emeritus at Georgetown University and former President of the National Strategy Information Center.

1. **Culture of Lawfulness** is a culture in which the overwhelming majority is convinced that the rule of law offers the best long-term chance of securing their rights and attaining their goals. Citizens believe that the rule of law is achievable and recognize their individual responsibility to build and maintain a rule of law society. In a culture of lawfulness, most people believe that living according to the rule of law (respecting the rights protected by law, fulfilling the duties codified by law) is the best way to serve both their public and private interests.

Rule of Law: While there are many definitions of the rule of law, most contain the following elements: Every citizen has an opportunity to participate in making, overseeing, and modifying the laws and the legal system; the laws apply to everyone, including the rulers; and laws protect each individual as well as society as a whole. The laws provide a formal means of enforcing the law and sanctioning violators with established punishments.

The *U.S. interagency definition* (U.S. Agency for International Development, U.S. Department of Defense, and U.S. Department of State) reads: "Rule of Law is a principle under which all persons, institutions, and entities, public and private, including the state itself, are accountable to laws that are publicly promulgated, equally enforced, and independently adjudicated, and which are consistent with international human rights law." Supplemental Reference: Foreign Assistance Standardized Program Structure and Definitions, Program Area 2.1 "Rule of Law and Human Rights," U.S. Department of State, October 15, 2007.

For *the United Nations*, the rule of law refers to a principle of governance in which all persons, institutions and entities, private and public, including the State itself, are ac-

tle reason to follow its principles whenever they believe it is not in their interests to do so.

This belief system is not immutable. Culture matters and it can be changed.

There is an important role for the next President, as well as Congress and major sectors of society such as education, law enforcement, and the media, if we want to foster a culture much more supportive of the rule of law. After all, America has done this in the past, and other regions of the world, under much more difficult circumstances, have shown that with leadership their culture can be changed for the better, thus enhancing public security and economic and social development.

* * *

The Problem

Every day, we come into contact with individuals—from all social classes—who feel and express little reason to follow the laws and institutions that we have created—and seek to enforce at considerable expense and even, sometimes, loss of life. We see this daily on television and other media. For many, this is also their daily experience on the speedways we call public highways and roads. For others, criminality is an all too common experience in their neighborhoods and in particular institutions—such as urban street corners, campus parties, in schools, and the darker side of the Internet. Many of those who violate the law seriously harm many thousands of others, or themselves, and have little respect for our laws or the institutions we have created to oversee and enforce them.

---

countable to laws that are publicly promulgated, equally enforced and independently adjudicated, and which are consistent with international human rights norms and standards. It requires, as well, measures to ensure adherence to the principles of supremacy of law, equality before the law, accountability to the law, fairness in the application of the law, separation of powers, participation in decision-making, legal certainty, avoidance of arbitrariness, and procedural and legal transparency.

There is *relatively little data* on Americans' contemporary belief in a culture supportive of the rule of law. Limited survey data does indicate that many Americans have a stronger commitment to the rule of law than some other liberal democracies. However, it should be noted that when following the law is juxtaposed with some other values, or there is a cost to following the law, it is not clear that Americans will so readily choose the law. It should also be noted that there appears to be more support for legal constraints on government as opposed to constraints on the behavior of individuals. Gibson, James L. "Changes in American Veneration for the Rule of Law." DePaul L. Rev. 56 (2006): 593.

Some are raised in environments where their parents, even if they are present in their lives, know little about the rule of law, and have little faith in the justice system. These individuals may have been abused at home, on the streets, or in prison, and therefore are unlikely to pass on the norms of the rule of law. The schools, for those who attend and pay reasonable attention, have few teachers and curricula that discuss the principles and benefits of the rule of law, and that it is the rule of law and not majority rule that daily protects minorities and the weaker elements of society. They thus do not have an opportunity to learn that it is the rule of law that provides major mechanisms to reduce injustices in our society and evolving opportunities to enhance our quality of life. With some exceptions, there are also far too few discussions in school settings about how and why to resist illegal temptations and narratives that are so prevalent in the lives of young people throughout the country. This runs the gamut from obeying driving and traffic regulations, to cheating on exams, to stealing intellectual property (e.g. music), and selling drugs, committing sexual and other types of assault, or becoming white collar entrepreneurs who exploit illegal opportunities, such as cybercrime, frauds and scams.

Every day, they also see or hear about even well-paid sports figures, celebrities, as well as business and religious leaders who succumb to temptation and violate civil and criminal law. Further, they personally experience or learn about the lawless acts of police and law enforcement personnel as well as elected and other government officials—all of whom either participated in making the law or are paid to uphold it.[2] Sometimes, those who have or are suspected of violating the law are mistreated and do not receive due process, which usually makes them increasingly hostile to the law in the future.[3]

This, of course, does not mean that all youngsters as adults have completely negative views about the rule of law. Many do not. They are aware that the laws provide many benefits. But when faced with the personal choice of following

---

2. See, for example, studies by the US Department of Justice and by academics which document which states and which branches and sectors of public officials are perceived to be most corrupt based on convictions and other indicators. In the last two decades more than 20,000 public and private officials have been convicted of crimes relating to corruption and 5,000 more are awaiting trial. Oguzhan Dincer and Michael Johnston, "Measuring Illegal and Legal Corruption in American States: Some Results from the Corruption in America Survey." Safra Center for Ethics, Harvard University, March 16, 2015. There does not appear to be a similar overall national study of police misconduct. However, the Cato Institute has a National Police Misconduct Reporting Project which compiles statistics. See their 2010 Annual Report, http://www.policemisconduct.net/statistics/2010-annual-report/.

3. One of the best empirical studies of why procedural justice is important to rule of law legitimacy is Tyler, Tom R. *Why People Obey The Law*. Princeton University Press, 2006.

the law in particular circumstances or gaining what they perceive to be the benefits of not doing so, they all too often succumb to temptation. Unless they have been educated or trained to resist temptation many continue to slip. The culture is working against them.

This culture can be changed. We have been able to do this in the past, sometimes very slowly, as with the abolition of slavery, the drive to institutionalize women's rights, to reduce smoking, and to promote environmentally-sensitive behavior.

It is past time to address the culture that too often tolerates and sometimes even fosters illegality. If we do, at a minimum this will help to reduce the many thousands of victims each year, and the large numbers of deaths and injuries, as well as the huge human and material costs of incarceration, hiring of more and more police, and the deployment of expensive police technologies. It will also increase the sense of fairness and the salience of dynamic opportunities in our society to oversee the performance of the law and to bring about requisite changes in the law and its procedures. This is a national as well as a local issue.

What Can be Done to Minimize the Problem at Low Cost

Perhaps the single most important way that this can be accomplished is through national and local leadership that leads to formal and informal education about the culture supportive of the rule of law.

This education can take a number of different forms. One of the most important is through school-based education reinforced by other sectors of society. Next to parental influence, school systems, if committed and prepared, are in a position to influence the next generations of youngsters. "Committed" means that school leadership has been persuaded that they can make a difference if they use a limited but significant number of their personnel and school hours to affect the knowledge, skills, and attitudes of their students about the rule of law.[4]

---

4. There is a considerable literature in traditional legal scholarship and more contemporary theoretical and empirical social science on the effectiveness both of cognitive learning and school-based education, as well as on environmental factors, in influencing behavior in developed democracies. In the more contemporary literature, see for example, Cohn, Ellen S., and Susan O. White *Legal Socialization: A Study of Norms and Rules*. Springer, 1990; Finckenauer, James O. "Legal Socialization: Concepts and Practices." *Trends in Organized Crime* 4, no. 2 (1998): 30-40; Grant, Heath B. *Building a Culture of Lawfulness: Law Enforcement, Legal Reasoning, and Delinquency Among Mexican Youth*. LFB Scholarly Pub. LLC, 2006.

"Prepared" means that the schools' professional teachers themselves would have to be trained to pass on the requisite knowledge and skill sets to their students. This subject is not rocket science. But like other subjects taught in schools, it does require some specialized training—perhaps a week or two. Teachers would need to be able to teach about the rule of law and why it outweighs the perceived benefits of illegal behavior for students, their siblings, families, friends, communities—and for our country. These norms cannot be passed on by diktat or "just say no" campaigns that have been launched to reduce crime, drugs, and gangs—usually led by local police in schools or after-school programs.

It has to be taught by professional and properly prepared teachers in the classroom and other formal school settings. Ideally, children should be exposed to the subject for the first time in primary school, but it is in junior high school when most adolescents will be directly exposed to the dilemmas, temptations, and also the positive opportunities that will be with them for much of their lives. It is in the seventh or eighth grade that they will start to make these choices daily. And it is here—for twenty to forty hours—that we want to increase their knowledge about the rule of law and its benefits, and what happens when the rule of law breaks down. This is illustrated so well in William Golding's famous novel Lord of the Flies and the movie "Goodfellas"—which children this age love to read, see, and discuss in classroom settings. We also need to prepare students to reason through the moral and legal dilemmas they will face, and to address them with critical thinking and decision-making skills. This includes, for example, when a poor person has no money and is hungry and steals food from a store, or steals an iPhone from a person in the subway, or on a more topical issue, whether they should cheat on an exam if they believe they will not get caught.

The skills to handle even more complex questions can be honed through multiple classroom scenarios and discussions. Hence the need for dedicated school time and for teachers prepared to handle the discussion that will ensue. We know from experience in the US and abroad that many students will welcome the opportunity to discuss the petty and more serious crime and corruption they see in the media, in the streets, or even in their own schools and homes. There will be debates in the classroom, in the school cafeteria, and at home about what was discussed in class. Not all students will agree— particularly with the disconnect and conflict between rule of law ideals and the reality they see in their daily lives. But for many youngsters, this will provide the first, and maybe the only opportunity to participate in a serious discussion of the subject before they are faced with real-life temptations. Where this approach has been tested, it has produced positive and measurable results.[5]

Fortunately, again if the schools are committed and prepared, there can be another opportunity to re-engage and reinforce the discussion in high school. Here students are at a stage where they can begin to understand that their personal behavior has implications for their community and their country. Again, some will not be convinced that following rule of law principles trumps criminality in almost all situations and dilemmas. No society has been able to achieve this level of moral and legal reasoning. But, particularly after the second round of formal education, it will be possible to measure a change in their knowledge and skills at handling the choices they will be facing over their lifetime.

---

5. Since the 1990s, there have been promising efforts to introduce this school-based approach in Palermo, Sicily; Hong Kong; and major Colombian cities. To determine if these efforts could be replicated, faculty in criminal justice, anthropology, and political science at John Jay College of Criminal Justice, Rutgers School of Criminal Justice, and Georgetown University's Government Department, all under the umbrella of the nonprofit National Strategy Information Center, teamed up with Sicilian, Colombian, and Mexican educators to introduce educational initiatives on school-based culture of lawfulness in their respective countries. They developed detailed curricula and prepared junior and senior high school teachers to teach 20 to 40 hour pilot courses.

Following the pilot courses, various instruments were used to ascertain if the curricula had been taught as designed, and to see what effect the course had on student knowledge, attitudes, and skills. With the exception of San Diego County, few US school systems were willing to devote time and resources to the project. After they received the results of evaluations of pilot programs, Colombian and Mexican educators adopted the approach. Since then, it has spread and become institutionalized in a number of cities and regions in the Caribbean Basin.

For several of these evaluations, see, Godson, Roy, and D. Kenney. "Fostering a Culture of Lawfulness on the Mexico-US Border: Evaluation of a Pilot School-Based Program." *Transnational Crime and Public Security: Challenges to Mexico and the United States*, John Bailey and Jorge Shabat, eds. (La Jolla, CA: Center for US-Mexican Studies, University of California, San Diego, 2002); Grant, Heath B. *Building A Culture Of Lawfulness: Law Enforcement, Legal Reasoning, and Delinquency Among Mexican Youth.* LFB Scholarly Pub. LLC, 2006, pp. 103-126; Marco Antonio Carrillo Meza and Martín Manuel Martínez Gastélum, *Programa de Cultura de la Legalidad: Revisión, Análisis y Resultados de Evaluación en Alumno de Tercer Grado de Secundaria en B.C.*—Reporte de investigación 2006 (Baja California, México: CETYS Universidad and Gobierno del Estado Baja California, 2006).

Reinforcing School-Based Education

School-based education will likely be even more effective, however, if it is re-inforced by education outside the classroom. It is particularly important that law enforcement set a good example and does not undermine the culture of legality. In addition to sanctions for their illegal behavior and incentives for following rule of law principles, the police too need rule of law education. Most training for police is heavily technical—how to drive safely, how and when to use force effectively and consistently with police rules of engagement. But with exceptions, there is very little education and training for police about a culture supportive of the rule of law. When crime goes up, or the police are condemned for improper or corrupt behavior, the "solution" all too often is either hire more police, increase their powers and technological capabilities, or replace them with new recruits. Then there is very little education and training for the new recruits in fostering a culture of lawfulness. Few police have been exposed to these "resistance" techniques in their formal school or professional training. There is too little effort directed toward developing the skills that would enable them to connect with the dilemmas of youngsters growing up with substantial lawlessness in their neighborhoods.

Another sector that could make a difference and reinforce a change in the overall culture is the media. There is an important place for the media to report on crime and corruption and to uncover "bad" behavior in society and the government of the day. But there are also ways for media professionals to contribute positively through creative reporting, narratives, and videos on those trying to overcome the obstacles and temptations that confront society. We have more than enough positive, exciting stories, events, and people, who are attempting to foster a culture of lawfulness. Youngsters could be helped to relate to these experiences and the opportunities available to them and not only to the negative narratives that tend to dominate in our modern day society. Such positive media stories can also be commercially profitable.

Illustrations of Change

If this had not already been done, then these educational efforts could be dismissed as unrealistic or overly idealistic. But it has been done to an impressive extent—even in cities and towns with high degrees of criminality and corruption in various parts of the world, such as Palermo, Sicily; Hong Kong; Botswana in Southern Africa; and in cities in Colombia such as Bogota, Medellin, and Pereira. There is a drive now underway in Mexico to replicate these experiences. These urban areas had never had a culture of legality. Organized crime was much more threatening than in the US. High and low levels of corruption were the order of the day. But these cities overcame many of these considerable obstacles and shifted the culture. It took leadership—mostly in the Executive agencies—to mobilize various sectors, and particularly schools, the media, and law enforcement.

What the President Can Do

In the United States, school systems are more pluralistic and less centralized than in these countries. Education to foster the culture of lawfulness requires support of local school systems. But if we want to reach schools across the nation in the next few years, then only the bully pulpit can do so. The next President can lead, both through highlighting the importance of the subject and underlining the national importance of changing cultural attitudes about illegal behavior and the rule of law. The President can also introduce both educational and material incentives to do so. But the President can't do it alone. He will need support from Congress and from state and local leadership in securing the commitment and preparation of the schools, law enforcement education, and media interest in the subject.

What is not being suggested here is that the President and next Administration seek to control either the content of education or the training of schoolteachers, students, policemen and women, and media professionals. There is an important distinction between leadership and control. What is being proposed here is that the President play a limited but important public role in addressing a national problem—the missing dimension of culture strongly supportive of the rule of law. The President can raise the salience of the issue and the various ways in which it might be addressed in educational arenas. He can open a national discussion on ways to meliorate a problem that has frustrated us for many years.

Once, not so long ago, our Founders considered this age-old problem. They recognized that people by their nature were neither devils nor angels, and that we could begin to design practical ways to manage the problem of order and opportunity in our society. Their answer was self-government and the rule of law, accompanied by the habits of civic virtue, informed by education—for no one is born knowing or believing in the rule of law.

About the Author

Dr. Roy Godson has been a professor of Government at Georgetown University for more than four decades. He has been an innovator and implementer of educational change in college, university, and school curricula focused on the security of democratic society and the rule of law. Dr. Godson has also served as a consultant to various agencies of the US government, the UN office on Drugs and Crime, and the Organization of American States. He is the author, coauthor, and editor of more than thirty books and monographs.

Part Four:
Questions for
the Candidates

Questions for the Candidates

The American presidency is a tremendous responsibility. It encompasses a vast range of powers and deals with issues encompassing both domestic and foreign policy. This preeminent constitutional position truly calls for our national best; our best in leadership, experience, knowledge, wisdom, strength, and humanity. Reflecting on even a few of the principal contemporary challenges facing the presidency, the larger-than-life nature of the requirements for the office immediately becomes clear. A list of contemporary challenges illustrating this point, prepared in the form of questions for the candidates, includes:

Major Focus

- What is the single most important issue facing the Nation?
- What are the five most important issues facing the Nation?
- What are the qualifications for the ideal American President? Which of these do you have? Which of these do you lack?
- Are you prepared to be Commander-in-Chief of the United States military?
- Do you believe presidential debates should be an effort to clarify for the American people how the candidates would address major national problems?

National Security

- What specifically would you do to deal with the global threat posed by ISIL, Al-Qaeda, and other radical Islamist terror groups? At minimum your response needs to include your policy toward ISIL in Iraq and Syria, as well as both the political/ideological and military dimensions of your response to these groups.
- Given the likelihood that the political/ideological dimension of the struggle against radical Islamist terror groups can be most effectively engaged

with the help of the vast majority of Islamic countries and peoples, how would you propose to reach out to Muslims in the United States, as well as to member states of the Islamic Conference, to mobilize an ideological response to ISIL and other such extremist groups both within the United States and internationally?

- How, if at all, would you strengthen the United States military? Specifically, how would you strengthen the Air Force, the Army, the Navy, the Marine Corps, and the overall war-fighting capability of the United States?

- What criteria would you use to determine when, where, and how United States armed forces should be committed abroad?

- During any period in which United States armed forces are engaged in combat, would you meet regularly with professional military leaders, including the Chairman of the Joint Chiefs and the Combatant Commanders, to take full account of professional military advice?

- How would you strengthen the Federal Bureau of Investigation and the intelligence community against domestic and foreign threats?

- How would you strengthen the National Security Council system to more effectively integrate through the NSC interagency process the resources and knowledge base of the full United States Government? To use a military reform analogy, the Goldwater-Nichols legislation sought to make the warfighting capability of the United States a more unified service effort; it added a more focused "purple" dimension to cooperation in combat operations across the services. Should we work more effectively in the always combined politico/military challenges to go more "red, white, and blue" in integrating skills and resources of the full United States Government, for example, through more effectively integrating a State Department "governance structure" component in operations such as Iraqi Freedom?

- How would you address the growing threat, nationally and internationally, of cyberattack and cybercrime?

- Would you support an enhanced missile defense shield for the United States, whether fixed land-based or mobile sea-based?

- How would you work to reduce nuclear proliferation and to prevent nuclear weapons from falling into the hands of terrorists?

Restoring Economic Growth

- Our Nation has become mired in low growth. What specifically would you do to increase the growth rate?

- How, if at all, would you change the current corporate and individual income tax systems? What effect would your changes have on the national growth rate?
- How would you address American energy policy, including energy independence and sustainability?
- Do you believe that America is over-regulated? If so, how would you control the "regulatory state?"
- Do you support free-trade agreements? If so, what criteria should be used to determine a good agreement?
- How would you strengthen small business in America; the backbone of the economy and employment?
- How would you address the Nation's eroding infrastructure?
- How would you encourage greater participation of women in the workplace?
- What changes, if any, would you make to strengthen the Nation against future financial crises? Do you believe that any of the legislation or regulations adopted after the 2008 financial crises were a mistake; if so which ones and why?
- Do you support continued independence of the Federal Reserve Board in carrying out monetary policy? What should be the goals of monetary policy?

The Deficit and Entitlements

- What specific measures would you take to address the looming debt crisis and to bring the deficit under control?
- What changes, if any, would you make in the Social Security system? Would you support "Social Security optionality" if it were shown to enhance retirement returns for working Americans and significantly reduce the wealth gap?
- How would you control the rapid growth of expenditures in federal health entitlements, including Medicare and Medicaid?

Health Care

- What changes, if any, would you make in federal health care programs, including the Affordable Care Act/ "Obamacare", Medicare, Medicaid, and NIH funding for basic research?

- Would you support a substantial increase in federal funding aimed at curing and reducing the disease burden of particular diseases, such as those in the arthritis complex, if it can be shown that the cost of the research would be returned many times over in reduced federal expenditures for health care?
- Would you support a more robust national response to mental illness? If so, how?
- What would you do to lessen the risk of global pandemics and enhance the capacity of the United States to deal with any such pandemics?

Foreign Policy

- Other than the threat from Islamist terror groups what do you regard as the most important foreign policy challenges facing the Nation, and how would you deal with them?
- How would you propose to strengthen cooperation between the United States and our NATO allies?
- Should the United States make clear to Iran, in the aftermath of the "nuclear agreement," that if Iran violates the agreement in ways suggesting movement toward a nuclear bomb, the United States will take whatever actions are necessary to prevent Iran from obtaining the bomb?
- How would you deal with Iranian terrorism and secret warfare around the world?
- How would you deal with the Syrian Civil War?
- How would you deal with Russian aggression against Ukraine?
- How would you deal with China's aggressive actions, including its' "nine-dashed-line" in the South China Sea?
- How should the United States deal with the continuing conflict in Afghanistan?
- How would you deal with the North Korean gulag and its nuclear program?
- What posture would you take toward the Israeli/Palestinian conflict?
- Would you support Senate advice and consent to the Law of the Sea Convention following its successful renegotiation meeting all of the conditions set by President Ronald Reagan, as urged by every American President of both parties, every Chairman of the Joint Chiefs of Staff, and a unified American industry?
- How should the United States interact with the United Nations? What UN reforms would you support? Should the United States seek to strengthen the Community of Democracies as a UN caucusing group?

Should it support an integrated ready reaction force from member state military units to deal more effectively with humanitarian disasters? Should it work to achieve greater focus on deterrence, rather than depending on a hoped for after-the-fact response? Should it work capitals more effectively in important UN votes?

- Would you support democracy and the rule of law around the World? If so, how?
- How should human rights, democracy and the rule-of-law be implemented toward major powers such as Russia and China, friendly nations such as Saudi Arabia, and authoritarian regimes actively setting aside democracy such as Venezuela under Chavezism?
- Would you support an initiative previously funded by the Congress in a feasibility study and explored by Freedom House pursuant to the congressional mandate (Freedom House being a non-partisan organization founded, among others by Eleanor Roosevelt, to fight Nazi extremism and promote democracy) to establish a democracy/rule-of-law training center for Africa funded jointly with the European Union in order to support more effective training for democracy in Africa?
- Should the United States have insisted on greater improvement on human rights in Cuba, as well as return of the American "hellfire missile" in Cuban hands, before proceeding toward a normalization of relations?
- How would you strengthen the Foreign Service and the Department of State for more effective United States diplomacy?

Immigration Reform

- What changes, if any, would you make in current immigration law and policy, and why?
- How would you strengthen United States borders?
- How would you strengthen the system for preventing visa overstays?
- How, if at all, should the Nation change its priorities for legal entry?
- In working out a comprehensive solution would you favor legalization or full citizenship to deal with the substantial number of long-term workers in the United States who are not lawful residents but who have otherwise complied with the law?
- What policy would you support toward refugees and asylum, including refugees from Syria and Iraq?

The Criminal Justice System

- What changes, if any, would you make in the federal criminal justice system?
- Are too many Americans in prisons and jails? If so, specifically, what should be done?
- Have we overused criminal penalties? If so, what changes should be made?
- Have we adopted unnecessarily harsh penalties in some settings? If so, what changes should be made?
- Have we failed to more effectively address alternatives to prison or jail time as alternatives in criminal convictions? If so, what changes should be made?
- What changes, if any, should be made in our criminal process to reduce wrongful convictions of the innocent?
- How would you address the crisis in community/police relations?
- How would you address "the war on drugs?"
- It is widely recognized that significant segments of American society do not understand their stake in upholding the rule-of-law. What would you do as President to change this?
- Would you support programs in the public schools educating against drugs and crime and supporting the rule-of-law?
- Consistent with the Second Amendment, what changes in the laws, or enforcement of the laws, would you make to reduce the chances of firearms in the hands of terrorists, criminals, or the mentally ill?

Education Policy

- What changes, if any, would you make in federal education programs?
- What is your position on "common core?" Why?
- Should the federal government encourage Internet programs available to all for education as desired? If so, how would you encourage such programs?
- Should the government work through partnerships with industry to encourage training in needed skills? If so, how would you set up such partnerships?
- What is the role of school-based education in fostering the development of a culture supportive of the rule-of-law? What steps would you take to encourage educators to help address this issue?

The Environment

- Do you believe that climate change poses a problem? Why or why not? If you believe that it is a problem how would you address it?
- Would you support a mix of cost-effective measures to reduce greenhouse gas emissions, including nuclear and enhanced technologies for burning fossil fuels, as well as solar and wind?
- Do you support the Keystone pipeline? Why or why not?
- Leaving aside climate change, what would you do, if anything, to protect and preserve the environment?
- Given the BP uncontrolled blowout in the Gulf, would you task your Administration with reviewing the adequacy of environmental and safety regulations for offshore oil and gas development? Would you support the use of Probabilistic Risk Assessment as a tool to lessen risk in outer shelf oil and gas development?
- Would you eliminate the mandate for ethanol in gasoline?

Civil Liberties and Civil Rights

- Do you support equal opportunity for all Americans, regardless of nationality, religion, gender, or race? What actions have you taken that would demonstrate this?
- There has been too much scapegoating within our national politics with one faction blaming our shortcomings on "wall street" and "billionaires," and another blaming "the media" and "illegal immigrants." Would you serve as President for all Americans, or continue this unproductive scapegoating?
- How would you balance the civil liberties of Americans against the need for intelligence collection and other modalities for protecting American lives against security threats?
- What measures, if any, would you take to support women's rights and enhance opportunities for women in the workplace?
- What actions, if any, would you take to protect and enhance religious liberty?
- Would you respect the Supreme Court's decision in *Roe v. Wade*?
- Would you respect the Supreme Court's recent same-sex marriage decision in *Obergefell v. Hodges*?

The Family

- What actions would you take to strengthen the American family, the foundation of personal and national strength?
- Would you eliminate the marriage penalty in the income tax code?
- Would you reduce or eliminate the estate tax which raises little revenue and favors consumption over family? Would you give a taxpayer's children the same estate tax exemption as their spouse?
- Would you eliminate any provisions in the "safety net" which are serving as disincentives to marriage?

Freedom and Authority: The Role of Government

- How would you "right-size" the federal government?
- What is your view as to the principal roles of the Presidency?
- What is your view as to the proper use of Executive Orders and signing statements?
- What congressional reforms do you believe are needed to enhance the functioning of the Congress in its appropriating and law-making roles?
- What is your view as to the role of the federal government versus that of the states? Do you support a robust federalism?
- What is your view as to the meaning of the Tenth Amendment to the Constitution which provides: "The powers not delegated to the United States by the Constitution, nor prohibited by it to the States, are reserved to the States respectively, or to the people?"
- What criteria would you support in appointing federal judges, and particularly Supreme Court Justices? Would you support a continuing active role for the Court in policing the constitutional fundaments of democracy; fundaments including separation of powers, bill-of-rights protections of the individual from the state, federalism, protection of the integrity of the electoral process, and a robust free press?
- Do you believe that "textualism;" that is, an approach focusing *solely* on the language of a statute, is the proper mode of statutory interpretation? Or do you believe that statutory language, like all use of language, must be interpreted in its fullest context, and thus, where known, "legislative history" should be at least a part of that interpretive process? Given the inherent semantic and syntactic ambiguity of statutory language taken to the Supreme Court, do you believe that "textualism" properly defers to legislative authority? Given the large number of statutory provisions the

Supreme Court must interpret, would this important issue be part of your criteria for selection of Supreme Court Justices?
- In your opinion how much of the 2008-09 financial crisis was caused by government action? How much was caused by the private sector? Specifically what do you view as the contributing factors from each?

Your Administration

- How would you lead the Nation? Please describe your leadership style.
- How would you select your vice-presidential running mate?
- How would you select senior level officials for your Administration?
- Do you believe that the Congress should streamline laws and regulations for presidential appointments to facilitate more timely transitions?
- What would you do to facilitate greater cooperation between you as President and the Congress?
- Would you respect the independence of the courts?
- Would you respect the independence of the Federal Reserve?
- How frequently would you hold press conferences with full opportunity for press Q and A?
- Would you serve as President for all Americans, regardless of their economic status, race, religion, or party?
- Would you put the interests of the Nation above party or personal advantage?
- Can you, without private reservation, take the constitutionally designated oath of office: "I do solemnly swear (or affirm) that I will faithfully execute the Office of President of the United States, and will to the best of my Ability, preserve, protect and defend the Constitution of the United States."